HISTORICAL RESEARCHES INTO SOME ASPECTS OF THE CULTURE AND CIVILIZATION OF NORTH-EAST INDIA

HISTORICAL RESEARCHES INTO SOME ASPECTS OF THE CULTURE AND CIVILIZATION OF NORTH-EAST INDIA

G.P. Singh

GYAN

Historical Researches into Some Aspects of the Culture and Civilization of North-East India

Rs. 890

ISBN: 978-81-212-1012-6

Published in 2009 in India by
Gyan Publishing House,
23, Main Ansari Road Darya Ganj
New Delhi-110002
Phones : 23282060, 23261060
Fax : (011) 23285914
E-mail: books@gyanbooks.com
Website : http : // www.gyanbooks.com

Laser Typesetting by : Quick Media, Delhi
Printed at : Young Art Press, Delhi - 92

Contents

Preface

This volume is a collection of my papers, published in various journals and books, and unpublished, relating to some of the aspects of culture and civilization of North-East India. Some of the papers written in early 1980's have been thoroughly revised and enlarged in the light of further study and research in the subject. I have put them together in one volume for the readers' easy accessibility to all the materials embodied in it. I believe they will be of some use to them.

I crave the readers' indulgence for any errors of omission and commission, which may be discovered by the discerning eye, although no pains have been spared to make the account lucid, accurate and comprehensive. The subject dealt with here is vast and complicated. I am, however, conscious of limitation of my knowledge of it.

G.P. Singh

Abbreviations

ABORI	*Annals of the Bhandarkar Oriental Research Institute,* Poona.
AQ	*Assam Quarterly,* Gauhati.
ARASI	*Annual Report of the Archaeological Survey of India.*
AR or As. Res.	*Asiatic Researches* (Comprising History and Antiquities, the Arts, Sciences, Ethnology and Literature and Asia), Calcutta, New Reprint, Delhi.
ASB	Asiatic Society of Bengal, Calcutta.
BPP	*Bengal Past and Present* (Journal of the Calcutta Historical Society).
CR	*Calcutta Review,* Calcutta.
DAB	*Deodhai Assam Buranji.*
DEB	*Descriptive Ethnology of Bengal.*
DHAS	Department of Historical and Antiquarian Studies, Gauhati.
EHK	*Early History of Kāmarūpā* .
EI	*Epigraphia Indica,* Delhi.
HCPA	*History of Civilization of the People of Assam to the Twelfth Century AD.*
IA	*Indian Antiquary* (Journal of Oriental Research in Archaeology, History, Literature, Language, Folklore, etc.), Bombay.
IGI	*Imperial Gazetteer of India.*
IHQ	*Indian Historical Quarterly,* Calcutta, New Reprint, Delhi.

JARS	*Journal of the Assam Research Society,* Kāmarūpā Anusandhān Samiti, Gauhati.
JASB	*Journal of the Asiatic Society of Bengal,* Calcutta.
JBORS	*Journal of the Bihar and Orissa Research Society,* Patna.
JBRS	*Journal of the Bihar Research Society,* Patna.
JIH	*Journal of Indian History,* Trivandrum.
JPASB	*Journal and Proceedings of the Asiatic Society of Bengal,* Calcutta.
JRAI	*Journal of the Royal Anthropological Institute of Great Britain and Ireland,* London.
MASB	*Memoirs of the Asiatic Society of Bengal,* Calcutta.
MASI	*Memoirs of the Archaeological Survey of India.*
MI	*Man in India* (A Quarterly Anthropological Journal), Ranchi.
PAHCI	*Place of Assam in the History and Civilization of India.*
PASB	*Proceedings of the Asiatic Society of Bengal,* Calcutta.
PNEIHA	*Proceedings of North East India History Association.*
RATA	*Report of the Archaeological Tour in Assam.*
SAA	*Statistical Account of Assam.*
SAB	*Statistical Account of Bengal.*
SHK	*Social History of Kāmarūpā*.

1

Some Newly Discovered Sources on the History and Culture of North-East India

In the arena of research, the presentation and delineation of subject-matter concerned presupposes a critical evaluation of all the sources at our disposal. An investigation should not only be confined to those sources which have been adequately churned and copiously used rather repeated attempts should be made for discovering some new sources in the hope of bringing some new ideas, facts and data into focus. Every research should aim at reconstruction and not reproduction. Most of the researches of today are regrettably merely repetitive, not qualitative or productive. The historical validity of all the conventional explanations should be fully and fairly tested before blindly supporting and quoting them. There should be an honest attempt to collect, as far as practicable, source-material available in different languages. Language, whichever it may be, should not be allowed to stand as a barrier in the way of discoverer of truth and seeker of knowledge. On the combined testimony of various sources containing variegated mosaic of information we can expect better result than the absolute dependence on isolated or fragmentary source-material. The present paper is nothing more than a discovery of some of those sources which have not yet attracted the serious attention of scholars engaged in study or investigations of various aspects of history and culture of north-east India. The sources highlighted here, if properly exploited, will definitely go a long way in filling up some existing gaps in our knowledge about the subject concerned.

Hindi

Jaychandra Vidyalankar's *Bhāratabhumi aura uske Nivāsi* (Bombay, 1925), which can be fairly considered as one of the valuable antiquarian records, provides a graphic picture of the origins, migration, settlements, antiquity, etc. of primitive Himalayan and Sub-Himalayan tribes of north-east India with little reference to their relations with contemporary rulers of various kingdoms roughly upto the seventh century A.D. Equally important is *Prāchin Bhāratiya Paramaparā aura Itihāsa* by Dr. R. Raghava (Delhi, 1953), which deals, to a considerable degree, with ethnological, socio-economic, religious and cultural aspects of various tribes of this region in pre-historic, proto-historic and historic times. *Bhārata Kā Mukti Saṅgrāma* by Ayodhya Sing (2 vols.) is of inestimable value from the standpoint of exhaustive description which it provides about the anti-British Resistance movements and liberation struggles of the Khasis, Jaintias, Garos, Nagas, Lushais, Singphos, Akas and other tribes during eighteenth, nineteenth and first half of the twentieth century. *Sanskriti Ke Chār Adhayāya,* (Delhi 1956) one of the monumental works of the National poet Ramdhari Singh Dinkar is a very dependable source for tracing out the various stages in the contribution of the non-Āryans of this region to the evolution of Indian religion, culture and philosophy.

Travellers' Accounts

Ibn Battuta[1] a celebrated Arabian traveller who visited India in the 14th century has left behind an interesting account about the subject concerned based on his personal experience. While dealing with Indian Archipelago, Bengal, China and Thubbat (Tibet) he has made a passing reference to the origins of Indo-Chinese population of this region with Monogolian characteristics as well as the religious and magical practices of the people of 'Kamaru' corresponding to Kamrupa or modern Assam. For further verification, corroboration and examination of the correctness of this statement the graphic description of Sir Henry Yule[2] (a popular authority on the Travels of Marcopolo, a Venetian traveller who visited India during 13th century), can be safely and profitably relied upon.

The rare and curious narratives of European travellers are also worthy of attention for our purpose. Ralph Fitch[3], the first English traveller, who came to India on political mission in 1584 during Akbar's reign, fifteen years before the East India Company procured the first Charter from Queen Elizabeth of blessed memory, and remained here upto 1590-91, has shed considerable light on Tripura's war with the Mughals in the 16th Century. Rev. Samuel Purchas (1575-1626) who published in the year 1626 first famous collection of voyages and travels undertaken by various English travellers under the caption *Samuel purchas's pilgrimage*[4], has also made incidental references to Tippara's War with Mogors (Mughals) in the 16th and 17th centuries within a reasonable compass. His *pilgrimage*—a trustworthy historical document - also records the brief political history of Cooch Behar, Bengal, Tipperah, Bhutan, etc.

Remonstrantie or Report of Francisco pel-Saert[5] a faithful Dutch record based on his seven years' (1620-27) experiences in India is also of some value from the point of view of little light it throws on the developments in north-east India during Jehangir's time. The narratives of another Dutch Sailor Glanius[6] definitely merits our attention for the description it provides about Mirjumla's War in Assam during the reign of Aurangzeb. The Accounts of two Portuguese travellers Father Stephen Cacella and Father John Cabral[7], who visited Assam between 1626 and 1630, are important only for trade relations of Assam with South Bihar. *Six voyages en persect Aux Indes* pub. in 1676 by J. B. Tavernier, a 17th century French traveller provides a glimpse into trade relations of Tripura with contemporary Eastern Kingdoms.

Portuguese Sources

The Map of Bengal compiled in 1660 by Mattheus Vanden Broucke[8], governor of Choromandal (1658-1664) and *History of the most memorable things that took place in the East Indies and the countries discovered by the Portuguese* written by Portuguese Father Pierre du Jarric[9] based on the account of Father Monserrates Relacam "de Equebar Roi des Mogares" (1580) can also be of some help for Mughal relations with Tripura during 16th and 17th centuries.

Classical (Graeco-Roman) Sources

Ammianus Mercellinus' *Resgestae'*[10], *"Remark on the Sequel to the periplus of the Erythraean sea and on the Country of the Seres as discovered by Ammianus Marcellinus"* by James Tylor (Calcutta 1847), *Le periple de la Mer Erythec'*[11] and *Arriani utferture periplus Maris Erythraei* by anonymous writer translated into another text *Geographi Grocoi Minores*[12] are some of those dependable classical records which can be of great help regarding the origins, identifications, ethnography, arts and crafts and other economic institutions of the tribal people of north-east India, only when we use them in all seriousness and with meticulous regards for the truth.

French

Sylvain Levi's *Le Nepal etude historique d'um Royaume Hindou*[13] characterised by all its precision and accuracy can definitely be taken as reliable treatise on the origins of Indo-Mongoloid tribes of the Himalayan region of north-east India, their migrations to Nepal in post-Bharata War period invasion of Nepal by the Kirātas of Assam of great antiquity, their political and cultural triumphs over indigenous Austro-Asiatic tribes and Indo-Āryans of Nepal in ancient times anterior to 6th century BC etc.

German

W. Schmidt's *Die Monkhmer Volker,* (1906) and *Die Gliederung der austrdlischen sprachen* (1919) also contain some kernel of historical truth about the origin of the Khasis based on the comparative analysis of linguistic structures.

Notes and References

1. H. A. R. Gibb, *Ibn-Battuta's Travel in Asia and Africa,* 1325-1354, London, 1929.

2. *Cathay and the Way Thither,* Vol. IV, (ed) H. Cordier, Hakluyt Society, London, 1916.
3. Ralph Fitch Ryley, *Narratives,* p. 98 ff.
4. J. T, Wheeler, *Purchas's pilgrimage and the Travels of Van Linschoten,* (Calcutta, 1864), pp. 1 114.
5. P. Geyl and Mereland, 1925.
6. *Relation of a unfortunate voyage to the Kingdom of Bengal,* 1682, pp. 140-161.
7. J. C. Wessels, *Early Jesuit Travellers* in *Central Asia,* 1924.
8. *Beschryfing van choromandel in Francois Valentyn's Ouden Niewoost Indien,* Vol. V, Amsterdam, 1728 (A. S. B. Lib, N. 2266).
9. Pt. II, BK. IV. Ch. 8, Bordeaux, 1608, 1610 and 1614.
10. 3 Vols., London, 1935-1939.
11. (Ed). H. Frisk-Goteborg, 1927.
12. (Ed). C. Muller, Paris, 1855. See also *Journal of Oriental Research,* 1879.
13. 3 Vols., Paris, 1905-1909.

2

Researches into the Origins, Antiquity, Nature and Functions of the Pre-Historic Megalithic Cultures of the Hill People of North-East India

The primary object of this paper is to throw new light on various aspects of the megalithic cultures of North East India in the Pre-historic Age. It is indeed an undeniable truth that the subject under review has attracted the attention of various ethnographers, archaeologists, antiquarians and other noted scholars like Mortimer Wheeler, Haimendorf, J. H. Hutton, J. P. Mills, R. T. Bloch, J. D. Hooker, H. Yule, C. B. Clarke, Godwin Austin, H. D. Sankalia, H. C. Dasgupta and P. R. T. Gurdon[1], but the picture which emerges out of their researches is neither graphic nor complete. Their accounts are more of descriptive nature than analytical. Moreover, several broken chains have been noticed in their accounts which need not only restoration but also fresh evaluation and interpretation. Further more, no systematic survey of the prehistoric relics and monuments of unknown antiquity of the aboriginals of North-East has been conducted so far nor has any extensive archaeological exploration been undertaken. However, in order to obtain a clearer picture of the subject reliance has been placed on the available archaeological Reports, Census Report, imperial records, indigenous sources, personal tour diary, contemporary accounts and other standard historical texts.

The duty of a historian is not only to investigate higher civilization but also the primitive civilization, for the latter constitutes the bedrock of the former. In historical reconstruction of the early history of mankind the sober method of research should follow.[2]

The master key to the investigation of primitive culture of primaeval antiquity is the monumental evidence of the Stone Age. The pre-historic remains and relics not only testify to the living condition of the people in different ecological settings, but also provide some clues for determining the stages and extent of progress in the realm of civilisation. Voltaire had reasonably insisted on making enquiry into the various steps by which men passed from barbarism to civilization. These monuments also cast reflections to a considerable degree on the knowledge, beliefs, arts, technology, customs etc. of the primitive people of hoary past. The Megalithic structures of Asia, Europe, Africa and Australia are the legacy of the races of mysterious past.

These Megalithic monuments have served as a Museum of early history and culture.[3] Prof. Nilsson in 1843 had affirmed that the antiquities of the human race of by-gone age are the "fragments of a progressive series of civilization"[4]. While adopting more or less the same line of enquiry Will Durant[5] had observed that the surviving records of the Stone Age are highly impressive. The people of the Neolithic Age laid another foundation of civilization.

The term Megalithic[6] are applied to structures or monuments of rudimentary character consisting of huge rough undressed stones as well as elaborately dressed stones of sophisticated kind popularly known as Menhirs, Dolmens, Cromlechs, Stone Circles, Stonehinge, etc.

The beliefs of the tribal people concerned in the doctrine of transmigration of soul or life after death and their socio-religious practices, ceremonies and customs constituted the basis and further promoted the growth of Megalithic cultures. The Megalithic monuments used to fulfil the three - fold functions, funerary, commemorative and religious.

The statement made by B. C. Alien, E. Gait, G. H. Alien and H. F. Howard[7] that "Assam is somewhat destitute of archaeological remains" is not tenable. An archaeological characteristic of Assam of world-wide fame is its wealth of Megaliths comprising sepulchral monuments like cairns, dolmens, menhirs, cromiechs, upright stones, flat and horizontal stones, male stones, female stones and some stones depicting carving and Jesigns on them.[8]

One of the most prominent and striking aspects of the history and culture of the Khasis, the Jaintias, the Nagas and the Cacharis is the age-old practice of erecting various kinds of monumental stones which are scattered generally on every ways in side. These are mysterious, solitary and clustered monuments of remote antiquity. These remarkable monuments abounding in this region are similar to that found in Europe and western Asia. Some of them are puzzling and delightful for antiquarians. The megalithic stones were erected at different periods of history. But historically this practice can be traced back to pre-historic age.

We find traces of wide spread megalithic culture in the Khasi and Jaintia Hills. The tall upright stones, known as menhirs representing Mao Shinrang or male stones are always uneven numbers varying from three to nine. The highest one is placed in the centre and the lower one on each side. The highest pillar which is the centre-monolith is occasionally crowned with a circular disk or covered with a round flat stone and to right and left they gradually diminish. In front of each set of three stones is placed one flat horizontal stone called by the English antiquarian "Cromlech" which rests on three or four small upright stones. This represents Mao kynthai or female stones, sometimes five menhirs and two dolmens have been found. The dolmens associated with human remains erected by a clan to commemorate member of the clan represent Mothers. This is for commemorative purposes. Memorial stones of considerable significance were classified into two categories:

(*a*) Stones erected by the family or Kur in accordance with the Khasi custom of ancestor worship, and (*b*) Stones which are erected by children in honour of the deceased parents. Both classes of stones are merely Cenotaphs or Masoleums of ancestors.

According to indigenous sources[10] after cremation the charred bones were collected in an earthen pot and eventually placed in the common sepulchre of the clan. Bones were placed under the cover of flat stones. Large upright stone groups were erected in honour of the dead. The philosophy behind the practice of erecting commemorative stones was that their spirits will be gratified by these memorials and their souls will be in eternal peace without being affected by supernatural forces. The installation of memorial stones preceded the performance of dance and music. This practice was based on certain social and religious norms. The erection of monoliths was associated with sacrifices of oxes, pigs, etc. Edward Gait while corroborating the account in his Census Report[11] pointed out that similar monuments are found amongst the Hos, the Mundas, the Kiratas and the Naga tribes. Gurdon[12] found a striking similarity between these monuments and those of England, Britanny, Denmark and Scandinavia.

C. Von Purer Haimendorf[13] has rightly observed that the Khasis and the Nagas alike erect single standing stone (menhirs) or alignments of stone in honour of the dead who are thereby encouraged to help their living kinsmen. The setting up of menhirs dolmens and stone circles links the Khasis and the Nagas with the Gonds of Bastar, the Mundas of Chotanagpur and Orissa tribes. The Khasis indeed approach more nearly to the dominant Megalithic custom of Peninsular India in that they collect periodically the bones of clan members and deposit them in a free standing cist as big as small house, built of enormous single slabs.

The Imperial records[14] bear witness to the truth that some inscribed memorial stones were found at Mawphlang in 1918-19. The memoral stones at Laileucote has been considered by the British antiquarians as the great work of archaeological interest. Several Megalithic monuments have been found near Cherra, Jowai, Nartiang and Laitlyngkote in pair menhirs or dolmen circles and other forms.

The eye-witness account of Lt. H. Yule[15] who visited the Khasi and Jaintia hills between 1838 and 1844 reveals the truth that the tallest pillar was in the market place of Nartiang in the Jaintia hills. The biggest menhir which still stands there measured 26 feet in height. A flat table stone or cromlech near the village of Sailankot elevated five feet from the earth measured thirtytwo feet by 15 and two feet in thickness. In other instance the monuments is a square sarcophagus composed of four large slabs-resting on their edges and well fitted together and roofed in by a fifth placed horizontally. The sarcophagus is often found in the form of a large slab accurately circular resting on the heads of many little rough pillars closely planted together through whose chinks one may descry certain earthen pots containing the ashes of a family. In Mausmai deep in the forest he saw great collection of such circular Cinerairies so close that one may step from slab to slab for many yards. A simple Cairn or a pyramid some twenty feet in height as seen by him sometimes remind us of the common notion of the Tower of Babel or pyramid of Saccara in Egypt. He further observes that in Bell's Circassia a drawing of ancient monument existing in that country which is an exact representation of the thousand such in the Khasi Hills and nearly as exact a description of referring to the relics on the eastern bank of Jordan may be read in Irby and Mangles's Syrian travellers.

J. H. Hutton[16] while visiting the Jaintia Hills in 1925 saw some dolmens as reminiscemce of Manipur. At Nartiang Bazar he saw single highest monolith twenty six and half feet long raised from the ground level to the top six feet to six inch in breadth and 2 ft. to 8 inch in thickness and enormous flat stones in the form of dolmens at its bases. The Nartiang Bazar is wonderful collection of manhirs or dolmens. Near Laitlyng he noticed dolmens in which bones of the dead were buried. This memorial stones represented the males in the right side and female to the left. He also witnessed quite a good number of menhirs and dolmens at Malynglang near Jawdaija and a stone circle like an Angami Tehuba Cromlech. Further near Mosniang he saw burial cist flanked by a menhir and broken dolmens.

Suniti Kumar Chatterjee[17] also refers to this popular custom of the Austric Khasis.

The Mon-khmer speaking people of North-East no doubt made a distinctive cultural contribution to the evolution of the Megalithic culture.

Equally significant is the Megalithic culture of the Nagas. A good deal of varieties are to be observed among the Naga tribes in their use of Monoliths. Some are of considerable size and others massive set up from time immemorial for commemorating the death, raids, hunting, conceptional valour or prowess and other utilitarian and ceremonial purposes. The Angamis, the Aos, the Semas, the Lothas, the Rengmas and the Konyak Naga tribes erect the memorial stones of great architectural merit. The Angami Monoliths are without carving or ornamentation, whereas on the other hand the Lothas ornament their monoliths with rough designs. The Sema Nagas perpetuate the memory by shallow circles of flat stones met in the ground. The Kacha Nagas build similar circle for the same purpose. The Ao Nagas also used to erect upright stones (Menhirs) like the Dusums of Borneo and Tinguian of Philippines. The purpose of setting up stones by Rengma Nagas is purely commemorative like that of Medagascar. Dr. T. Bloch[18] during his archaeological tour in the Naga Hills found striking similarity between 'V' shaped pillars and memorials used by the Naga tribes.

L. W. Shakespear[19] presents a very authentic account of the Megalithic cultures of the Nagas. The Angamis and Maramis have been in the habit of setting up huge stones right from the early days. The Nagas of Maram in Manipur territory set up in the past the largest and the most remarkable "Stonehenge". The gigantic Monoliths at Togwema has been referred to by him and by Hutton in 1923. The Konyak Naga erect small Monoliths for ceremonial purposes.

J. H. Hutton[20] suggests that the Angamis' Tehuba Cromlech bears resemblance to the stone circles of the Jaintias. The Angami Nagas always put the big end of the stone in the earth. The Kacha Nagas followed the Khasi plan and installed prominent large stones at Lakema. He also refers to carved stones at Kigwema in the Naga Hills associated with fertility symbols like that of Khonoma. J. P. Mills[21] refers to stones of Kacha Naga village of peisa with a carved female figure associated with a cult of fertility. The popular tradition and the actual practice of erecting the monoliths point to a highly developed stone cultures of the Naga tribes.

Both commemorative and funeral stones roughly fall into three groups i.e. ossuary pillar, Dolmen stone circles and ritual stones. Memorial stones can be broadly classified into two categories - Quadrilateral and Verticular.[22]

The stone monuments of the Naga tribes of Manipur consisting of Monoliths not as large as that of the Khasis and Jaintia were found either singly or arranged symmetrically in rows, avenues circle or ovals, cairons or heaps of stones, single smaller stones or flat stones. The huge stone Monoliths or 'Y' shaped structures found in Mao and Maram areas really appear as architectural monuments. The sepulchural monument erected by some of the minor Kuki tribes in honour of rich women after her death are also interesting architectural objects .[23]

Significantly enough, the Megalithic monuments at Salangthel near Moirang in Manipur engraved with the symbol of genital organs of female and some flat horizontal stones bearing the engravings of foot prints are of great architectural interest.[24]

The hallowed monoliths of North Cachar Hills were used for depositing ashes of the dead as a proto-type of the Khasis. J. H. Hutton and J. P. Mills both noticed solid and hollow monoliths in North Cachar hills in 1929.

While comparing the pre-historic dolmens, cromlechs and other monuments of the Khasis and Nagas with Gadabas, Bondus of Orissa and Gonds of Bastar and tribes of the Deccan, Haimendorf[25] was not struck by any resemblance. More important are the differences in function and meaning of the monuments. The Megaliths of the tribal folks of today are with comparatively few exception, memorials connected with graves or burning ground. But those of pre-historic times are closely associated with graves.

One of the noteworthy features of the megalithic culture of North East India is that it represents a living tradition of entirely unknown antiquity, whereas the South Indian Megaliths came to an end in the first century A.D.

It is worthwhile to note that all these monuments of N. E. India were brought under the Ancient Monuments Preservation Act, VII of 1904 passed by Lord Curzon.[26]

One of the curious features to be noted here is that these Neolithic stone Monuments are associated with the cult of fertility, ancestor worship, theory of sacrifice, and worship of Phallus-Linga and Yoni, later personified as the mother Goddess and Siva principles of Saktism. G. Bertrand has emphatically asserted that "the Khasi Monoliths comprising memorial stones, menhirs and dolmens like those of Western Europe, Northern Africa and Western Asia are doubtless the emblems of that phallic cult of standing stones which were so spread in ancient times. These monoliths in the shape of Linga found in India are associated with the worship of Siva".[27]

One remarkable fact which has not yet been acknowledged by many competent authorities is that the tribal notion of life after death and idea of the plurality of souls gave a new line of speculation to the Vedic Aryans and Brahmanical thinkers who had no acquaintance with the doctrine before. Sir Mortimer Wheeler, a celebrated archaeologist has correctly stated that "The Buddhists, Jains and Hindus imitated free-standing structures in cutting their cave temples and monastries ... ."[28]

It remains to be examined whether the megalithic culture of North East India represent Northern Black Polished (N.B.P) ware associated with Iron objects or painted Grey ware associated with copper or Bronze implements. Since the black and red ware associated with iron objects or other metals like copper and bronze like that of Central and Southern India have not been discovered in the megalithic burials of the North-East, it can be fairly admitted that this region had not reached the level of distinctive ware culture.

In North Eastern India the Khasis were the only tribes who acquired the knowledge of Iron ore. This is very puzzling question whether their megalithic monuments of the neolithic age was associated with iron object or copper. It can be fairly stated that they acquired, the knowledge of iron in post Neolithic age. S K Chatterjee[29] attempted to prove that the Khasi or Mon-Khmer group of Austro-Asiatic were in the neolithic stage of culture and, learned, the use of copper and Iron. Lt. H. Yule[30] observed, that the Khasi Iron ore is two thousand years old. But this is a plausible hypothesis not correct discovery. Pliny[31] in his National History ascribes its antiquity to the first century A.D. The tradition also confirms the remote antiquity of the Iron technology of the Khasis. It can be positively affirmed, that their megalithic culture began in the Neolithic Age, but comparatively at later stage it became associated with the Copper, Iron phase of culture.

The questions relating to the origins and antiquities of the megalithic cultures still remain unsolved. The divergent views and many hypothetical theories have made the confusion worth confounded. The closer links and affinities of the tribal megaliths of N. E. India with those of the megalithic monuments of South-western coastal strip of India, South-East Asia, Philippines, Formosa, Megagascar, Africa, Iran, Mediterranean world and pacific world, Asia minor, Western Asia, France, Britain, Scandinivia and Denmark in respect of method and purpose, of course, stir our imagination. But they can never represent a single cultural phase as supposed by Mr. Peet. Prof. Panchanan Mitra suggested that there arose Indo-Erythraean culture complex and in the north-east srong culture stream came by sea-board which later passed over to another zone. This is a fanciful notion.[32]

Dr. J. H. Hutton[33] while delivering a lecture in the Indian Museum at Calcutta in 1923 observed that its origin was from Indonesia and the Mon-Khmer speaking Khasi tribe or Australoid or Austro Asiatic or Pre-Mediterranean Khasis introduced this culture.

S. C. Roy[34] and Haimendorf[35] are inclined to recognise that Megalithic builders were proto-Dravidians. A. H. Dani[36] dates back this culture to simply pre-historic age. He has made a futile attempt to associate this culture with the stone tools of Neolithic Age. It reached its highwater marks comparatively at later stage.

As a matter of fact, the Megalithic culture of the North-East is an essence of both indigenous and foreign elements. It would be absolutely wrong on our part to truce its origin and growth only under the external influence. The identity of custom and striking similarities between the various practices do not always necessarily hint at their common origin. The contemporary geographical factors and natural environments in the different countries conditions the evolution of the Megalithic culture in different ways. The antiquity of this culture may tentatively be ascribed to the Neolithic Age (7000-4000 B.C.). Thus pre-historic times of pre-Aryan period proved to be a cultural watershed in the early tribal history of N. E. India.

Haimendorf[37] as a protagonist of the theory of its foreign origin observed that "they belong essentially to South-Eastern Asia-Indonesia, Oceania, the Philippines & Formosa". Whatever be the truth underlying this statement, it is almost certain that this culture was introduced in N. E. India by Austro-Asiatic immigrants (the Khasis) as clearly stated by M. Wheeler.[38]

Notes and References

1. Wheeler, (1947, 147-310; 1968, 150-53); Haimendorf (1945, 73-86); Hutton (1926, 133, 333-46); Mills (1930, 34-35); Bloch, (Report on the Archaeological Tour in Assam, 1905); Hooker (1854, 66ff); Yule (1844, 617-18); Clarks (1874); Austen (1874 1-6); Sankalia (1962, 100-2); Dasgupta (1931,1-96); Gurdon (1914, 145f; 1904, 64-65)- all have dealt with the Megalithic cultures of North East India without solving the problems relating to their origins and antiquity.
2. Henry Maine strongly advocated the cause of sover research for proper understanding of the Primitive culture (Lowie, 1949, 423).
3. Tylor (1903, 38f, 61f) suggests that the megalithic structures of Asia minor, Egypt, Palestine, China, England, France, Algeria and indigenous tribes of India are of great antiquarian interest.
4. Prof. Nilsson emphasised the need of understanding the significance of the antiquities of the past (Ref. to Tylor, 1903, 61-62).
5. Durant (1954, 97f) has rightly pointed out that the Neolithic Age marked the second foundation of civilization.
6. The term Megalith is derived from the Greek words Megas i.e. great and lithos, i.e. stones. This term was "originally introduced by antiquarians to describe easily definable class of monuments in Western and Northern Europe." (*Ancient India*, 1947-48 No. IV, p. 5)

7. (1879, 40) In both the valleys and hills of Assam large number of remains of archaeological interests have been discovered.
8. *Journal of the Assam Research Society* (J. R. A. S), April 1933, Vol. I pp. 4-5; J. E. A. S. April 1939, Vol. VII, pp. 10-18.
9. Allen, 1905-8, 53-54, 124; Gurdon, 1904, 64-65; *Journal of the Asiatic Society of Bengal*, 1879, Vol. VIII, 133-137; Yule, 1868, *Calcutta Review,* Vol. 274; K. L. Barua, 1939, 4-12, 35-40. All these sources throw considerable light on the Megaliths of the Khasis.
10. G. Costa (1937, Ch. XX, 63-72) deals with the customs of thirty Khasi Kings.
11. Gait (1891, 261)
12. Gurdon (1914, 145f)—some of his observations are subject to further verification.
13. Haimendorf (1945, 73-86). See his comparative analysis.
14. Pol. Dept. B. Progs Jan. 1919 N. 479-87 File o. Ill, M-15 of 1918. The Report is based on the Tour Diary of D. C. K & J Hills; Letters Issued to Govt. Vol 35. 1867-68. Both these records are very important from archaeological point of view.
15. Yule (1844, 617-18) presents an exhaustive account of the subject. See also his *Calcutta Review,* 1868, Vol. XXXVIII, 274f.
16. Hutton (1926, 333-461) presents a trust worthy account of the Meghaliths of the Jaintias. I had the opportunity to see quite a good number of Megalithic monuments in Khasi and Jaintia Hills.
17. S. K. Chatterjee (1969, 37-38) makes an incidental reference to the megaliths of the Khasis.
18. Bloch (1905, Report on the Archaeological Tour in Assam) presents a very valuable and reliable account. See also *Imperial Gazetteer of India,* 1908, 586.
19. L. W. Shakespear (1929, 260-62) extensively traversed through the Hills of the North Eeast and obtained the

first hand information of the subject. See also *Journal of the Royal Anthropological Institute* (J.R.A. I) 1965, Vol. 95,28.

20. Hutton (1926, 333-46); See also his account in J. R. A. I. LVI, 7 If. and Man in India, 1926, 74.
21. Mills (1930, Man in India, 34-35).
22. Bareh (1970 67-68) has made a very scientific analysis of the subject.
23. Hodson (1974 86ff) gives a clear description of the Megaliths of the Naga tribes of Manipur. See also Geographical Society 1904, 31-32 and *Journal of the Society of Arts.* Vol. LXXX, 559.
24. I visited this site in June, 1985.
25. Haimendorf (1945, 73-86) has drawn his conclusion on the basis of a comparative study of the subject.
26. Proceedings of the Hon'ble Lt. Governor of Eastern Bengal and Assam, June 1910, Arch. Deptt.
27. G. P. Singh (1981, 25-26) ; Bertrand (1958, 134-35). The histiorical authenticity of the statement has been carefully examined.
28. Wheeler (1968, 158-59); G. P. Singh (1981, 25), The Contribution of the tribal people to the evolution of the philosophical thoughts of the Hindus, Buddhists and Jains has not yet received the serious attention of the scholars.
29. S. K. Chatterjee (1969, 37).
30. Yule (*Calcutta Review* 1868, Vol. XXXVIII, 278). See also *Imperial Gazetteer of India* Vol. VI, 73; Vol. XV, 262-63; *U Nongpynim,* Naiwang Nov. 1937, 3-5; *U Khasi Mynta,* Risaw Oct. 1902; J. A. S. B. 1832, Vol. I, 150ff; Hooker (1854, Vol. II 66ff) Yule, J. A. S. B., 1842, Vol. XI, 853. All these sources are important for the detailed study of the knowledge of the Khasis about Iron Technology.
31. Taylor (J. A. S. B. 1847, Vol. I 68-69, 73). On the authority of Pliny he tried to prove that the Khasi iron is not earlier than the 1st century A.D.
32. For detailed study see K. L. Barua, 1939, J. A. R. S. Vol.-VIII, April, 1939, No. I, 1-18; *Ibid.,* July 1939, 35-40.

33. Cf. Bagchi (1929, Introd. XVII, XVIII). He has focussed on this matter on the basis of the extracts of J. H Button's speech.
34. Barua (J. A. R. S. July 1939, 35) has discussed the views of various scholars without striking any balance between them. Nor has he drawn any plausible conclussion.
35. Haimendorf (1953, New aspects of the Dravidian problem, Tamil culture -II)
36. Dani (1960, 41) has mainly discussed the problems associated with Neolithic Stone tools, not the Megaliths.
37. Haimendorf (1945, 73-86).
38. Wheeler (1968, 150). Both Haimendorf and Wheeler, no doubt made sincere attempt to understand the problems associated with the subject, but some of the ideas as presented by them need further investigation.

Bibliography

Allen, B.C. 1905-8 : *Assam District Gazetteer,* Vol. X.

Allen, B.C., Gait, E.A., Allen, H.H. & Howard H.F. 1879 : *Gazeetteer of Bangal and North-East India.*

Austen, G. 1874 : *Journal of the Asiatic Society of Bengal,* Vol. XIii, Pt. 1.

Barua, K.L. 1939 : *Journal of the Assam Research Society,* April, Vol. Vii, July, Vol. Vii. N. 2.

Bagchi, P.C. 1929 : *Pre-Aryan and Pre-Dravidians in India,* Calcutta.

Bareh, H. 1970 : *Nagaland District Gazetteer.*

Bertrand, G. 1958 : *Secret Land Where Women Reign,* London.

Bloch, T. 1905 : *Report on Archaeological Tour in Assam.*

Chatterjee, S.K. 1969 : *Indo-Aryan and Hindi,* Calcutta.

Costa, G. 1937 : *Ka Riti Jong Ka Riti Laiphew Syiem,* Shillong.

Dani, A.H. 1960 : *Pre-History and Proto History of Eastern India,* Calcutta.

Dasgupta, H.C. 1931 : *Journal of the Asiatic Society of Bengal,* Vol. XXVII.

Durant, Will, 1954 : *The Story of Civilization, Pt. I, Our Oriental Heritage,* Newyork.

Gait, E.A. 1891 : *Census of India,* Assam Census Report, Vol. 1.

Gurdon, P.R.T. 1914 : *The Khasis,* London.

— 1904 : "Notes on the khasis, Syntengs and allied tribes inhabiting the Khasi and Jaintia Hills Dist. in Assam," *Journal of the Asiatic Society of Bangal,* Vol. LXXIII, Pt. IV, (Calcutta, 1905).

Haimendorf, C.V.F. 1945: "The Problem of Meghalithic Cultures in the Middle India," Cf *Man in India,* Vol. XV.

Hooker, J.D. 1854 : *Himalayan Journals.* Vol. 11, London.

Hutton. J.H. 1922 : "The meaning and method of the Erection of Monoliths by the Naga tribes". Cf. *The Journal of the Roy. Anthropological Inst.* LII.

— 1926 : "Some Megalithic work in the Jaintia Hills" *Journal & Proceed of the Asiatic Society of the Bengal,* Vol. XXII (Calcutta. 1928).

— 1926 : "The use of stones in the Naga Hills", *The Journal of the Royal Anthropological Institute,* Lvi.

— 1926 : *Man in India,* Ranchi.

Hudson, T.C. 1974 : *The Naga Tribe of Manipur.*

Lowie, R.H. 1949 : *Primitive Society,* London.

Mills, J.P. 1930 : *Man in India,* Ranchi.

Shakespear, L. W. 1929 : *History of the Assam Riffes,* London.

Singh, G.P. 1981 : "The Genesis and Growth of of Tribal Culture and Civilization in North East

India (from pre-historic times to the 12th fcentury A.D.", *Journal of the Institute of Social Research,* Vol. I No. 1, Shillong.

— 1980-81 : *The Quarterly Review of Historical Studies,* Vol. XX, No. 4, Calcutta.

Sankalia, H.D. 1962 : *Indian Archaeology Today,* Bombay.

Tylor, E.B. 1903 : *Primitive Culture,* vol. 1, London.

Yule, H. 1844 : "Notes on the Khasi Hills and People, *Journal of the Asiatic Society of Bengal,* Vol. XIII, Pt. 2, Nos. 151-6.

— 1868 : *Calcutta Review* Vol. XXXVIII.

Wheeler, M. 1968 : *Early India and Pakistan,* London.

— 1947 : *Ancient India (Bulletin of the Archaeological Survey of India,* No. 4.)

3

A Glimpse into the History of Evolution of Tribal Civilization in North-East India in Ancient Times

The early history of the tribal people of North-East India from the pre-historic times to the 12th century A.D. is still shrouded in mystery. It is a completely unrecorded period and the most obscure phase of their history. Both oriental and occidental scholars have left this subject to remain as hidden treasure. No serious attempt has ever been made to portray the vivid picture of the subject on a scientific basis. Some stray accounts furnished in interspersed narratives are not only meagre but are also unreliable and unauthentic. From antiquarian standpoint the subject is a very interesting field of historical inquiry. Though in the absence of any trustworthy historical evidence it is difficult to record any fact with great amount of certainty and confidence, yet on the basis of some facts which may be gleaned from epigraphical records, some dubious and fragmentary references in the early classical literature, native chronicles, traditional and mythological accounts, documentary evidences, discovery of archaeological remains and other collateral evidences we can venture to re-construct the history of the period under review.

Though it is an undeniable fact that the dawn of the Neolithic Age really marked the beginning of tribal civilization in North-East India and the first flower of this civilization blossomed in the garden of the tribes belonging to Austro-Asiatic groups, yet the positive evidence of the remains of various caves in the Khasi-Jaintia Hills, the Garo Hills, North Cachar Hills and Mikir Hills testifies to their habitation anterior or much earlier to this Age. J.P. Mills (1) suggests that both the traditional and physical characteristics of some of the hill tribes bear the clear evidence to this fact that the earliest inhabitants of Assam were of Negrito stock. "There is strong tradition however that the remnants of the race were blocked into a cave near Haflong by a Kachari King". The stone celts and megaliths associated with burial urns erected in the memory of their deceased representing the phallic worship, the use of iron implements, the developed hunting, fishing, animal husbandry, the growth of clans and the marriage system, the erection of thatched buildings, the formation of groups under the leadership of headman, the art of cultivation, the primitive system of jhum cultivation, the introduction of matriarchal principles in the matter of administration and inheritance, the belief in the immortality of the soul or the spirit, the practice of worshipping the mother cult led to the foundation of the Khasi-Syntong cutlure and civilisation in the Neolithic Period. Dr. S.K. Chatterji (2) has rightly observed that they were in the Neolithic stage of culture and perhaps in India they learned the use of copper and later on they developed a primitive system of agriculture employing their primitive weapon. This truth has been also more or less further corroborated by Dr. R.C. Majumdar (3). Thus the tribes belonging to Austro-Asiatic or "Finno-Ugrian Austro-Asiatic" group Pre-Mediterranean-speaking Mon-Khmer and allied languages once covered a large part of the globe and gradually occupied various parts of India. The Khasi-Syntengs affiliated to this group have made several distinctive cultural contributions in the field of Neolithic shouldered hoe, megalithic burials, art of cultivation, iron-smetting totemic religion and matriarchy—all indicative of advanced culture and civilization. The stone celts and megalithic monuments found in the Garo Hills, the North-Cachar Hills, the Mikir Hill, the Naga Hills, Manipur and Upper Assam establish their racial and ethnological links with South-East Asia, Wetern Asia, Pacific and

Mediterranean world and Europe during prehistoric period. As a sequal to the arrival of the successive hordes of tribes known as Tibeto-Burmese the intermingling of races, languages and cultures in North-East India followed. According to K.L. Barua (4) the Bodo tribes came into contact with the Mediterranean Pundras of Northern and central Bengal who had the same chalcolithic civilization as that of the dwellers of the Indus valley. They first came under the civilizing influence of the Mediterranean, then of the Alpine and lastly of the Vedic Aryan colonists in North Eastern India about 1000 B.C., if not earlier. To quote him (5) "The earliest Prehistoric culture in Assam, so far known, was not a Paleolithic but a Neolithic culture spread throughout the length and breadth of the province as indicated by the wide distribution of Neolithic celts. We do not know who the original authors of this culture were. Perhaps ages after came a people much more advanced in cutlure who introduced the shouldered Neolithic hoe, terraced rice cultivation, megalithic burials, ophiolatry and matriarchy. These people began with a Neolithic culture but latterly they acquired the knowledge of iron-smelting. We do not know whether they developed this art themselves or borrowed it form others. They were speakers of a language which belonged to a family very widely distributed all over the owrld. In course of time however they were displaced and submerged, in most places by horde of new comers from Tibet, Burma and Yunan. These new comers may have been actually inferior to the Mon-Khmer peakers in culture when they debouched from the hills on the North and settled on the plains of Northern Bengal and the Assam valley but gradually they came under the cultural influence first of the Mediterranean Pundras of Bengal, then of the Alpines and lastly of the Aryans by which time the historic period began."

The fabric of tribal civilisation has been woven by both internal and external threads. The economic, religious, cultural and other factors as well as their contacts with the outer world largely affected the course and currents of their civilisation. During the Maraka period in the Epic Age the migration of Aryans from Mithila to Assam greatly influenced the Austric and Bodo culture. Placing our reliance upon native chronicles (6) as wells as other evidence (7) we can state that during the early period right from the time of Yudhisthira (about 5 thousand years ago) the Jaintias were under the influence of Brahmanical rulers, as a result of which they accepted Aryanised faiths and practice. Their religious customs, ceremonies and priesthood system are strikingly similar to those of Hindus. The cult of Saivism and Tantrikism further developed among the Khasis, the Jaintias and the Garos (8). From the Epic Age to the 12th Century A.D. the relations of the Khasis and the Jaintias with the rulers of Kamarupa, Bengal and other neighbouring areas moulded their way of life. Both the Brahmin and Buddhist priests from Bengal as a result of their frequent visits to their places and cultural fellowship certainly might have influenced the various grades of their culture. The Garos, relations with the rulers of Kamarupa between 7th and 13th century gradually shaped their sociocultural pattern.

The early rulers of the North-Cachar Hills maintained their relations with the Epic Heroes and the rulers of Hill-Tipperah by borrowing various cultural traits. On the basis of the literary evidences, (9) native chronicles (10) and other historical evidence (11) we can unfold this latent fact that the Hill cacharis had close contacts with Epic Heroes and Aryan rulers. As a result of this contact the process of their Hinduisation soon followed which can be proved on the basis of numerous evidences (12). In the Mikir Hills innumerable archaeological finds of Hindu temples and images prove that they were under the control of the Varman, the Mlechha and the Pala dynasties. The political and cultural relations of the Tipperah Kings with the rulers of Kamarupa, Bengnl and with several Brahmins from Mithila greatly determined the shape of their early culture and civilisation. On the basis of some valuable evidences (13) we can affirm that as a result of the relations of Tipperah tribes with Aryan rulers as well as the neighbouring Kingdoms, the process of Sanskritization soon began which gradually put its indelible imprint on the tribal beliefs and practices.

The vertical stone Monoliths set up by the Nagas (known as Negroids) in the Neolithic Age remind us of the cultural traits of the people of Indonesia, Phillipines, Sumatra, Malanesia and Polynesia. Their contacts with the rulers of civilized countries in plains in connection with trade and Manipur to the south and Kamarupa to the west influenced their culture, trade, industries arts and crafts, language and warfare. The imperial records (14) furnish the evidence of Naga trade relations with plains of Assam, Burma, Manipur and other places which went a long way in changing their ways of life. The Nagas are also traditionally believed to have established their early contacts with the Epic Hero Bhima and the Kachari Kings. It is very difficult to specify the particular period. A. G. Macall (15) has unravelled this truth of great historical value, hitherto completely unknown that the Lushais were also deeply influenced by varied contacts with predominantly stronger civilisation through the earlier ages. He expresses the doubt that it remains a matter of considerable curiousity that they never "fell to the teachings of Buddha, Confucious or other great preceptor, with whose disciples they must have been in intermittent contact all through the ages." About Manipur C. J. Lyall (16) rightly remarked that "I have always taken a lively interest in the singular oasis comparative civilisation and organised society set in the midst of congeries of barbarous people over whom its rulers exercise an authority."

The politico-cultural contacts of North-Eastern frontier hill tribes with Burma, China, Bhutan, Tibet, Northern and Eastern Asia and Gangetic India contributed to the growth of composite culture and civilisation. As a result of the contacts of the early settlers of the frontier areas with the Brahmins of the several Aryan colonies set up there, some sort of synthetic culture-Aryo-Mongoloid—culture developed. The crude form of Saivism, the cult of Tantrikism with esoteric beliefs, Vaishnavism and Buddhism—all the prominent schools of religion—developed and co-existed for centuries. On the basis of archaeological records (17) we find the evidence of the prevalence of Hinduism and its impact on non-Aryan way of living. Both tradition and epigraphy confirm this truth. According to Pandit Vidyavinod (18) tradition records that a colony of Brahmans was set up in Sadiya region near the city of Kundin by Parasurama. Kaundinya, well known as the founder of the Kingdom of Kamboja belonged to this Brahmin colony. The existence of Aryan colony in North-Eastern frontier region and the impact of Aryandom on Mongoloid elements can never be denied. The Gauhati Copper-Plate inscription of Indra-Pala-Varma-Deva (Circa-1038 A.D.) deciphered by Dr. Heornle (19) also reveals the identical truth.

It is worthwhile to note that when the process of Aryanisation set in the North-Eastern region tentatively between third millennium B.C. and 1000 A.D, the hill religion, culture, language, manners and customs, beliefs and practices, arts and crafts were greatly modified. Their early contacts with both the Alpine and Vedic Aryans which profoundly contributed several factors to the synthesis of culture cannot be denied. It is generally believed that the Alpine Aryans coming from Iran to the Eastern India before Bharata War of 3100 B.C. across the Himalayas diffused advanced culture known as "Vratya culture" before the advent of the Vedic Aryans. After the coming of Vedic culture the synthesis of both the cultures emerged which was complete about the time of Buddha. During the early centuries of Christian era and 5th century AD they introduced the Aryan language of Pisachi family and popularised the propitiation of both the natural objects and malevolent spirits. The Assamese term Deo or Deva signifying an evil spirit or a malevolent god was probably applied by the Magian immigrants to the Gods of aboriginal

Tibeto-Burmans who had to be appeased by crude worship and sacrifices. Hence the priestly class of Bodo tribes like the Chutiyas and the Tipperah later came to be known as Deoris or Deorais. The Alpine traits are discernible among the Nagas, the Bodos, the Lushais, the Manipuris and others who are racially Tibeto-Chinese speaking Mongoloid coming from North-East (20).

Dr. B. Sahni (21) writing on the "The Himalayan Uplift since the advent of Man" exposes this fact that there is evidence of contact between early human cultures on the two sides of the main Himalayas. Migration across mountains was possible in Palaeolithic times. The Himalayas were not a barrier to the migration of Palaeolithic or even the Neolithic men. Direct contact was established not only with China but also with Iran across the Himalayas since the dawn of human existence. "The migration of Alpine in India is believed to have taken place before the advent of the Vedic Aryans and towards the close of chalcolithic civilisation in Sind or nearly 5000 years ago." H. C. Chakladar (22) also refers to the contacts of Vedic Aryans with the people of Bengal and Assam. The Vedic Aryans settled in Assam about the beginning of Christian era. The Greek source (23) also supports this view. R. M. Nath (24), also holds the view that Maithili culture also "influenced the Austric and Bodo cultures sometimes by annihilation and sometimes by assimilation. Some of the Bodos and the Austrics held their own ground in the hill areas sometimes as vassals and sometimes as independent rulers. The Austric Ka-Meikha and the Bodo U-Mei-Ludai were gradually assimilated to the Hindu pantheon and became goddess Kamakhya and Siva Umananda." According to Pauranic evidence (25) Kuru, Panchala, Eastern Country, Kamarupa, Pundra, Kalinga, Magadha, Dakhisna had established their mutual contacts in the early period. Actually the eastward movement of the Aryans through Bihar and North Bengal towards this region paved the way for the fusion of the Aryan and Mongolian cultures. According to native chronicle (26) "Debaka, one of the principal habitatantes of the Mikirs upto this day is believed to be a fragment of the Devaka kingdoms forming part of the empire of the Imperial Guptas as we learn from the Allahabad Pillar inscription of Samudra Gupta; and the remains of old buildings and sculptures in the adjoining areas point to the existence of a flourishing Hindu state during the time of Samudra Gupta and his successors."

The contact of North-Eastern India with the rulers of Bengal, Orissa, Mithila and Magadha is a unique feature of Eastern Himalayan civilisation. Right from the time of Ashokan period to the Satavahan Age the cultural contacts among various racial groups were established in the regions stretching from Assam to China, which probably continued till the 13th century.

The various tribes belonging to the Austric group, Negroid group, Bodo group, Tibeto-Burman group and semi-Aryanised group evolved a mixed civilisation and developed various theological and philosophical doctrines which contributed to the growth of Hindu religion and culture known as Proto-Hinduism. The assimilation of non-Aryan religious beliefs and practices within the fold of Aryan culture and vice versa later became the twin pillars of composite Indian culture and civilisation. This period also witnessed the progress of aboriginal art in North-East India. Their monolithic marvels dating back to later Neolithic Age, Pre-historic finds, ancient monuments and relics of pre and post Christian era scattered all over the region, architectural remains, sculptural and iconographic arts, decoration and paintings undoubtedly testify to their attainment of high degree of artistic perfection. The observance of traditional ceremonies and festivals accompanied by music, songs and dances also formed an integral part of their civilisation. As a result of the political and cultural intercourse amongst the various racial groups a common pattern in respect of the society, economy, polity, art and architecture and religious beliefs can be noticed.

Whatever fragementary and recorded and unrecorded evidences we have got at our disposal, can certainly help us to form a general idea about the genesis and growth of tribal civilisation which reached its culmination to a considerable degree through the various processes. Further research may radiate more lights on the subject. Here we cannot fail to quote Atkinson (27) "The hill-tribes of Northern Himalaya-Khasa-Nagas, Kiratas and Cinas had attained to certain degree of civilisation in some respect superior to that reached by the Aryans of the Vedas. They lived in forts and walled towns."

Notes and References

1. J.A.R.S. (*The Journal of the Assam Research Society*), Apr. 1933, Vol. I, No. I, pp. 4-5.
2. *Indo-Aryan and Hindi,* pp. 37-38, Calcutta, 1969.
3. *History of Ancient Bengal,* pp. 251 f, 1st Edn. 1971.
4. J.A.R.S. July 1939, Vol. VII, No. 2, pp. 38, 39.
5. Ibid. pp. 40-41.
6. *Deodhai Assam Buranji*, pp. XXII, XXIV, XXV, XXVI, pp. 169-175, Gauhati, 1932; *Jaintia Buranji,* pp. 1-10, Gauhati, 1937.
7. J.A.R.S., July 1935, Vol. III, No. 2, p. 69.
8. B. K. Kakati, *The Mother Goddess Kamakhya*, pp. 10-16, Gauhati, 3rd Edn. 1967; R. M. Nath, *The Background of Assamese Culture*, pp. 4, 17, 95, Shillong, 1948.
9. *Skanda Purānā* (Kalyan Series), pp. 178-80 ; The *Mahābhārata, Adi Parva*, pp. 452-461, Verses-2-5.
10. *Deodhai Assam Buranji*, pp. 162-68, XXI.
11. W. W. Hunter, *The Statistical Account of Assam*, Vol. II, pp. 403-4, London 1879, Reptd. Delhi, 1975.
12. Montgomery and Martin, *Eastern India*, Vol. V, pp. 665, 690, Reptd. Delhi, 1976; Assam Sec. Private Sec. Office, Arch. Branch "B" Progs, June 1910 No. 7-9. *Proceedings of Lt. Governor of Eastern Bengal and Assam* June 1910, No. 18; J.A.S.B. 1900 Vol. LXIX, p. 45.

13. W. W. Hunter, *Statistical Account of Bengal*, Vol. VI, pp. 357-8, 463, London, 1876; H. H. Wilson, *Vishnu Purāṇa*, Ch. XVII, p. 354, Calcutta, 1961; *Vishnu Purāna* (Kalyan Series) p. 732; Pargiter, *Ancient Indian Historical Tradition*, Ch. IX, p. 109, Reptd, Delhi, 1972; Aitchison, *A collection of Treaties, Engagements and Sanads*, Vol. II, p. 173; Calcutta, 1930; K. L. Barua, J.A.R.S. Octo. 1935, Vol-III, No. 3, pp. 90-97; *Imperial Gazeetteer of India* 1908, p, 606; Report of E. F. Sandys Cf. S. Playne & C. *Bengal and Assam, Bihar and Orissa*, pp. 460 F. London, 1917; *Mahābhārata, Adi Parvan* Verses-35, pp. 2 3, 261-62.
14. Letters received from Govt. Vol. 8, Al. 1832. p. 368 ; Letters issued to Govt. Vol. II, No. 78, or 6, p. 265; Vol. of Letters received from Misc. Officers Vol-5 (a) 1840; *Proceedings of Chief Commissioner of Assam* (Foreign Dept.) 1890 No. 513.
15. *Lushai Chrysalis*, pp. 34-35, London, 1949.
16. J.A.R.S. July 1935, Vol-III, No. 2, p. 68.
17. D. T. Bloch. *Report of the Archaeological Tour in Assam* Jan. Feb. 1905; S. F. Hannay, J.A.S.B. 1848, Vol XVII, pp. 466-67, 471-72.
18. *Kāmarūpa Sāsanāvali*, p. 27 (Introd) Cf. J.A.R.S. July 1939, Vol. VII, No. 2, pp. 60-61.
19. J.A.S.B. 1897 Vol. LXVI, Pt. I, p. 129, First Plate, Verse-13.
20. J.A.R.S. Jan. 1936, Vol. Ill, No. 4, pp. 115, 131-132; J.A.R.S. July 1938, Vol. VI, No. 2, pp. 48-52.
21. Vide *Current Science,* Vol. V, No. 2 Aug. 1936 Cf. JARS July 1938 Vol. VI, No. 2, p. 46.
22. *The Aryan Occupation of Eastern India*, pp. 78 ff., Calcutta, 1962.
23. W. H. Schoff, *The Periplus of the Erythraean Sea*, p. 253, London 1912.
24. *Op. Cit.*, p. 27.
25. *Vishnu Purāna* (Kalyan Series), p. 671.
26. *Deodhai Assam Buranji*, pp. 209-14.
27. *The Himalayan Gazetteer*, Vol. II, Pt. I, p. 363, Delhi, 1973.

4

Āryanisation, Brahmanisation and Sanskritization in the Valley of Manipur in North-East India : A Historical Reappraisal

The beginnings of the process of Āryanisation in the valley of Manipur can be traced back to the Vedic age. There are some positive evidences to establish that one of the branches of those Āryans who migrated from Mithilā or Videha (north Bihar) and settled in the Brahmaputra valley towards the end of the later Vedic period entered Manipur through Surma or Barak valley where they disseminated Vedic religion, culture and philosophy as a result of which a large section of the non-Āryan Meitei population came within the pale of Āryanism[1]. The expansion of Āryan culture in Assam known in ancient times as Prāgjyotisha and Kāmarūpa, Manipur and Tripura from Videha region in the Vedic and post-Vedic times is a widely acknowledged fact[2]. Atombapu Sharma, a noted Sanskrit scholar of Manipur, has categorically stated that the Āryans came from Mithila and settled in the valley of Manipur in the Vedic age. He has emphasized again and again that the archaic religion of Manipur called "Sanātan Dharma" is of the Vedic antiquity[3]. This can further be corroborated by the statements of three other native scholars of Manipur, W. Yumjao Singh[4], L. Iboongohal Singh[5] and R.K. Jhalajit Singh[6]. They all have advocated the coming of several groups of Āryan to Manipur in the Vedic age and the diffusion of Vedic culture and civilisation there. It is said that those who became Āryanized became popularly known as "Ariwa" (represented by so-called high class Manipuris of today)[7]. The people in the valley gradually came under the influence of Āryan culture.

And Manipur became "a large Āryan colony in ancient times". However, the general statements of the former two scholars that the Meiteis are descendants of the Āryans of the Vedic age[8] are not beyond question[9]. Only a section of them can at best be taken as of Āryan origin because of Āryan settlements in the valley of Manipur but not the whole community. This fact can not be lost sight of that they by and large belong to Tibeto-Burman family of the Mongoloid race. A number of scholars have admitted that they belong to both Āryan and Mongoloid stocks[10]. The former is mainly represented by Manipuri Brahmanas. Their commingling and cultural fellowship led to the evolution of a synthesis of two different cultures - Āryan and Mongoloid which may also be called Sanskritic culture. Suniti Kumar Chatterji has rightly called it "The composite Ārya-Kirata culture of Manipur"[11]. The Aryanisation, in fact, marked the beginning of the process of Sanskritization.

The expansion of Āryan culture in the valley of Manipur in the Vedic age can very well be proved by the system of worship which prevailed there. The propitiation of Vedic gods, viz., Indra, Varuna, Agni (fire) and Sun, identified with old Manipuri gods - Soraren, Wangbaren, Mei and Numit respectively, show the influence of Vedic religion and culture on the traditional religious system of the people in the valley[12]. The archaeological discovery of stone sculptures of images of Vedic gods like Indra seated on Eirabat (elephant) in anthropomorphic form and Agni in a seated posture on the Vãhana (carrier) depicting two heads and three legs, kept on display in Mutua Museum, Imphal[13], also confirms the prevalence of Vedic faith there. The Meiteis' mode of worshipping fire in their dwelling houses was almost identical with that of the Vedic Āryans *(Rigveda,* VI, 1, Suktas 1-5). The striking similarity between the religious system of the Vedic Āryans and that of the Meiteis leaves no room for doubt about the coming of the latter within the fold of Āryan culture. The religious system of the valley people like that of the early Vedic Āryans was very much based on the doctrine of polytheism. The rituals and sacrifices which were followed by the later Vedic Āryans also formed part of their religious practices. The culture which flourished in Manipur in early times was purely of Vedic origin. J.T. Wheeler has rightly placed Manipur within the geographical limits of Vedic India[14]. The early phase of Aryanisation proved to be a milestone towards the foundation of Hinduism in Manipur. The non-Āryan inhabitants of Manipur valley assimilated many Āryan ideas in their primitive or animistic religious beliefs. The impact of Āryan religion, language, culture, manner and customs on the native population of Manipur set the stage for the growth of Hindu culture in the later period. Several elements of the Āryan culture which were introduced in the valley of Manipur seved as the base of Hinduism in the subsquent period of history.

There are some authentic evidences to prove that some sections of the Brāhmanas and Kshatriyas (representing ruling class) of "pure Āryan blood" from northern India including the Gangetic plains also settled in the Valley of Manipur in the pre and post Christian era while passing through it (being the safest land-route) to Burma and other South-East Asian countries for spreading their religion, languages (Sanskrit and Pāli) and culture by founding kingdoms and setting up colonies there[15]. Those Brahmanas and Kshatriyas who settled in Manipur were gradually absorbed in the original settlers of the land leaving behind the indelible imprints of their religion, culture and philosophy on them. The incorporation of some Brahmi and Devanāgari letters in the archaic script of Manipur, which came into use as early as the eight century A.D., bears the stamp of the system of writing of the speakers of the Sanskrit and Pali languages the details of which have been provided in the MS *Mayek Laisak Khangba* (study of the alphabets). Manipur Brāhmanas were known to the Burmese as "Ponnas" and Kshatriyas as "Kathe" (Kathians of classical geographers and historians)[16]. It is striking to note that most of the Manipuri kings belonged to Kshatriya class. The tradition preserved in the Burmese chronicles also affirms the Kshatriya colonization of Manipur and Burma dating back to several centuries before Christ[17]. According to the *Mahar*ā*j*ā*vamsa,* the royal chronicle of Burma, Dhajaraja, a king of the Sãkya race (of Kshatriya clan) settled at Manipur about 550 B.C. and later on conquered upper Burma[18]. There are some incidental allusions to the brahmanic rule in Manipur before the dawn of the Christian era[19].

The period extending from the fourth to the seventh century A.D. was very eventful so far as the brahmanical influence in Manipur is concerned. There are some fragmentary evidences to show the visits of Brahmin priests from Bengal and other places to this ancient land at regular intervals. They were, of course, absorbed in the Meitci population and lost their identity as Brahmanas but left behind some traces of their culture[20]. The worship of goddess Durga in Manipur in the fifth century A.D. as stated by L. Iboongohal Singh[21], might have been introduced by this group of Brahmanas. However, this was a passing phase. The coming of Brahmanas from Bengal to Manipur in early period does not strike any wonder in view of the fact that from Mithtã and Kãmarupa (the two main centres of Nagar Brahmanas) many Brahmanas immigrated to eastern India and Bengal between the fifth and seventh century A.D.[22]

By the end of the eighth century A.D. Manipur came under the influence of Hindu culture to a considerable extent which can be proved by an epigraphic evidence. A copper plate inscription in archaic Manipuri script dated Saka 721 (A.D. 799) issued by king Khongtekcha (A.D. 765-799), which was discovered by Yumjao Singh (a pioneer archaeologist of Manipur) from Phayeng village, about 9 miles west of Imphal, and also deciphered by him, testifies to the prevalence of worship of Siva, Durga, Hari, Ganesh and other brahmanical gods and goddesses[23], which marks the transition from Vedism to Brahmanism. The popularity of

Shaivism, Shaktism and Tantricism, the three sects of Hinduism, in early Manipur can also be proved by other reliable evidences[24]. S.K. Chatterji observes : "The Meitheis or Manipuris appear to have entered the Hindu fold at least as early as the 8th century when Vaishnavism spread among them...."[25]. In the eighth century A.D., the Hindu influence in Manipur is believed to have spread from Kāmarūpa after a band of people came from that place with venecer of Hinduism at the request of the said king and settled at Bishnupur named after their tutelary deity, Vishnu, which they carried with them[26].

The Meiteis, in fact, came under the influence of various cultures in ancient times which gave fillip to the process of Sanskritization in the valley of Manipur.

The later half of the fifteenth century marked the opening of a new chapter in the history of evolution of brahmanical culture in Manipur. The immigration of Brāhmanas into Manipur from different parts of India in successive waves began during the reign of the famous king Kyamba alias Chintamani (A.D. 1467-1508) and continued till the time of Gambhir Singh (A.D. 1825-1834). During the period a large number of Brahmanas migrated from Mathurā, Vrindāban, Nandagrāma, Kānyakubja or Kanauj, Kanpur and Prayag in U.P., Magadha in Bihar, Nabadvipa, Nadiya, Krishnagar and Shantipur in West Bengal, Shrihatta or Sylhet and Dhaka in erstwhile east Bengal, Puri in Orissa, Assam, Tripura, Nepal, Gujarat, Lahore and other places to Manipur, settled in its valley, got social recognition, enjoyed royal patronages, received different family titles and married local women whose offsprings became the progenitors of many Brahmin families of today, as recorded in the native chronicles (published)[27], an unpublished genealogical record[28] and other collateral sources[29] of great historical value. As the Muslim rulers of Bengal and U.P. in medieval times adopted intolerant religious policy, the Brāhmanas there could not profess and propagate their religion freely. Thus in order to enjoy complete religious freedom they migrated from there to Manipur. The reasons of migration of Brahmanas from other parts of India and Nepal are not known to us. However, they became part and parcel of the Meitei community. And they began to propagate the brahmanical religion and culture on a large scale which paved the way for the rise and growth of Hinduism which was declared as state religion in the early eighteenth century.

In the wake of brahmanization the Vaishnava Missionaries of different schools also came to Manipur to preach their respective Vaishnava faith and to carry on proselytizing work. The king Charairongpha (1697-1709) was converted to Vaishnavism in 1704 by a Brahmin priest named Krishnacharya from Shweta-Ganga, Puri (Orissa), as recorded in one of the royal chronicles of Manipur[30]. He embraced Gaudiya or Chaitanya Vaishnavism and adopted the Sanskritized name - Pitambar Singh. Garibniwaj (1709-1748), one of the renowned kings of Manipur, was formally initiated to Vaishnavism in 1717 by his Guru Gopal Das. A Vaishnava preacher named Shantidas Goswami, who belonged to Ramanandi school, came to Manipur from Sylhet sometime between 1720 and 1728 to popularise the worship of Rama, Sita and Hanuman. Initially he achieved remarkable success in his mission as the king along with his followers accepted his faith. But the king ultimately embraced Chaitanya cult of Vaishnavism which laid great emphasis on the worship of Shri Krishna as the Supreme deity and that of his consort, Radha[31]. This cult was based on the doctrine of bhakti or devotion and Bhagavata tradition. As a matter of fact, during the time of this king both the schools of Vaishnavism, Chaitanya school and Ramanandi school, flourished side by side, but the former triumphed over the latter. The king finally declared the Vaishnava form of Hinduism as the state religion[32]. A large number of the people (Meiteis) were brought within the fold of Hinduism[33]. This was a very important phase of Sanskritization. However, the fact remains that this religion was popularised by him more by imposition than by persuasion. W. McCulloch, one of the authorities on the history of Manipur, has also remarked that "Hindu religion has been professed not from conviction, and it is but a fashion"[34]. But this is only partly correct. It may be added here that the Meiteis of today are the non-tribal Hindu population predominantly inhabiting the valley of Manipur. Bhagyachandra Singh (1759-1798), another famous king of Manipur, also popularised the Chaitanya cult of Vaishnavism. This cult further retained its popularity during the times of his successors.

The spread of brahmanical religion and culture had far-reaching impact on the contemporary society, religion and culture, art and architecture, sculpture and iconography, coins and inscriptions, language and literature, dance, drama and music.

As a result of introduction of brahmanical culture the traditional social customs and rites and rituals were gradually modified. The rites of birth, marriage and death were performed in conformity with the Hindu ideals and practices. The sacred thread was adopted by both Brãhmanas and Kshatriyas. The Brãhmanas performed religious ceremonies and conducted the rites and rituals along with the old family priests called Maibas and priestesses called Maibis. In fact, they were the joint custodians of socio-cultural tradition. McCulloch's view that the Brãhmanas did not command any respect and their doctrines were not accepted[35], can be disposed of. The Brahmanas no doubt occupied an important position in the Meitei society but their supremacy was never acknowledged. As they represented the upper class, the feeling of low and high emerged in the society, and social distinction was maintained to some extent. But the caste rule was not applied. In fact, the classes and castes as such did never exist in the Meitei society.

The spread of brahmanical culture led to the transformation of old aniconic form of worship into an iconic form of worship. The worship of icons of Hindu pantheon began from the fifteenth century onwards. The images of Hindu gods and goddesses were carved on stones and woods and installed in the newly constructed temples and at other sacred and historically important places for their worship which helped in the propagation of Hinduism. The image of Vishnu was first installed in the Vishnu temple at Bishnupur, about 18 miles south-west of Imphal. A brick temple dedicated to Lord Krishna was constructed by Charairongpha at Brahmapur Guru Aribam Leikai which is still in excellent state of preservation. During the time of Garibniwaj the images of Rama and Hanuman - (or Mahabali) were carved and placed in the temples at Wangkhei. A temple dedicated to Shri Krishna was also built during his time (probably in 1722). Bhagyachandra Singh installed the wooden image of Shri Govindaji (a manifestation of Krishna) for its worship which is now in the Govindaji temple within the palace compound of the Maharaja. All those Hindu temples were looked after by the Brahmanas. Gambhir Singh was also a true devotee of Shri Krishna. It was during his reign that the images of Lord Jagannath, Balabhadra and Subhadra were installed for the first time in Manipur. Besides, the images of Krishna and Balaram were also installed. He introduced many important religious festivals like Rathayãtra, etc.

Most of the coins which were struck between the seventeenth and the nineteenth century bear Sanskrit legend in Devanãgari script. The inscriptions of the same period also contain some Sanskrit words.

The importance of the study of Sanskrit language and literature steadily increased for which the credit goes to Brahman Pandits. During the time of Garibniwaj the whole Kritivasi *Rãmãyaṇa* (in Bengali version) and the *Ãdi* and *Ashvamedhika* Parvans of Gangadas Sen's *Mahãbhãrata* composed in the sixteenth century, were rendered into Manipuri. Later, the *Rigveda,* the *Bhãgavat Purãaṇa*, the

Bhãgavad Gitã, *Gita Govinda* of Jayadeva, etc. were translated into Manipuri with parallel original Sanskrit verses. *Dharani Samhitã*, a Sanskrit text, was compiled during the time of Gambhir Singh. It is also worthwhile to mention that from the middle of the eighteenth century onwards the Bengali script was adopted in place of the archaic Meitei Script.

Manipuri dance, drama and music also felt the impact of brahmanical culture. A new form of dance known as *Rãsalila*, which is intimately connected with Chaitanya School of Vaishnavism, became very popular during the time of king Bhagyachandra Singh. This dance later got recognition as one of the six prominent Schools of Indian classical dances. However, old pre-Hindu ritualistic dances like the Lai-Haraoba (the rejoicing of God) did not lose its importance. A New school of drama also came into being which was fundamentally based on the Vaishnavite themes. It was staged under different names. The Brãhmanas made significant contribution to the development of Manipuri classical music known as 'Nat' based on six *ragas* and thirty-six *raginis* expounded in the Sanskrit texts on Indian classical music. The Brãhmanas well versed in musicology composed various types of song, including the devotional ones, both in Sanskrit and Bengali. The process of Sanskritization reached its culmination by the end of the nineteenth century. All these developments accelerated the pace of Hinduisation.

It is significant to note that despite all the changes that took place in the social and religious life of the Meiteis following the rapid expansion of brahmanical culture, as noted above, their age old customs, traditions, religious beliefs and rites and rituals continued to survive. Their traditional religion based on animistic cult flourished side by side with Hinduism. The worship of their primitive gods and goddesses like Sanamahi and Panthoibi went on with that of Hindu deities or divinities (of mainly Shaiva, Shakti and Vaishnava sects) like Vishnu, Shiva, Durgã, Kãli and Krishna. More or less the same system continues till today. T.C. Hodson is also of the view that the Meitei religion represents the synthesis of animism and Hinduism[36]. This marks the syncretism of two different faiths. This is generally described as a syncretic form of Hinduism. The Vedic, Purãnic, Brahmanic and Vaishnava doctrines got assimilated or harmonized with the old faiths and beliefs of the Meiteis. J. Shakespear has correctly stated that the progress of Hinduism in Manipur was achieved through compromise with ancient faith, non-Hindu cults, etc.[37]. This can best be qualified in the words of Suniti Kumar Chatterji: "Manipur Hinduism gradually became a synthesis of the old Meithei religion with gods and goddesses and myths, its own legends and traditions, its social customs and usages, and its priests and ceremonials, and of Brahmanical Hinduism with its special worship of Radha and Krishna"[38]. This also shows the religious and cultural integration of Manipur[39].

Notes and References

1. H.C. Chakladar, *The Aryan Occupation of Eastern India* (Calcutta, 1962), pp. 78, 188; "Aryans in Eastern India in Rigvedic Age", *Modern Review* (Calcutta, Jan. 1930), pp. 40-44; "Eastern India and Aryavarta", *Indian Historical Quarterly (*herein after abbrev. as IHQ), IV. pp. 84-101; J. Johnstone, *My Experiences in Manipur and the Naga Hills* (London, 1896, reptd., Delhi, 1971). p. 130; R. Brown, *Statistical Account of the Native State of Manipur and the Hill Territory under its Rule* (Calcutta, 1874, reptd. Delhi, 1975), p. 21.

2. For details see R.C. Majumdar, *Expansion of Aryan Culture in Eastern India* (Imphal, 1968), pp. 27-32, 35, 39-40; V.R.R. Dikshitar, "Aryanisation of East India-Assam", IHQ, XXI (1945), pp. 29-33; D.R. Bhandarkar, "Aryan immigration into Eastern India", *Annals of the Bhandarkar Oriental Research Institute,* XXI, pp. 103-16; N.K. Dutta, *Aryanization of India* (Calcutta, 1925), pp. 5ff; R.C. Dutt, *Ancient India* (2000 B.C. - 800 A.D.): *Epochs of Indian History* (Delhi, 1980), p.7; S.S. Tunga, "Aryanisation in

North-East India", *North-Eastern Affairs* (a Quarterly study of trends & events), III, 4 (Shillong, 1975), pp. 17-32.

3. *Rigveda,* pt. 1 (Imphal, 1960), pp. 24-43; *Manipur Ka Sanatan Dharma* (Imphal, 1951), pp. 20-25; *Meitei Hareimaye* (tr. into Eng. by A. Dorendrajit Singh, Imphal, 1934), pp. 1-20.
4. An *Early History of Manipur* (Imphal, 1966), pp.13-27, 63-72.
5. *An Introduction to Manipur* (Imphal, 1963), pp.14-16.
6. A *Short History of Manipur* (Imphal, 1965), pp.11-12, 21-24.
7. Iboongohal Singh, *op.cit;* pp. 11-12, 14; Jhalajit Singh, *op.cit.,* p. 11.
8. Atombapu Sharma, *Rigveda,* pp. 24ff; Yumjao Singh, *op.cit.,* pp. 13ff, 63ff.
9. See Ch. Manihar Singh, *The Meitei: Origin and Affinity* (Imphal, 1984), pp. 9-25; G. Kabui, *History of Manipur,* Vol. I (Delhi, 1991), pp. 12, 15-16.
10. Johnstone, *op.cit.,* pp. 80-1; Brown, *op.cit.,* p. 57; E.W. Dun, *The Gazetteer of Manipur* (1st edn. Shimla, 1886, reptd. Delhi, 1975), pp. 6, 15, notes; B.C. Alien, E.A. Gait & Co., *Gazetteer of Bengal and North-East India* (Delhi, 1979), p. 614.
11. *Kirata-Jana-Krti* (Calcutta, 1974), p. 156.
12. Yumjao Singh, *op.cit.,* pp. 63-69,71-84; Iboongohal Singh, *op.cit.,* pp. 14-17, 27-31; Jhalajit Singh, *op.cit.,* pp. 21-25; S.K. Chatterji, *Religious and Cultural Integration of India* (Imphal, 1967), pp. 41ff; K.B. Singh, *Himalaya, Man and Nature,* III, 5 (Octob, 1979), p. 11.
13. *Sculptures of Manipur,* Bulletin of Mutua Museum, Imphal, No. 2, Dec. 1982.
14. *India of the Vedic Age* (Delhi, 1973), pp. 148-9.
15. Majumdar, *op.cit.,* pp. 47-49; *Hindu Colonies in the Far East* (Calcutta, 1944), p. 14; *Ancient Indian Colonies in the Far east,* Vol.1 (Dhaka, 1927), pp. 13-4; R.B. Pemberton, *Report on the Eastern Frontier of British India* (Calcutta, 1835, reptd. Gauhati, 1966), pp. 51, 55-6; A. Phyre, *A History of Burma* (London, 1883), pp. 3-4, 15; G.E. Harvey,

History of Burma (London, 1925), p. 9f; Johnstone, *op. cit.,* pp. 80-81, 97; Dun, *op. cit.,* p. 6, note; Abdul Ali, *Notes on the Early History of Manipur* (Calcutta, 1923), p. 3; J. Roy, *History ofManipur* (Calcutta, 1973), p. 5; Yumjao Singh, *op. cit.,* pp. 29-30, 118, 124-26; Iboongohal Singh, *op. cit.,* pp. 56-7.

16. Yumjao Singh, *op. cit.,* pp. 21-24.
17. A letter dated 30th Sept. 1950 written by S.K. Chatterji to Yumjao Singh also throws some light on the subject concerned.
18. G.E. Gerini, *Researches on Ptolemy's Geography of Eastern Asia* (London, 1909), p. 745.
19. *Ibid.,* p. 33; E.A. Gait, C.C.H. Alien & H.F. Howard, *Gazetteer of Burma,* Vol. I (Delhi, 1983) pp. 236-7.
20. Chatterji, *op.cit.,* p. 28; Jhalajit Singh, *op. cit.,* p. 44; Roy, *op. cit.,* pp. 22-23; N. Khelchandra Singh, *Ariba Manipuri Sahityagi Itihasa* (Imphal, 1969), p. 67; S.N. Paratt. *The Religion of Manipur* (Calcutta, 1980), p. 103.
21. *Op.cit.,* p. 31.
22. See D.R. Bhandarkar, "The Nagar Brãhmanas and the Bengal Kayasthas", *Indian Antiquary,* LXI (1932) pp. 41-55, 67-72.
23. *Report on the Archaeological Studies in Manipur,* Bulletin No. 1 (Imphal, 1935), pp. 40-43, App. 1.
24. Chatterji, *op. cit.,* pp. 42-44, 48; Yumjao Singh *The Religious Belief of Ancient* Manipur (Imphal, 1966), pp. 28-9; *Vijay Panchãli* (History of Manipur in English), ed. by M. Jhulon Singh, Pt. 1, (Imphal, 1936), p. 14; J. Shakespear, "The Religion of Manipur", *Transactions of the Folk-Lore Society,* XXIV, 4 (Calcutta, 1913), p. 19.
25. *Kirãta-Jana-Krti,* p. 48.
26. R.M. Nath, *The Background of Assamese Culture,* (Shillong, 1948), pp. 86, 88.
27. *Bamon Khunthoklon,* ed. by H. Ibopishak Meitei (Imphal, 1987), pp. 3-11; *Cheitharol Kumbaba* (herein after abbrev. as CK), ed. by N. Khelchandra Singh and Iboongohal Singh (Imphal, 1967), pp. 36, 56-58, 64f, 122,129 : Vijay *Panchali,* pp. 85-87.

28. *Bamon Meihaobarol* (without any page number).
29. Iboongohal Singh, *op. cit.*, pp. 31-33, 207-11, Jhalajit Singh, *op. cit.*, pp. 82, 90, 95, 104, 113-16, 138, 167, 206; also his "The Migration of Brahmins and its Impact on the Culture of Manipur", Proceed, of the NEI Hist. Assoc. (Imphal, 1982), pp. 84ff; W. Ibohal Singh *A History of Manipur* (early period) (Imphal, 1986), pp. 574-81, 606-7.
30. CK, pp. 56-58, 60.
31. *Ibid.*, pp. 83, 85-87; *Vijay Panchali*, p. 65.
32. *Ibid,*, pp. 64-66, 69; T.C. Hodson, *The Meitheis* (London, 1908, reptd. Delhi 1984) p. 45; *Encyclopaedia of Religion and Ethics,* VIII (1964), pp. 402-3.
33. C.U. Aitchison, *A Collection of Treaties, Engagements and Sanads Relating to India and Neighbouring Countries,* Vol. XII (Calcutta, 1931), p. 102.
34. *An Account of the Valley of Manipur and of the Hill Tribes,* (Calcutta, 1859), pp. 17-8.
35. *Ibid.*, p. 18.
36. *Op. cit.*, pp. 95 & 97.
37. *Op. cit.*, pp. 414 & 451.
38. *Op. cit.*, p. 153; see also his "A Manipuri Purana",' Manipur Public' Library, Annual No. 1954, p. 6f.
39. See S.K. Chatterji, *Religious and Cultural Integration of India,* pp. 19ff. 41-49.

5

The History of Rise and Growth of Hinduism and Buddhism among the Tribal People of North-East India

This paper aims at presenting as far as possible a historical account of the rise and growth of Hinduism and Buddhism among the tribal people of north-east India.

The four-fold sub-divisions of Hinduism - Saivism, Saktism, Tantricism and Vaishnavism-emerged as popular religious cults, coexisted with the aboriginal forms of worship and further flourished after the coming of a large number of tribes within their fold. This gives us some idea of the growth of tribal religio-cultural and philosophical system. It is worthy of note that the slow infiltration of the Āryan ideas, Aryanised Gods and mode of worship, the proselytizing activities of the Brãhmanas, and assimilation of the brahmanical doctrines into the non-Āryan faiths, beliefs and practices paved the way for the evolution of the synthesis of the Indo-Mongoloid and Indo-Āryan cultures as well as set in the process which eventually gave birth to intermittent character of Hinduism popularly known as "proto-Hinduism". The antiquity, variety and vitality of Hinduism that prevailed among the tribal people also deserve our notice.

The rise of new faith-Buddhism of both Hinayana and Mahayana schools - which was imported from Magadha, Tibet, Burma and other neighbouring Buddhistic kingdoms between the seventh century and the eighteenth century was another remarkable event in the tribal religio-cultural history. This faith was accepted by the sizeable section of the tribal population.

The subject under notice has been neither properly explored nor thoroughly investigated. The study of the subject is based on literary evidence, archaeological evidence (numismatic, epigraphic, ruins and remains), native chronicles, Persian annals, historical records, documentary evidence, popular traditions, and some contemporary sources.

While dealing with the rise and growth of Hinduism, some light can be thrown on the characteristic features of the major religious cults and some other minor religious cults that gained popularity among the tribal people. Among the principal sub-divisions of Hinduism, Saivism and Saktism are generally reckoned as prominent religious group. It is true that outline of Śaiva cult is found in Vedic writing but later centuries added new features to it, the chief among which is the worship of column known as the linga emblem under which Śiva is now most commonly adored. The phallic worship among the aboriginal tribesmen in ancient times is historically a proven fact. The old theory that it was borrowed from Dravidians is no longer valid. The royal patronage was extended to the propagation of Mother Cult but Saivism continued to be the popular religion among the tribal people. The Saktism identified with the active female principle *(Prakriti)* of Sankhya philosophy or with the Maya of Advaita philosophy, defined as energy and co-existent with Brāhmanas, was manifested in one or other form of worship of Śakti under various names, Devi or Pārvati, Durgā and Kali, in accordance with the rites prescribed in the Tantras. Though the Śakti is theoretically one, yet she assumes many forms. Sometimes many deities are combined into one and sometimes a sovereign is attended by a retinue of similar female spirits. Among such forms we find the ten Mahāvidyas, or personifications of her super-natural knowledge, the Mahamatris, Matrikas or the Great Mothers, allied to the aboriginal goddesses, the Yoginis or sorceresses and Dakins. But the most popular of her mainfestations are Durgā and Kāli. The forces of nature are identified under separate personalities known as Divine Mother and old ideas are revived with fresh and more impure association. The ritual of the sect prescribing blood offerings and other abominale libidinous rites found in the Tantras embodying cruder form of belief are as old as Athrava Veda but that has subsequently developed. Later, probably in the post Harsha period, it left its indelible mark on Tantrik Buddhism. North-Eastern India was decidedly teh birth place of Saktism. Along with Satism Tantricism - a system of magical or sacramental ritual—also became popular. The Sakti cult gained more popularity than the Tantric one among the tribal people of north-eastern India. The system of propitiating the female deities adhering to the doctrine of Saktism was prevalent among some of the tribes in ancient and medieval times. The Vaishnavism, one of the major religious cults, acquired influence among some of the tribal people in early medieval period. The doctrine of Bhakti greatly influenced them. The tribal minor religious cults largely based on their indigenous faiths or traditional beliefs co-existed with those major religious cults within the fold of which they came.

According to *Kālikā Puāana*[1], before the advent of Naraka (a Mytho-historical figure) in pre-Yudhisthira period the whole of Prāgjyotisha was inhabited by the aboriginals known as the Kirātas. In the heart of Pragjyotish, the Mother-Goddess Kāmākhyā ("the Goddess of sexual desire" and chief sanctuary of Saktism) was Nāyikā of Kāmarūpa. After being subjugated and annihilated by Naraka in a war, the Kirātas were driven away towards the Dikkaravāsini and Lalitakāntā in the east where they later settled. The whole Pragjyotisha (later known as Kāmarūpa) was bounded on the east by Dikkaravasini. On the basis of some reliable sources,[2] mainly the literary and classical, the Kirātas can be identified with the Khasis and the Jaintias (the Austrics), the Garos, the Kacharis, the Chutiyas and Hill-Tipperahs (the Bodos), the Nagas, the Mikirs, the Akas, the Idu Mishmis and probably the other tribes belonging to Indo-

Mongoloid group having the admixture of both Aryan and non-Āryan bloods living at present in different hill regions of north-east India. At the time of dispersing in different groups from Kāmarūpa into the hills the Khasi-Jaintias, Kacharis and Chutiyas carried away with them the Cult of Mother Goddess as replica of the past life. D.C.Sircar[3] locates Dikaravāsini temple near Paya in Lohit District of NEFA (present Arunachal Pradesh) and associates Lalitakāntā with hill-streams of sandhya Lalita and Kanta not far from Kāmākhyā temple in the ancient city of Prāgjyotisha. The Paurāṇic account is supported by varied sources. H.H. Wilson[4] has also referred to the Naraka episode of Prāgjyotisha. In another faithful record[5] it is clearly mentioned that the Kāmākhyā temple of Śakti (Śiva's consort) very famous in ancient time was a great centre of bloody or sensual form of worship as inculcated in the Tantras. Probably it had its origin in Kāmarupa. *Yoginitantra* furnishes the evidence that the religion of Yogini Pitha (Kāmākhyā) was of Kirāta origin *("Siddhesi Yogini Pithe Dharmah Kairatajahmatah")*[6]. No wonder, the Kāmākhyā was an embodiment of the fusion of the Āryan and non-Āryan beliefs and practices. Charles Eliot has rightly observed that it claims to be a revelation from Siva himself but from historical standpoint "it appears to be compound of Hinduism with un-Āryan beliefs. It acquired great influence both in the courts and among the people of North-Eastern India but without producing personalities of much eminence as teachers or writers."[7] Saivism or Saktism as testified to by these trustworthy accounts was certainly the prevailing religion of the above mentioned Kirata people especially the Khasis, the Jaintias, the Garos, the Kacharis and Tippera tribes in both pre-and post - Naraka period.

The history of Saivism, the most ancient living faith in the world, dates back to the Chalcolithic Age. According to B.K. Kakati, Śiva worship was the most popular form of religion in early times both amongst the aboriginal and the Aryanised people. In the pre-historic legendry period, Śiva appears to have been the popular God amongst the aboriginal people. It is quite probable that aboriginal Kirātas were under the protection of Śiva. Saivism in some gross form associated with wine and flesh was the prevailing religion of the aboriginal Kirātas. "The Aryanised conquerors held this religion in disdain and placed it under a ban. At the same time to secure easy recognition by aboriginal people they brought to prominence, another local cult—the cult of Mother Goddess— worshipped in the Yoni symbol as opposed to the cult of Śiva worshipped in the phallic symbol. The mother cult of Kāmākhyā must have belonged to certain matriarchal tribes like the Khasis and the Garos."[8] Saivism as testified to by this account was certainly the prevailing religion of the Khasis, the Jaintias and the Garos before the advent of Naraka in Assam in Pre-Yudhisthira period. At the same time, the Khasi-Jaintias in particular had faith in the worship of Mother Goddess. They used to worship Kāmākhyā Devi before coming to their present home in Meghalaya. The worship of Kāmākhyā was no doubt tribal in origin. Later, the Hindu mode of worship was adopted. This statement is further confirmed by R.M. Nath, who holds the view that Kamei-Kha was the Austric name and later on it was called Kāmākhyā by the Hindus. "The Bodos installed the Phallic emblem of their worship near the Austric Kameikha. The Austrics termed this emblem by the name Umei-Ludai-Fia (a sign of masculine gender, Mei = Mother, Ludai = male genital organ, Fia = pha = God). This name underwent transformation to Umaluda—Umanuda and is now known as Umananda—a Śiva-Lingam on the peacock island in the middle of the Brahmaputra opposite Gauhati, traditionally believed to be the consort of Kamakhya. The Bodos called the Austric Kameikha the genital organ of Mother Earth, Kamei-Fria (Fria=Famale God)."[9] The Khasis and Syntengs lived containing the holy-Shrine of Kameikha. He further points out that "As a proto-type of Kamei-kha which was the holiest shrine of the Khasis and the Jaintias, a similar shrine was eatablished in the southern slope of the Jaintia Hills where a natural spring flowed round a rock... This was named Griva-Kāmākhyā and was represented as the shoulder of the Śupreme Mother. Near this rock was installed a massive Śiva-Lingam and it was named Hatakeswarat."[10] Jayanta, one of the Jaintia kings, established another Kamakhya in the south-estern part of the kingdom on the slope of the hill near kanaighat and nemed it Bama-Jangha-Pitha or the left thigh shrine and the stone emblem was identified as the left thigh of the supreme Mother from its shape. Ram Singh—II (1790-1832), a great devotes of Śiva, constructed a sky scraping Śiva Temple on the top of the hillock of Dubi near the Shari bridge.

In the Jaintia Hills Hinduism also flourished through royal patronage which can be proved on the basis of epigraphic records. The Jaintiapur Copper-Plate Inscriptions of Mahadevi Kasasati, wife of king Badagosayi of Jaintiapur dated Śakābda 1710 (A.D. 1788), 1723 (A.D. 1801) and 1725 (A.D. 1803) bear an eloquent testimony to the prevalence of the worship of the Gods and Gddesses like Vishnu, Kali, Brahmā, Durgā, Rādhā and Krishna. These Copper Plates record three grants issued from time to time. The first inscription dated Sakābda 1710 (A.D. 1788) records a grant of twenty halas of land by this queen of Jaintiapur to the Goddess Kālikā established in Shri Lilapuri Sannyas's abode (Matha) apparently at Jaintiapur. Two halas of lands were granted to Brāhmanas and oil presser attending the Goddess Kālikā and temple. The grant formed a part of royal domain. Two halas of lands in Nayavanakhala of Devipur was given to Shri Vishnu for the pleasure of Vishnu. Another grant dated Śakābda 1723 (A.D. 1801) Ashadha records that land measuring two and half halas, that is thirty Kedaras, in village (Purvaphanda attached to Nayavana) was given for the pleasure of Goddess Durgā and Kāli. Later on, in Śakābda 1725 (A.D. 1803) two halas of land, that is 24 Kedaras, lying in village Ḍalaikandi was given for the pleasure of "Sri Rādhā-Krishna" and ceremony of Doljatra in the Kalika Matha and at Ujaninagara.[11] This can be corroborated by other sources[12] also. The Goddess like Kāli representing Śakti and procreative force manifested in the female form worshipped by tribesmen and other Goddess like Bhairavi are not product of purely Hindu imagination but representating earlier stage of amalgamation in which Hindu and aboriginal ideas are clearly compounded. According to Syed-Sayeed-ud-din Ahmad, it was in the epic age that Jaintiapur was occupied by the Āryans and Brāhmin kings. "In the reign of Zoodhisthir several Brahminical Kings occupied the throne of Jaintiapur. Towresh-Khaynehray at that period was a prince (The Raja of Jaintia and Brāhman)".[13] The religious and ceremonial rites were completely Hinduized under the priesthood of the Brāhmaṇas.

It may be noted here that there were several stages of the growth of Hinduism among the Jaintias. Their capital Jaintiapur was situated in east Bengal and included twenty-two parganas of the modern Sylhet district. They came under the influence of Hindu religion and culture of Bengal. The Jaintia Rajas were strong champion of Hinduism. They were followers of the Śakta sect of Hinduism. Nartiang and Jaintiapur were the two strongholds of Hindu culture. The Durgā Bāri at Nartiang and Mahādeva, Than at Syndai were established in the fifteenth century and Bengali Brahmins were appointed as the temple priests by the Rajas. Of all the cults of Hinduism, Tāntrik Śakti cult was the most popular among the Jaintias. Human sacrifices were prevalent in the Durgā temple at Nartiang and the Kāli temple at Jaintiapur. Hinduism had reached the height of its progress in the Jaintia hills before the coming of the British. It is recorded that three British subject were sacrificed by the Raja of Goba, a vassal or feudatory of Jaintia, wich furnished the pretext for the British to annex Jaintia hills in 1835. The Jaintia kings of Sutnga also embraced Hinduism. The Hindu kings of Jaintia had encouraged the performance of Hindu rites and ceremonies.

The last Jaintia king Rajendra Singh (1832-35) adopted Vaishnava form of Hinduism. He is credited with having composed devotional songs on Radha-Krishna in Bengali.

There was some impact of Hinduism on the Pnar Khasis (Syntengs) because of their frequent contacts with the Hindus of the plains. They had, in fact, territorial proximity. In the beginning of the 19th century, a Vaishnava Ashram was in existence at Shella, one of the Khasi states contiguous to the Sylhet plains. The worship of the Hindu deities like Śiva, Durgā, Kāli, Lakshmi and Ranachandi was in vogue among the Khasi-Jaintias.

Śiva is said to have adopted the appearance of the Kirata and considered the special deity of that race. The Himalaya born Goddess Umā and Gangā have the nick-name of Kirāti.[14] This view can also be corroborated by a classical author.[15]

The tradition certifies that right from the epic age till the period unknown the Khasis (living at present in the Khasi Hills of Meghalaya)used to worship the Jyotilinga of Shilanath in a cave temple. Later it was installed in a temple built at comparatively modern time in Shillong. The Śaiva-Śakti cult was practised by the non-Āryans under Brahmanic auspices. It formed no part of the Aryan religion. The scriptures, *Kālikā Purāna,* and *Yoginitantra* set the guide lines for the further practice of the cult. Thus, on the basis of all recorded evidences and popular tradition this fact can undoubtedly be admitted that Saivism and Saktism were the popular forms of religion among the non-Āryan tribes in Pre-Vedic or Pre-Āryan period. In one of the sources,[16] it is wrongly mentioned that the Mother Cult arose in Eastern Bengal or Assam about 5th century A.D. and was opposed by the Vaishnava reformer. This date can be outrightly rejected.

Dealing with the Garos (living at present in the Garo Hills), Montgomery Martin Categorically stated that some of them were also converted to the worship of Vishnu[17].

According to *Rigveda,* Brahmā, Vishnu, and Rudra or Śiva are the different attributes of the same. Actually Śakti worship was common to both Śaivas and Vaishnavas. Vishnu himself is believed to have permitted Naraka to worship the Goddess Kāmākhyā. Saktism was associated with the principle of toleration and liberalism. The Terracota Fragments (belonging to 5th, 6th, 8th, 9th and 12th centuries) collected by G.N. Bhuyan[18] from Bhaitbari in the Garo Hills show that the Garos worshipped the Śivalinga in the temple, and also the other Gods and Goddess like Ganesha, Manasa and Kartikeya.

Śaivism also flourished in North-Cachar Hills. The earliest account available shows that Vikramaditya-pha (1410-1469) installed the first Vana-Lingam Śiva image in a temple on the bank of the tank named the city Vanpur after the deity. Later on, the stone image of Vishnu was installed. In the 18th century when process of Hinduisation started the temples of Śiva were set up in different parts of the country. The rock-cave temple of Hara-Pārvati on the Bhubaneswar Hill originally constructed by the Tipperah Kings was kept up in glorious condition while the Vishnu temple at Chao-Bang (Subang) near Vikrampur oginally constructed about the seventh century A.D.... was allowed to fall into decay."[19] This is further supported by archaeological evidences which refer to Śiva temple on a low hill Chandragiri near Sonai[20] and Śiva-Tila in Tulagram in Maibong known as Rock-cut temple.[21] L.A. Waddeli also points out that they have adopted many of the externals of Hinduism.[22] Regarding the 'V' shaped chessman monoliths of Dimapur, L.W. Shakespear[23] observes that they were huge "Lingam" (Śiva-Śakti Principle) stones believed by some savants to be and evidence of ancient phallic worship. According to R.M. Nath, "Hidimba or Dimapur with its phallus like mushroom ruins may reveal unexpected facts. It became associated with Kāmākhyā and attained the distinction of the Piṭhas and Upa-Piṭhas. Hidimbai Pada along with Mahamaya and Goddiyana became famous place for worship".[24] The numismatic evidence also testifies to the prevalence of Hinduism in Kachar hills. The silver coins from Haflong dated Śaka 1503, Śaka 1524, Śaka 1594, Śaka 1536, and Śaka 1537 prove that much before the shifting of capital to Dimapur and Maibong the Hindu culture was adopted by the rulers. The coins indicate that the rulers themselves were patron of Hari-Hara and Hara-Gouri or Śiva-Vishnu[25]. S.K. Chatterjee[26] thinks that Hinduisation in the Kachar Hills was started as early as 15th century.

W.W. Hunter has presented a very elaborate and authentic account of the progress of Hinduism among the Kachari tribes. According to him, the Kachari Kings were certainly influenced by Brāhmin Priest. It was universal tendency of all partially civilized tribes in India to accept Hinduism and thereby to increase their superiority over the surrounding barbarians. The process of conversion went on slowly both at Maibong and Khaspur. Brāhmins from Sylhet lived in capital for several generations under the royal Patronage and enabled many to embrace Hinduism. In 1790, Raja Krishna Chandra together with Gobindra made a public profession of Brahmanism with certain expiatory rites. "When a hill people take up Hinduism they adopt that form of it which bears most resemblance to their own ancient worship. Thus the Cacharis having practised a gloomy demon worship adopted the rites of Kali, in their most horrible form and identified her with their own female demon Ranchandi. The wild tribes profess the Hindu religion but the principal objects of their worship are the spirits who have authority over the powers of nature".[27] Ranchandi was their tutelary Goddess. The Cacharis also used to worship the Goddesses Lakshmi, Durgā, images of Visnu and Ganesha. Mr. Frank[28] has referred to the worship of Ganesha, Hanumān and Pārvati. The images were destroyed by the Nagas. Fisher[29] in his Memoir of the countries on and near the Eastern Frontiers of Sylhet has stated that in Cachar, Kāli, Jagannath and Vasudeva were the principal deities. Both Śakta and Vaishnava forms of Hinduism were prevalent. The Cacharis, the Lalungs and the Mikir tribes are also believed to have accepted Hinduism during the time of Koch rule in medieval period, probably the 16th century.

The Tripuris, the largest tribe of Hill-Tipperah (Tripura) also came under the influence of Hinduism. Tribal religion was greatly modified by Hinduism. The cult of Śiva was the state religion of Tripura. Somerset Playne's Report[30] illustrates the truth that the influence of Vaishnavism since Chaitanya's time (1485) was also discernible. When Lord Śiva promised Tripur's widowed Rani a son, he stipulated that Surya and Chandra or the Sun and the Moon as well as the Chaturdas Devatas (fourteen Gods and Godesses) should be duly and regularly worshipped. The fourteen Gods identified with Brahmanical deities worshipped by them were the following:— (*a*) Hara or Śiva—the destroyer in Hindu trinity, (*b*) Umā or Durgā—the consort of Śiva, (*c*) Hari or Vishnu - the preserver in the Hindu trinity, (*d*) Mā or Lakshmi—the consort of Vishnu and the Goddess of prosperity, (*e*) Bāni or Sarasvati - Goddess of Knowledge, (*f*) Kumāra or Kārtikeya - the God of war and the commander-in-chief of the Gods, (*g*) Ganapa or Ganesha - the God of Wisdom, (*h*) Biddhu or Chandra - the Moon, (*i*) Ka or Brahma - the creater in Hindu trinity, (*j*) Abdhi - the God of ocean or water, (*k*) Gaṅgā - the most sacred river of the Hindus, (*l*) Sekhi or Agni - the God of fire, (*m*) Kama - the God of love and (*n*) Himadri - the Himalaya mountain.

The religion of Tripuri tribe is a curious mixture of Hinduism and animism. Actually, their tribal religion like that of other Bodo groups was much modified by Hinduism. Their Hindu way of the religious rites are performed by Brahmin Pandit and the tribal way of religious rites by tribal priests. Sacrifices form an important part of their religion. According to the local tradition preserved in the *Rājamālā* — royal chronicle of Tripura—the Chaturdas Devatas were first worshipped by king Trilochana, a contemporary of Yudhisthira. The temple of Chaturdas Devatas is situated at old Agartala, about 5 miles from present Agartala. This temple was built by Krishna Manikya sometime in the latter half of the 18th century. It is believed that the original temple was situated at Udaipur, the old capital of Tripura. The images are made of an alloy of eight metals. Human sacrifices prevailed in Tripura from very ancient times. The sacrifices were performed at the altar of gods and goddess. The worship of Siva in Tantric form and the Sakti cult also acquired influence among the Tripuris. During the time of Deva Manikya, a Tantric Brahmana of Mithila visited Tripura. The Tantric form of worship and human sacrifices received some fillip. However, the system of human sacrifice was done away with in the latter half of the 17th century. The Tripuris still worship Chaturdas Devatas.

K.L. Barua opines that "the Bura devata, the chief of the fourteen devatas of the anicent Bodo king, was a horned God like the one depicted in a Mohenjodaro Seal and which Sir Johan Marshall claims as a prototype of Siva Pasupati"[31]. It was during the time of Ratna Manikya (14th century) that Hinduism became popular religion but actually the Hindu Gods and Goddesses were worshipped by the Tripuris along with the tribal Gods and Goddesses. Dalton on the basis of extracts of General Report of the Tippera district states that among the Tripuri tribes the prevailing religion was form of Hindu idolatry. It was during the reign of Dharma Manikya (15th century) that the process of conversion to Hinduism began. The coming of Brahmins from Bengal greatly modified the religion of the Bodo and Indo-Mongoloid tribes of Hill Tipperah. But both Hinduism and traditional religion went on together. This dualism became noticeable among other tribes also who imbraced the Hinduism.[32] This statement has been supported by S.K. Chatterjee. To quote him, "this led to the close approximation of both the royal family and ranks and file of the Indo-Mongoloid people of Tripura to the Bengalis in religion and culture."[33]

On the basis of some reliable sources[34] it can be pointed out that the Chakma tribes of Hill Tipperah and Mizo Hills, inspite of being basically the Buddhist, used to believe in both Hinduism and animism in the past. The Hindu God Siva and Goddess Kāli were worshipped by them. The influence of Hinduism is evident from the fact that they like the Hindus depended very much on the Brahmana priests regarding certain matters.

D. Sharma is of the opinion that the Aryans imbibed Dravidian culture and religion. The cult of Linga and Yoni is certainly of Pre-Āryan Dravidian origin. In support of his view he has referred to the views of John Marshal who ascribes the discovery of Saivism to Mohenjodaro and Harappa.[35] K.L. Barua also suggests that the Bodo tribes gradually established the contact with Mediterranean Pundras of Northern and Central Bengal and adopted the same Chalcolithic civilization which the dwellers of Indus valley did.[36]

In North-Eastern Frontier Region (now Arunachal Pradesh) also the influence of Hinduism can be traced out. There are some archaeological evidence to show the prevalence of both Saivism and the cult of Mother Goddess in this region. Archaeological discoveries show the existence of crude form of Saivism in this region before the emergence of the mother-cult. The discovery of a Sivalinga (Phallic symbol) with round base of black stone and with its temple base in the course of an excavation carried out at Paya in the heart of Dikkaravasini (now in Lohit district) by L.N. Chakravarty (former Deputy Director of Research, Research Deptt. Arunachal Pradesh Administration) in 1965-66 is an irrefutable proof of the prevalence of this non-Āryan faith. Twelve lines of bricks at this site perhaps provided the foundation of a temple there. The said Śivalinga is now installed in a newly built temple at Tezu. Śiva-linga temple may be ascribed to 14th-15th century A.D. Parasurāma-kunda, a famous holy place for pilgrimage quit adjacent to it, is held as a champion of Saivism and the associated legend has its hold even now. Pandit Vidyavinod observes that, according to tradition, a colony of Brāhmans was set up at this place during the time of Parasurama.[37] It may be added here that the Akas (one of the tribes of Arunachal Pradesh), progenitor of Bāna, were ardent devotees of Lord Śiva.

In the course of archaeological excavations carried out by L.N. Chakravarty at Malinithan near Likabali (now in Siang district) in 1970-71 and 1973 the ruins of a Hindu temple (constructed of huge block of stones), several stone pillars with carved lotus motif on them and sculptured images of popular gods and goddesses of Hindu pantheon, such as Dasabhuja Durgā, Ganesha, Kārtikeya, Sarasvati and magnificent Bull-Nandi (the vehicle of Śiva) scattered all around the place mostly in broken portions, and numerous erotic relief figures were discovered. This discovery is taken as an unmistakable proof of the prevalence of two popular cults of Hinduism Śaiva and Śākti or Mother Goddess.[38]

The findings at Malinithān (a Pithasthān in ancient times) may be dated to 9th-14th or 15th century. The Hindu culture must have flourished in and around Malinithan during the period. The Hinduised Indo-Mongoloid empire had already come into existence in North East Frontier Region about the middle of the seventh century.

A striking feature of the remnants of Malinithān is the frequent occurrence of Maithuna figures in various postures. The erotric sculptures are no doubt the survivals through Tantricism of the fertility cult of the primitive tribal society upholding the Mother principle as the procreative power of nature. According to B.K. Barua, "the occurrence of these figures mainly in Śiva and Śakta temples as suggested by Sir William Rothenstein was a part of the Tantric attitude which was characteristic of Indian religious philosophy between the 10th and 12th centuries; it appears that these erotic sculptures have the support of the traditional practices of centuries of temple building and have been enjoined by the sacred texts such as the Kāmasūtra."[39]

The Archaeological Report of T. Bloch shows that in Sadiya region the images of Surya and Kali dancing on Śiva and Saraswati were worshipped by Indo-Mongoloid people.[40] Here we find a cultural synthesis between Saivism, Saktism and Tantricism.

D.C. Sircar states that the encroachment of Hinduism in the tribal sphere of beliefs in this part of India cannot be denied. The medieval sites like Malinithān and the Paya Dikkaravāsini or Tamresvari temple inscription of Prince Muktadharmānārāyana dated Śaka 1364 (1442 A.D.) as well as the tradition locating the Vidarbha country constitute the monumental evidence to the fact.[41]

According to S.S. Barua, the second copper plate of 1401 A.D. found near Chilamora in North Lakhimpur Sub-Division indicates that at Sadhayāpuri, the old name of Sadiya, a old Hindu dynasty flourished in the 14th century and the Chutia tribes were greatly influenced by the Śakta-cult of non-Āryan origin. The Chutiyas living at Sadiya or Bhismaknagar region known as Vidarbha in ancient time were greatly influenced by Medieval Hindu culture of India. Tamreshwari temple with Phallic symbol of Śiva installed near by the Parasuramkunda was frequently visited by the present Idu Mishmi tribes living in the Hills.[42]

According to J.P. Wade,the Devalaya in North Lakhimpur Sub-Division with a temple of Kāmākhyā was frequented by the Hill tribes of Upper Assam for worshipping the symbol of female procreative principle of Śakti.[43]

On the basis of all the recorded evidence, we can plausibly conclude here that in North-East Frontier Region the mixed culture—both Āryan and non-Āryan religious elements—flourished which also proves the intercultural contacts. The theory of pre-Āryan Dravidian origin of the Śakta cult does not need any elaboration here.

It is to be noted here that from the 12th to the 16th centuries when Buddhism itself deeply infected with Tantricism was disappearing, Saktism was the most popular religion among some of the tribes of north-east region. After the beginning of 15th century Saktism was patronised by the Ahom rulers of Assam. But Saktism never inspired any popular or Missionary movement, rather it was directed against the Vishnuites. The strange inconsistencies of Saktism are in varied forms as a whole but the contrasts are more violent and the monstrosities more conspicuous than anywhere. The wild legends and metaphysics are both mixed together with the cult. There is no doubt that the worship of Goddess (especially the Goddess of fertility) was wide spread among the Egyptians and Semities, in Asiaminor, Greece, Italy and in Magadha and Bengal in the form of Saktist corruption of Buddhism but here it has got some unique features.

After Śaivism and Śaktism mixed with varied forms of Tantric rituals attained great popularity, the Tantrikism developed in full form among some hill-tribes of north-eastern India. It was a system of magical or sacramental ritual which professes to attain the highest aims of religion by such methods as magic, sorcery, witchcraft, exorcism, etc. Though it is the development of the Vaidik Karmakānda but practically it differs from the Vedic sacrifices in method rather than principle. After c. 630 A.D. it was infected with Buddhism. Many Tantras present it in a refined form Saktism and modified form of Saivism in conformity with ordinary Hindu usage. But other features are indubitably connected with aboriginal cults. K.L. Barua holds the view that "both Tantricism and the ghastly rites of the Kapālikas originated from Saivism and it is now accepted by most scholars that the Vedic Āryans coming into India found a crude form of Saivism associated perhaps with human sacrifices. The Bodos as well as the Austric people coming under the cultural influence of the authors of the Pre-Aryan Indus culture probably copied the custom from the latter with the priest. Subsequently, the Tantric form of Hindu religion got intermixed with the Vajrayana cult of Buiddhism."[44]

B. Bhattacharyya observes that it was during the Pāla's rule that Kāmākhyā became center of Tantric Buddhism.[45] According to Babu Nandlal Dey, Tantrikism as an offshoot of Buddhism of the Mahayana School developed about the ninth century under the Pāla rulers of Magadha. Pala King Dharma Pāla founded the Buddhist University of Vikramsila which became the centre of Tantrik doctrines and from this centre Tantrikism probably spread in Kāmārupā and Tibet.[46] But this view has been strongly contradicted by E.Gait who holds the view that it was Assam where Tantrik form of Hinduism originated.[47] The latter view is much more trustworthy than the former one. E. Gait further observes that "The old tribal beliefs are gradually being abandoned and the way in which Hindu Priests established their influence over Non-Āryan Chiefs and gradually drew them within their fold is repeatedly exemplified in the pages of Assam History".[48] He further confidently remarks that Saktism was the predominant form of Hinduism in this part of India. Its adherents base their observances on the Tantras, a series of religious works in which the various ceremonies, prayers and incantations are prescribed in a dialogue between Siva and his wife Parvati. The fundamental idea behind it is the worship of the female principle, the procreative power of nature, as manifested by personified desire. It is religion of bloody sacrifices from which even human beings were not exempted.[49]

Here some valuable information are brought to light. From the copper-plate inscription of the Pāla Kings (11th century) it appears that the North-Eastern Frontier of Assam was a Āryan colony.[50] *Yogini Tantra* also refers to the Kolva Pitha in this region where moral and secular laws were framed by the tribesman themselves. The people belonged to different sects of Hinduism; Hinduism seems to have spread amongst the aboriginals. In the biography of the Vaisnavite Saint Vamsi Gopāla Deva references have been made to "Mishmi Brāhmans". This region inhabited by the hill-tribes was called Saumera Piṭha. *Kālikā Purāṇa* refers to it a land under the command of Goddess - *Dikkaravāsini*. Tantrikism developed among some frontier tribes with all its esoteric beliefs and practices.

The Tāmreśvari (Dikkaravāsini) temple at Paya near Tezu (in the Lohit district of Arunachal) regarded as Kāmākhyā of the East was the famous centre of Shakti cult. The Chutiya tribe reigning at Sadiya at the beginning of the 13th century brought this cult into prominence. The TāmreŚvari Devi (Goddess of Copper temple) was so famous that it was at that time looked upon as a centre of worship for all the hill tribes on the North Eastern Frontier. The Goddess was popularly known as Keshai-Khati (eater of the raw flesh). She was worshipped in both Shakti and Tantric form. In one of the reliable sources, it is clearly stated that in that temple human sacrifices were annually offered by the Chutiya priest which continued for several centuries.[51] The temple was built in the 14th or 15th century. An inscription of Muktādharmānārāyana dated Saka 1364 (AD 1442) written in the Sanskrit language and Bengali-Assamese script of the 15th century found inside the temple records the construction of a boundary wall of bricks around the temple of Dikkaravāsini by Muktādharmānārāyana. The word *Śivacaraṇaprasadat* (i.e. through the grace of Siva's feet) with which the inscription commences indicates inclination of the ruler towards Saivism. This is further confirmed by his interest for the preservation of the temple. Dikkaravāsini, described as a form of wife of Śiva or Mahamaya in the *Kalikā Purāna,* was worshipped in eastern Assam in medieval times. She was variously known as Tāmresvari Mai and Keshai-Khāti because her temple had a roof of copper sheets and human sacrifices were offered to her. The Chutiyas, religious system was obviously a blend of Saivism, Saktism and Tantricism. This form of Hinduism continued to prevail till the overthrow of the Chutiya ruling family of the Sadiya region by the Ahoms in the 16th century.

An illustration of Tāmreśvari temple with an image of the said Goddess, carved stone gateway, ornamented pillars, and statue of an elephant has been provided by S.F. Hannay (JASB, XVII, 1848, p. 466, pl. xxx).

The remains of the famous Tāmreśvari temple (or copper temple) are located on the right bank of a small stream named Dewulpani, 8 miles east of present Sunpura within Arunachal Pradesh. They constitute the mute evidence to the prevalence of the Śakti cult of Hinduism among the tribes of Sadiya and adjoining regions. The contributions of Indo-Mongoloid tribes to the rise of Śakti cult or the worship of the mother goddess in the Tantric form can be proved by all the available evidences. The ruins of the Tāmreśvari temple is one of the evidences. The recent discovery of the ruins of a brick-built temple with a Phallic symbol of Lord Śiva in the vicinity of Tāmreśvari temple also testifies to the prevalence and eminence of Śiva-Śakti cult in the said region in ancient and early medieval periods.

The cult of Tantricism spread also amongst the Synteng tribe of the Jaintia Hills. A shrine was set up. The Jaintia Rajas were Saktas and adherents of Kapālika tenet which enjoined the immolation or human sacrifice. Jayantia has been mentioned in the *Yogini Tantra* as one of the sacred places to the Devi. Human sacrifices continued there down to 1835 when it was stopped by the British by disposing the king of his territory. The three British subjects captured are believed to have been immolated in 1832 at the Shrine of Kali in the Jaintia Hills. In Hill-Tipperah also Tantric rite of sacrifice was followed[52] E. Gait has also referred to the worship of various forms of Kāli by the tribal Priests of the Chutiyas and the prevalence of Saktism amongst the Jaintias. About the Hinduism of the Jaintia tribes he further states that "The Rajas belonged to the Śakta sect ... they were very particular in the observance of the ghastly system of human sacrifice laid down in the *Kālikā Purāṇa*".[53] This fact is further corroborated by documentary evidence[54] and other sources.[55] H. Yule has observed that the worship of Kali to a certain degree spread into Khasi Hills and a spurious Hinduism has been grafted on to the original demon worship of Kassiah. The groves, rocks and streams — a semi religious - were converted into the abodes or the actual personification of the gloomy Mahādeo.[56] The Ahom chronicle[57] refers to the worship of Mahāmāyā Bhagavati Goddess Durgā amongst the Jaintias. L.W. Shakespear[58] observes that "Tāmāsari Mai" was dedicated to Kamakhya and the Yone but Śiva and Lingam were also worshipped with barbarous rites and human sacrifice. M.S. Johri[59] has also pointed out that the worship of the female principle of Procreation - Saktism was the dominant religion of the people. The Tamreswari temple was located in the country of Mishmi tribes. The temple Priests were the Idu Mishmis. Human sacrifice was performed at the altar of the Goddess. Besides these temples, some other temples of Śiva were also in existence where animal sacrifice was performed. Thus we find that both Śiva and Śakta cult were prevalent among the frontier hill tribes.

The Tantrikism was associated with magic, witchcraft, animal and human sacrifices and occult practices and this cult was powerful till it received a check from the cult of Vaishnavism or Vaishnavite reformers of 15th century. The Sakti cult or female forms became popular due to Sankhya philosophical ideal of "Purusha and Prkriti". In a very valuable source,[60] the growth of both Sakta and Tantric form of Hinduism extensively associated with Magic, sorcery, witchcraft in bygone days in this part of India has been mentioned.

K.L. Barua has clearly stated that the Ranchandi and Mahāmāyā of the Kachari tribes, Tāmreśvari of the Chutiyas, Jaintesvari of the Jaintias and the fourteen Devatas of the Tipperas were worshipped by resorting to human sacrifices in medieval times.[61]

Dr. Stein's view that the practice of human sacrifices was imported into India from Asia Minor by the mediterraneans or their predecssors—the proto Austroloids[62] - can be very well disputed. In another source also, human sacrifice prevalent among the hill tribes of this region in medieval age has been referred to.[63] However it was undoubtedly a barbaric practice and Voluptuous aspect of Hinduism. This barbarous and immoral worship was looking glorious in their holy places, but so far as the theology and metaphysics are concerned, any defending argument is not plausible.

J.H. Hutton informs us that the Phallic worship is connected with that of Khmer of Java and of Japan. The Linga is simple cone and the Yoni is triangular prism. Both are somewhat though not very much realistically presented by the Angami Nagas of Kohima and in the pre-historic monoliths of Dimapur.[64]

N.N. Law has correctly stated that the Mother Goddess cult is pre Āryan elements in the Indian culture. The cult of Linga and Yoni (Śaiva-Śakta Principles) worshipped in anthropomorphic forms is older than the Chalcolithic age of Mohenjodaro. Phallus worship played an important part in the religious and magical ideology of the pre-Āryan and non-Āryan peoples of India. The cult of Linga became embedded in Brahmanism in the epic period.[65]

Showing the influence of remarkable religions known as Saktism (worship of Sakti or Śiva's spouse under various names, Devi, Durgā, Kāli, historically appearing as a compound of Hinduism with non-Āryan beliefs) and Tantrism (a system of magical or sacramental ritual) — both principal subdivisions of Hinduism - amongst the hill people of north-eastern India, Sir Charles Eliot has observed that "The birth place of Saktism as a definite sect seems to have been North-Eastern India. The population of these countries is not Aryan and is largely composed of immigrants from the North belonging to the Tibeto-Burman, Mon-Khmer and Shan families. In all this region we hear of no ancient Brahmanic settlements, no ancient centres of Vedic or even Puranic learning, and when Buddhism decayed nobody of Brahmanic tradition such as existed in other parts of India imposed its authority on the writers of Tantras, even at the present day the worship of the female spirits only half acknowledged by the Brahmans, prevails among these people and in the past the national deities of many tribes were Goddesses who were propitiated with human sacrifices. Thus the Chutiyas of Sadiya used to adore a Goddess called Kesai-Khati-the eater of raw flesh. The rites of these deities were originally performed by tribal priests, but as Hindu influence spread, the Brahmans gradually took charge of them without modifying their character in essentials... The language of mythology could not describe more clearly the endeavours of a plebeian cult to obtain recognitioin."[66]

After having the evidence of the prevalence of Saivism and Tantricism in gross forms here it is necessary to throw light on the slow progress of Vaishnavism amongst the hill tribes. Both Vishnu and Śiva are believed to have been the off spring of philosophic and poetic minds playing with a luxuriant popular mythology but the sectarian tendency is stronger in Vishnuism than Saivism. The doctrine of Bhakti is common to both very much similar to that of Sankhya and Vedants. The chronology fails in tracing the early history of this sect. However, it was due to the influence of Vaishnava movement of Shankaradeva in the 15th century that some tribes came under his influence. His creed was qualified monism as expounded by Ramanuja and it differed from absolute monism of Shankaracharya. Shankaradeva's philosophy of Vaishnavism brought some hill-tribes under his influence who ultimately became his disciples and great Vaishnava Preacher. Some of them known belonged to the Naga, the Garo and the Mikir tribes. Venerable preachers were Narottam of the Nagas, Govinda of the Garos, Balai of the Mikirs, Paramananda of the Miris, Ramai of the Kacharis, Damodar of the Bhutias and Aghona Chandra - Gam Dafla. They went as ambassadors of unity of the people of the hills and thse plains in every nook and corner of the hills and preached religious philosophy of Shankaradeva[67]. According to S. Johri, both Noctes and the Wanchoos, the tribes of NEFA (modern Arunachal Pradesh), were Vaishnavites and the Goswami of Baraghar Sattra near Nazira was their religious teacher. The devotional songs attributed to Lord Krishna and dances depicting various episodes in the life of Lord Krishna and Radha were becoming popular among the Noctes, one of the frontier tribes.[68] The Vaishnavism of both Noctes and Idu-Mishmi tribes has been mentioned in another source[69] too. To this day, the Noctes practice a form of Vaishnavism which they imbibed from the Vaishnava Satras of Assam.

After a detailed enquiry and investigation into the veneer of Hinduism amongst different tribe, we find that a gradual process of conversion of animistic tribes to Hinduism and other faith was taking place in this part of India.[70] Among the frontier tribes who came under the influence of Brahmanical philosophy of Hinduism as a whole were the Chutiyas[71] who adopted Hindu customs, the Akas[72] who started worshipping God Hari or Harideo and the Miris and the Mishmis who adopted Hindu rites and rituals. L.A. Waddell has stated that the Digaru Mishmis or Tain acted as guides to Hindu Pilgrims to the sacred Shrine — Brahmakunda - in NEFA.[73] E. Gait points out that the Kacharis, the Mikirs and other tribes came under the conversion process of Hinduism.[74] Dalton has also mentioned that the work of proselytism was carried by Hindu priest amongst the Kacharis and other cognate tribes.[75] R.M. Nath has referred to the Hinduised Mikir tribes during the Hindu regime and the influence of Hindu culture and worship of Śiva and Durgā as Bura and Buri and propitiation of the Goddess Kali and sacrifice of human beings at Her altar among the Lalungs who are very much like the Mikir tribe.[76]

J. Johnstone has revealed the historical truth that towards the middle of the 18th century a Hindu revivalist movement took place in the East of India. The conversion to Hinduism on the Eastern Frontier from Sadiya down to Chittagong was daily taking place. To quote him "A man belonging to Hill tribes, if the Raja chose at any time, received the sacred thread of twice born castes, and on payment of small sum of money was admitted as a Hindu and was thenceforth called Khetree (probably a corruption of Khatri). This privilege was not accorded to Mussulmans. I once asked a Manipuri why they received hill-men and not Mussalman, both being Mlecchas according to Hindu theory, he said it was because the hill-men had sinned in ignorance whereas Musulmans knew the evil of their ways."[77]

According to Ursula Graham Bower, Jadonang - a Kabui Naga of Manipur - enunciated such a religion which appears as a splendid blending of Hinduism and Christianity.[78]

Some tribes of Tripura also came under the influence of Hinduism. Roy Burman points out that the Magh tribe also professed Hinduism. Riangs went through a process of syncretism by which the Hindu deities, Shiva, Vishnu and Krishna, were identified with their own deities.[79] This is further substantiated by documentary evidence, according to which, out of Nowatiyas, Jamatiyas and Riangs-all Tipperah Hill tribes - the Riangs adopted some Hindu customs and worshipped Hindu deities.[80]

Assam Census Reports bear on eloquent testimony to the fact that a large number of the aboriginal tribes living in different parts of the north-east came within the fold of Hindu religion. The Khasis (inhabiting the areas adjoining Sylhet), Syntengs, Jaintias (of Nartiang), some Garos, Mikirs, Hajongs, Lalungs, Rabhas, Miris, Mishmis and Kacharis (especially of North Cachar Hills) are stated to have been proselytized or converted to Hinduism. North Cachar Hills witnesses a rapid progress of Hinduism. More than ten thousand Kacharis had already come within the fold of Hinduism as per census of 1881. The Chutiyas of Sadiya region were found fully Hinduized. The Saivism and Saktism - two important sects of Hinduism-were the prevailing form of religion among the Hindu converts.[81]

In his *Assam Census Reports* (1891), E.A. Gait observes: "The chances of successful research are fast passing away as many of the tribes concerned are rapidly losing their... religion and traditions, infact, their very identity in the folds of a steadily proselytizing Hinduism."[82] He further states that the Sakti cult with Tantrik form of worship originated in Assam, which was also a fertile field for propagation of neo-Vaishnava doctrines of Chaitanya. Saktism was modified by the Shamanistic tendencies of the non-Āryan converts. Some tribes on the frontier were under the influence of Hinduism; some belonged to the Hindus. A number of tribes (mentioned in preceding para) were absorbed in Hindu converts.[83]

Regarding progress of Hinduism among the tribes, Mr. Lloyd remarked in his Assam Census Report (1921) that border line between Hinduism and Animism in Assam is very vague owing to the continuance of primitive practice side by side with the Hindu ceremonies. In 1931, the Hindu Mahāsabhā (Assam Provincial Hindu Sabha) endeavoured to do away with the border line altogether and persuaded all the Animists to accept themselves as Hindus. In order to propogate the new faith-Hinduism - among the tribes, the leaflets were distributed among the Mikirs in Nowgong by the Hindu Mahāsabhā in which it was said that the Khasis, Jaintias, Garos, Mikirs, Kacharis, Chutiyas and other tribes living in Assam are really Hindus. The leaflet said that in 1921 all the Hindu tribes were recorded as Animists; the census officer enrolled the tribes as Animists and not as Hindus against the wishes of the tribals themselves. The leaflet was a true copy of Bengali leaflet issued by the Bengal Hindu Sabha and published in Dhaka. More than 50 different Missionary Societies from different countries of Europe, America and Australia were actively engaged in spreading Christianity amongst the simple hill tribes of Assam, Bengal and Bihar. In order to stem the tide of conversion to Christianity. The "Hindu Mission" (Central Office, Calcutta) commenced its work amongst the aboriginal tribes of Bengal, Bihar and Assam in 1926 and continued up to 1930. The Hindu ideals were propagated among several tribes. The success was phenomenal. During the period, over sixty thousand animist tribes including the Khasis, Kacharis, Mikirs, Lalungs, Miris, and Rabhas of Assam and some of the tribes of Bengal and Bihar were absorbed into the Hindu fold. The border line between animism and Hinduism was removed. A good number of tribes voluntarily came within the fold of Hinduism. Commenting on the work of Hindu Mission in his tour diary, D.C. Darrang said; "Though Hinduism is religion or rather a social system of very great antiquity, it is only in quite recent years that it has laid claim to the aboriginal. The propaganda work of Hindu Mission was certainly a great success in Assam from their point of view and had an enormous influence on the tribal people hovering in the borderland between Hnduism and Animism" The Hindu Māhāsābhā is said to have carried on an "intensive propaganda" to convert animist tribes to Hindusim. They started propagating that all tribesmen are genuine Hindus. In 1931. a vast majority of tribes in Assam including those of North Cachar Hills returned as Hindus as in 1921. All what we have stated above can be evidenced by C.S. Mullan's *Assam Census Report,* 1931. It is not correct to say that the conversion of the tribes (concerned) of Assam to Hinduism took place by fiction and not reality. It is a fact of history that the non-Āryan Kirātas1 God Śiva identified with Rudra in Hindu pantheon was worshipped by a number of tribes in Assam, particularly by those who were adherents of Śakti cult. The Hindu converts amongst the tribes had faith in both Śaiva and Śakti cult as noted before.[84]

We also learn from one of the reliable sources that the Khasis, Jaintias and Chutiyas in large number came under the influence of Hinduism. During the period from the beginning of the 18th century to 1830 a vast majority of the Kacharis came within the fold of Hinduism. The ruins of temples have also been found in the Kapili valley. A temple sacred to Durga stands on the hills immediately to the east of Silghat, a village in Nowgong district.[85]

The Persian source also refers to the little influence of Hinduism among the Hill tribes of Eastern India.[86] Here we cannot but quote S. Johri : "Before the arrival of the British the tribals of Assam were gradually and peacefully being assimilated into this civilization or culture... border line between Hinduism and animism is very vague for Hinduism manifests itself according to the mental development of its recipients. This vague barrier between Hinduism and animism was through the ages being dissolved... the process of converting the aboriginal tribes to Hinduism which is going on before our eyes today commenced long before the time of which we have any authentic record."[87] He also points out that the Noctes of Tirap - Vaishnavites - established five temples in Namsang area. Mishmis, believer in Majeedagarh - the God of destruction and equivalent of Śiva or Mahādev - were the rightful claimants of the offerings of Parasuramakund or Brahmakund.[88]

Johri further adds that the Mishmis were the descendants of Brāhmans and they followed the Aryan religion. The Abors 'and Hill-Miris', God "Jam" is the corruption of the "Yama" of the Hindus. The Dafla tribes of Subansiri visited the temple of Vasudeva founded at the confluence of the rivers Rangapjam and Kachikata in the native village of Madhav Dev in North-Lakhimpur district and their interest in Vaishnavism was increasing day by day. The Akas worshipped the God Hari (Vishnu) and Vaishnavism was not an unknown cult to them. They adopted the practice of flying prayer flags and erecting mannes like the Buddhists. The Bagini, the Nishis, the Sulungs, the Mishmis and the Adis — all frontier tribes (now in Arunachal) - used to worship the minor religious cults of Sun and Moon.[89]

In one British record, it is mentioned that in post-Hiuen Tsang period the aboriginal chiefs were converted to Hinduism and Brahmins were given land grants.[90]

It is significant to note here that the process of Aryanisation and sanskritizaion, the combined influence of the Vrātya culture of the Alpine Āryans and of the culture of the Vedic Āryans, the movement of the Brāhmanas between 2nd millennium B.C. and the 12th century A.D. and other unidentified factors greatly modified and transformed the early character of tribal Hinduism. From the Brāhmanic age to the end of the British rule the aboriginal and Hinduised practices went on together in some hill regions of north-east India. But the tribal people retained their traditional and age-old beliefs and did not completely submerge into the main currents of pure Hinduism like the Śakas, the Hunas, Yavanas, Tartars and some Mongols.

We find that the followers of all schools of philosophy - the Vedic, the Pauranic and the Tantric-thrived in northeastern part of India equally well and the Āryans and non-Āryans equally contributed to the building up of the socio-cultural fabric of the country. Their positive contributions towards making the composite culture and civilization of India, being the distinguishing hallmark, can be held as of Pan-Indian significance. This may be looked upon as an interesting and important line of historical enquiry in tracing the composite nature of Indian civilization. In the long historic process of giving the concrete shape to Indian civilization as a whole, the contributions of the Austrics, Indo-Mongoloids, Tibeto-Burmans and other Hinduised and Semi-Hinduised aboriginal tribes of this region can never be underestimated. On the basis of the above mentioned facts discovered from various sources all the theories presented so far discarding and ignoring the impact of Hinduism on the non-Āryan tribes and vice-versa can very well be disposed of.

We cannot deny the fact that the contacts between tribal communities and Hindu population have extended over countless centuries and we have every reason to believe that the concepts stemming from pre-Āryan civilization have found their ways into Hindu doctrines, thoughts and scriptures just as concepts of orthodox Hinduism have been assimilated by many of the primitive hill-tribes of our country.

The religio-cultural and philosophical patterns of the tribal people of north-east India distinctly appear as a curious blend or queer mixture of both the Āryan and non-Āryan elements. Both may be found combined into startling juxtaposition. The assimilation of tribal polytheistical beliefs, animistic faith, propitiation of both benevolent and malevolent spirits, supernatural objects, natural phenomena and other innumerable gods and goddesses having the anthropomorphic attributes based on magico-religious system, eschatological beliefs, doctrine of Atman or soul, and their ideas connected with monotheism (in the words of Max Muller henotheism), ritualism, priesthood, sacrifices, Saktism, Tantrism and other indigenous faiths into the religious system of the Āryans and later the Hindus is one of the cardinal features of Indian religious history. The concept of proto-Hinduism later emerged. It has been rightly said that "the bottles of Hinduism have always proved capable of holding all the wine poured into them". Several Upanishadic, Vedic and Pauranic doctrines and even the Vedantic philosophy have got pre-Āryan features to a considerable degree. The influence of non-Āryan religion on Hindu religion and philosophy is similar to the impact of Hinduism on Buddhism, impact of Buddhism on Christianity, and influence of Sufism and Greek philosophy on Islamic theology. The process of religious confraternity has moved in cyclic order through the millenniums and centuries.

It has been rightly observed by S.K. Chatterjee that "When the Aryans came into India, the country was not a no-man's land; it was already populated by some races or peoples which had risen to a high level of civilization... the non-Āryan contributed by far the greater portion in the fabric of Indian civilization and a great deal of Indian religions and cultural tradition. The ideas of Karma and transmigration, the practice of Yoga, the religious and philosophical ideas centering round the conception of the

Divinity as Siva and Devi and as Vishnu, the Hindu ritual of Puja as opposed to the Vedic ritual of Homa—all these and much more in Hindu religion and thought would appear to be non-Āryan in origin".[91] "These Kiratas or Indo-Mongoloids might very well have come to India before the Āryans and they contributed a great deal in the evolution of Hindu History and culture in North-East and Eastern India.[92]

Buddhism was a protest against developed brahmanical system of theology and in some respect was the development of the principles of Sāṅkhya school of philosophy.[93] One can see the growth of Buddhism at the expense of Brahmanism. Buddhism had definitely an earlier contact with Tantricism than other forms of Hinduism. Buddhism gradually assumed a debased style due to the influence of Tantric form of Hinduism— Sakta Hinduism - over it.

In the context of North Eastern Frontier Region, L.W. Shakespeare observes that primitive forms of Buddhism existed prior to the introduction of brahmanical Hinduism about the middle of the fifteenth century. He quotes Hannay who states that in the Sadiya region many temples of Buddhist origin were found.[94] In fact, no definite date of the advent or introduction of Buddhism among the frontier tribes can be suggested.

There are some positive evidence to prove the tribals, embracement of Buddhism. Quite a good number of hill tribes of North Eastern Frontier Region (now Arunachal Pradesh) embraced Buddhism. The main Buddhist tribes include the Monpas, Sherdukpens, Membas, Khambas, Zakhrings, Meyors, Khamptis, Singphos and Tangsas. The first six are followers of Mahayana school and the rest three of Hinayana (one of the eleven sects of *Theravada).*

Those tribes who follow Mahayana School of Buddhism regard Buddha as eternal without origin and decay. They worship the Stupas and images of Buddha and Bodhisatvas. The followers of Hinayana or Theravada School of Buddhism advocate the original idea of strict monastic life and rigid disciplinary rules or laws. They believe to attain perfection by becoming Monk following eight-fold path and other doctrines preached by Buddha. The diversities among the Buddhist tribes (both Mahayanists and Hinayanists) are immense. The priestcrafts, symbolisms, attitudes, beliefs and practices vary from group to group.

It is significant to note that when the Mahayana sect accepted the new Tantric system called Kalchakrayan which came with in the fold of Vajrayana in or about the tenth century A.D. it came to be called Vairayana. The Mahayana school was also called Vajrayana obviously due to the Tantric influence. The great Tantric Buddhist teacher and preacher of mysticism, Padmasambhava of Nalanda University (in Bihar) went to Tibet in AD 747 or about the middle of the eighth century in response to an invitation from its king Ti-Song-De-Tsen to preach the doctrines of Mahayana Buddhism. He also taught to the Tibetan people magical arts associated with Tantric form of Buddhism. In fact, he preached in Tibet the Buddhism which is nothing but mystical aspects of Hinduism which relates to charms, miracles and occultism. Later, Atisha Dipankara of Vikramashila University (also in Bihar) was invited by Tibetan king Chang-Chhup-Od to come to Tibet for removing doctrinal differences between Mahayana and Hinayana schools of Buddhism. He went to Tibet in AD 1042 and preached there Mahayana Buddhism with greater emphasis on Vajrayana. The form of Buddhism these two Buddhist scholars from Bihar preached in Tibet was accepted by the Monpas, Sherdukpens and other Mahayanist tribes in the seventeenth century.

According to the local traditions and beliefs of the Monpas and Sherdukpens (in the western and southern part of Kameng respectively), Lopon Rimpoche (local name of Padmasambhava) visited their areas in the eighth century. Many places are hallowed by his visit. It is believed that the conversion of the Monpas to Buddhism was started by him. The Nyingmapa, one of the three popular sects of Buddhism in Tibet, had a good following among them even before the twelfth century. The three Nyingmapa temples of Urgyanling, Sangeling and Tsorgeling were established at Tawang. The Karmapa sub-sect had a sizable following among the Monpas by the twelfth century as evidenced by the Karmapa temple established at Kimne, one of the sites hallowed by the visit of the Master. The Karmapa was the first to be established among the Monpas of central Kameng sometime between 1682 and 1742. The advent of the Gelugpa sect among the Monpas of Kameng can be traced back to the time of the second Dalai Lama, Gedun Gyatso (AD 1475-1543). We do not know the actual date of the conversion of Sherdukpens to Buddhism. Some manuscripts in the Tawang monastery bear witness to the fact that Meme Gyapten, whom the Sherdukpens regard as their ancestor came to their area as an associate of Tanpei Dronme sometime between 1475 and 1543. The Gelugpa was the first organized sect to work among them sometime around 1742.[95]

The form of Buddhism practised by the Monpas is basically of the Lamaist Mahayana school. Their important religious centres are at Tawang, Dirang and Morshing. The famous monastery at Tawang was constructed by Mera Lama sometime between 1643 and 1647 (or in 1650) at the initiative of fith Dalai Lama, Nag-wang Lobjang Gyatso of Tibet (1617-1682) who was himself a Monpa. Mera Lama built the monastery with the help of the people of Tawang and neighbouring villages. It is considered to be the largest Buddhist monastery in India. With the establishment of this monastery, the Tibetan Gelugpa sect gradually but steadily gained prominence and the other sects lost their hold.[96] The said monastery is important in the perspective of art, architecture and its library of old Buddhist scriptures. The Buddhist style of paintings, wood carvings and the Murals of exquisite beauty are unique art treasures of the Monpas which not only testifies to their religious activities but also their cultural heritage.

Monpas' *Chorten* is actually a stupa-shaped structure where prayers are conducted on certain occasions. Their *gompa* is a temple wherein they worship the image of the Buddha[97]. Every village has a *gompa*. All houses have small altars and chapels with statues of the Buddha. The stupas and gompas belong to either seventeenth or eighteenth century.

The Sherdukpens also worship the images of Lord Buddha in their *gompas*. Their religion is a blend or mixture of Buddhism and animistic belief.

The Khambas and Membas (in the Siang district) also profess Mahayana Buddhism as noted before. They very much resemble the Monpas of Tawang. The Khambas have a number of shrines and temples in their villages with images of the Buddha. The two other Mahayanist tribes are the Zakhrings and Meyors (in the Lohit district).

The *Theravada* or Hinayana form of Buddhism prevails among the Khamptis and Singphos of Lohit-Tirap belt. In the fifth century AD, the Indian Buddhist Missionaries from the eastern coast brought *Theravada* to Burma. The original homeland of the Khamptis and Singphos was Burma. The former belong to the Shan or Tai race and the latter to the Kachin clan. While in Burma, they used to practice the said form of Buddhism. In the eighteenth century, they migrated from there to Assam carrying with them their old religious experience. The Khamptis made their first settlement on the banks of Tengapani, south of Sadiya, sometime between 1752 and 1769. When a golden Buddha temple was erected there, the place came to be known as Chowkham. Their immigration and subsequent expansion in Assam continued over a hundred years. Some Khamptis and Singphos had settled also in Noa Dihing valley (now in Tirap district of Arunachal Pradesh). The Khamptis are settled in some twenty villages of the Lohit district of Arunachal and also found in two districts of Assam, viz. Lakhimpur and Dibrugarh. The Singphos made their first appearance about 1793 and settled on the Buri Dihing in the Namrup region and on the Tengapani, east of Sadiya. They are now in Lohit district of Arunachal Pradesh.

It is distinctly recorded in one of the reliable sources that the Khamptis, advanced of all the frontier tribes in knowledge, arts and civilization, and the Singphos followed the Hinayana School of Buddhism prevalent in Burma.[98] Pandit P.B. Vidyavinod has rightly pointed out that Buddhism was an exiled religion and found shelter in Ceylon, Indo-Chinese peninsula, China, Tibet and Nepal. Some of the mountainous tribes northeast of the Brahmaputra valley known as Bhutiyas and Khamtis became Buddhists as a result of their connection with Tibet and Burma respectively.[99]

It is also to be noted here that Burmese Buddhism during Pagan period (1044-1287) was mixed up with Hindu-Brahmanical cults, Vaishnavism in particular, Mahayanism and Tantricism as a result of cultural contacts between Burma and Magadha. However, modern researches connect Thaton Buddhism with Hinayana school.

As early as 1847, John Butler, while making a general statement about the Buddhist tribes of Assam, pin-pointed that they used to worship Gautama Buddha in their temples with the help of their priests. They also resorted to offerings to various gods in conformity with their animistic belief. He also referred to the prevalence of Buddhism in Khampti society.[100] The religion of Khamptis, no doubt, bears the stamp of Burmese *Theravada* school of Buddhism. In 1872, E.T. Dalton categorically stated that the Buddhist Khamptis regularly maintained their priesthood system. Their priests were well conversant with recondite mysteries of their religion.[101] Towards the close of the nineteenth century, Buddhism among the Khamptis was nothing but a strange or queer mixture of Theravada Buddhism and their indigenous faith and belief.

The Singphos also practice the Theravada form of Buddhism but at the same time believe in numberous spirits. In *Assam Census Reports* of 1881 and 1891, the Khamptis, Singphos, and other Buddhists of Tawang find mention. In the report of latter year, it is clearly stated that a great majority of Shan Khamptis in Lakhimpur, and the Singphos were converted to Buddhism.[102]

Following the Buddhist tradition the Khamptis used to construct *Viharas, Stupas,* temples and monasteries in their villages for different purposes. A number of Khampti monasteries were built in the nineteenth century in Lohit area. One of the oldest and biggest Theravada monasteries exists at Chowkham. One of the oldest Theravada temples is located at the village Momong at a distance of 22 km from Namsai. It is locally called *Momong Vihara.* The monastery was constructed in 1918 AD. It contains one of the earliest bronze images of Buddha brought from Burma sometime in the latter half of the nineteenth century. "The temple consists of a big and spacious prayer hall with an altar. On the left wall of the altar, mural paintings depicting stories from Buddhist *Jatakas* can be identified. The monastery has at present 2 *bhikhus,* 7 *sramanas* and 7 lay disciples."[103]

Archaeological explorations and excavations in some parts of Arunchal Pradesh have yielded a few Buddhist stupas (of both Hinayana and Vajrayana sects), relics and monuments.

Some of the discoveries in Noa Dihing valley in Tirap district throw light on the heritage of the tribes like the Khamptis and Singphos. The ruins of a Buddhist stupa was unearthed at Vijayanagar in the course of an excavation carried out there by Y.A. Raikar (one of the former Deputy Directors of Research, Arunachal Pradesh Administration) in April 1971. The stupa is brick structure or *Kangmu* as called by the Khamptis and Singphos. It is situated on the right bank of the river Noa Dihing, about 3 km west of Tirap. The architectural style of the stupa shows its affinities with the 10th-11th century Stupas in Burma such as those at Hmawza and Pagan. Vijayanagar Stupa is evidently of Hinayana sect, other important discoveries at the site comprise the Buddha images. One small image is made of quartz with metal plating and a thin gold wash. Small flat metal images are 50 in number, including those found after the excavation. Some fragments of an image in lacquer work have also been found. This could be a wood-lacquered figure, though the wood is decayed. All these images are in the sedant "witness attitude" which appears to be popular among the Khamptis and Singphos. The Stupa and other antiquities discovered at the site may be assigned to late eighteenth century. It is believed that after having migrated from Burma the Khamptis settled at Khomong in the tiny plateau of Vijayanagar for some time only in the latter half of the eighteenth century.[104]

The other important site in Noa Dihing valley is Miao Bum. A cylindrical stone structure about 250 feet in height was found there. Other stray finds connected with Buddhism were reported occasionally from the same area since 1942. In 1962, a bronze image of Buddha (8" inches in height) now installed in Assam Buddha Dham, Lekhapani, was discovered at Tirap gate in Tirap district. The discovery of a similar bronze statue was reported as early as 1942 from the same area. Another Buddha icon of sand stone, which was earlier on display at the Central Museum, Shillong, was discovered in 1950 near Jairampur, Tirap district. In the same year, one Buddha head of white quartz was collected from Nampong in the same district which was also kept in the Central Museum, Shillong.[105]

As stated earlier, the Tangsas (in Tirap district) are also followers of Hinayana form of Buddhism. The Akas (now in the Kameng district) came under the influence of both Hinduism and Buddhism, though they had their own religious system based on shamanistic - animistic belief. R. S. Kennedy notes that "their animism has every appreciable amount of Tibetan Buddhism mixed... as Tibetan Buddhism is to animism, so is Aka animism to Tibetan Buddhism. Near their villages are *Chortens*...the chants sung by the priests are undoubtedly imitation of Lama Chants... they have a Buddhist temple or *Chakang* with an idol in it"[106] C.R. Macgregor also refers to the acceptance of Buddhist tenets and philosophy by the Aka tribe.[107] Buddhism, however, did not make a lasting impact on them. In due course of time, they started showing an inclination more towards Vaishnavism of the saints of Assam than Tibetan Buddhism. The Mijis (also in the Kameng district) like the Akas came under certain amount of Buddhist influence. But it proved to be a passing phase. They like many other tribes follow the indigenous tribal religion.

Buddhism was in the most flourishing state in North Eastern Frontier Region in the late medieval period (17th and 18th centuries). It further flourished in the nineteenth and twentieth centuries. The Arunachal tribes mentioned above (except the Akas and Mijis) still profess Buddhism.

Buddhism could not make much headway in other parts of north-east India. However, there are some concrete evidence to show that there were some other tribes who also could not keep themselves away from the forces of Buddhism and ultimately came within its fold.

The two important Buddhist tribes are the Chakmas and Mags or Mughs. They immigrated into the Chittagong Hill Tracts from Arakan in Burma towards the close of the sixteenth century or in early seventeenth century wherefrom some time later the former's diffusion took place and a large section of them moved to Mizo hills (present Mizoram) and Hill Tipperah (present Tripura), settled there and in recent past some became the settlers of Lohit-Tirap belt in

Arunachal, and the latter came to Mizoram and Tripura. Both the tribes are mainly concentrated in Tripura.

The *Theravada* Buddhism of Chakmas has its roots in Burma or Chittagong. The Chakmas of Tripura, according to W.W. Hunter, were Buddhists. In every village, there was *Khyang* — Buddhist temple - and Monk, and the images of Buddha were being worshipped according to the established religious rites. The Monks were the pivot of Buddhist system of religion. At the same time they worshipped Lord Śiva and Kāli *vis-a-vis* traditional deities. Their religion on the whole appears to be mixture of Buddhist, Hindu and old tribal customs.[108] The Mughs follow the Buddhist religion and custom. The Persian chronicler, Muhammad Cazim, has also referred to the prevalence of Buddhist faith amongst the Mugh tribe of Tripura. At the same time, he has called them semi-Hinduized.[109] J.C. Ghosh has also given an indication that Tippera became a centre of Buddhism because of its contact with Sylhet in Bengal and Magadha in Bihar.[110]

The archaeological ruins in the southern part of Tripura testify to the fact that a Buddhistic kingdom was there in remote past. The Mags and the Chakmas are two Buddhist dominant communities of south Tripura. Rangamati (the present Udaipur in south Tripura) was the capital of the Buddhistic kingdom. It was situated on the southern bank of the Gumati river.[111]

Most of the Chakmas and Mags in Tripura still profess Buddhism. In the temple of Lord Buddha in a Chakma village, there are *Bhikkus* (Monks), *Rauless, Ojhas* and *Gankulies.* The *Rauless* perform the customary rites from cradle to grave. The *Ojhas* appease the evil spirits. The *Gankulies* sing religious songs from village to village. The supreme God of the Mags is *Phora* (Buddha). In each Mag village there is a *Kheyang* (temple of Lord Buddha). "It is a single roomed but thatched with a four sloped roof designed in the form of *Pagoda.* Inside the temple there is an image of Lord Buddha in Yoga-form which is made of mud. There is a priest for this temple who is known as *Shamphura.*"[112]

This may also be noted here that Tantric Buddhism found its way in Jaintia hills from Kāmarūpa (ancient Assam) and partly through Sylhet in the post-seventh century. It is said that "Griva Kāmākhyā of the Jaintias was named as Grivakali and the Jangha Kāmākhyā was named as Jangha Kali. Bancharu being profoundly influenced by the cult of Buddhist Tantricism introduced the sacrifice of human beings in the shrine of Jangha Kali.[113]

We learn from two faithful Tibetan historical records, *Pagsam Jon Zan* of Sumpa Khan-po, and *Kahbab Dun-dan* of Lama Taranath (the author of famous work, *History of Buddhism in India,* composed in 1608) that after the downfall of Magadha, one of the chief centres of Buddhism, and the destruction of Nalanda and Odantapuri Buddhist universities in Bihar at the hands of Bakhtiar Khilji (in AD 1197), a large number of Budhdists fled towards Nepal, Munad (Burma), Arakan and other places. Some of them dispersed in the plains and hills of Assam including Cachar, Sylhet and Tripura and propagated Buddhism. Towards the east, Buddhism spread more and more than before. A place called Nan-gata or Naingata (the Hill Tracts of Assam, Cachar and Tripura) was inhabited by the Buddhists and ruled over by Sundara-Hachi, one of the four sons of Bablasundar, a Buddhist king of Chittagong and Tippera.[114] During his rule some of the tribes of the said hill tracts might have come within the fold of Buddhism.

Regarding some influence of Buddhism on the Naga tribes, it has been pointed out that the tree and serpent worship of the old Nagas including those of Manipur was based on Buddhist beliefs.[115] But it is very difficult to affirm the veracity of the statement.

On the whole, we find that both Hinduism and Buddhism - the two prominent schools of religion - flourished among some of the tribes of north-east India during the period under notice.

Notes and References

1. Sanskrit text with parallel Hindi trans., ed. by Chamanlal Gautam (Bareli, 1973), Vol. I, Vs. 100-118, 125-26, pp. 497-501.
2. *Valmiki-Rāmāyana, Bāla Kānda* (ed. by Pt. Akhilanand, Amritsar, Vs. 2025) ch. 55. v. 3; *Vishnu Purāṇa* (Hindi edn.), p. 671; *Mārkandeya Purāṇa* (Hindi edn), pp. 154-55; *Brahma Purāṇa* (Hindi edn.), p. 308; Pargiter, *The Mārkaṇḍeya Purāṇa* (Eng. trans. Bibliotheca Indica Series) Vol. II, pt. II Canto—LVII, pp. 283-84, 322; W.H. Schoff, *The Periplus of the Erythraean sea* (London, 1912), pp. 252, 278f: McCrindle, *Ancient India as described by Magasthenes and Arrian* (ed. by R.C. Jain, Delhi, 1972), pp. 80f. App. 4, pp. 230-33; McCrindle, *Ancient India as described by Ptolemy* (Calcutta, 1927), pp. 191-94; Gerini *Researches on Ptolemy's Geog.* (London, 1909), pp. 28ff.
3. *Studies in the Geography of Ancient and Medieval India* (Delhi, 1971), pp. 162-63.
4. *Vishnu Purāṇa* (Calcutta, 1961), Book. V, ch. XXIX, p. 459.
5. *The Imperial Gazetteer of India,* Vol. VI, p. 23.
6. *The Journal of the Assam Research Society,* Vol. XVI, 1962 (pub. 1964), p. 61.
7. *Hinduism and Buddhism* (London, 1st Pub. 1921, reptd. 1957) Vol. II, p. 274.
8. *The Mother Goddess Kāmākhyā* (1st edn. Gauhati, 1948, 3rd 1967), pp. 10-16.
9. *The Background of Assamese Culture* (1st edn. Shillong, 1948), pp. 4, 17, 95.
10. *Ibid., pp.* 97, 99, 105.
11. K.M. Gupta, JARS, Vol. I, N. I, April 1933, pp. 6-9.
12. Dubi Copper Plate Inscription of Ramasinha, *Journal and Proceedings of the Asiatic Society of Bengal,* New Series, Vol. XVIII, N. I, 1922, pp. 73, 77-79. Daudig plate and Jaintiapur plate, JPASB, Vol. XIX. N. 8, 1923, pp. 323, 329, 331-35; E.A. Gait, *Report on the Progress of Historical Research in Assam* (1897), p. 16.
13. JARS, Vol. Ill, N. 2, July 1935, p. 67

14. E.A. Gait, *History of Assam,* (2nd edn. Calcutta & Simla, 1926) p. 12.
15. See W.H. Schoff, *The Periplus of the Erythraean Sea* (London, 1912), p. 254.
16. IGI, Vol. I, p. 427.
17. *The History, Antiquities, Topography & Statistics of Eastern India* (collated from original documents) (reptd. Delhi, 1976), Vol. V, pp. 665, 690.
18. JARS, Vol. XX, 1972 (Pub. 1972-73), pp. 8-13.
19. R.M. Nath, *op. cit.* pp. 71, 75.
20. Assam Sec. Private Sec. Office, Arch. Branch "B" Progs, June 1910, Nos. 7, 9.
21. *Proceedings of Lt. Governor of Eastern Bengal and Assam,* June 1910 No. 18.
22. JASB, Vol. LXIX, 1900, p. 45.
23. *History of Assam Rifles* (London, 1929), pp. 256 f.
24. JARS, Vol. IV, No. 2, July 1936, p. 38.
25. P.C. Choudhury, JARS, Vol. XIV, Sept. 1978, pp. 36-37, 41.
26. *Kirata-janakrti* (ASB, Calcutta, 1974) p. 123.
27. *The Statistical Account of Assam* (London, 1879, reptd. Delhi, 1975), Vol. II, pp. 400-01.
28. JASB, Vol. LXXI, Pt. Ill, 1902, pp. 36-37.
29. Cf. A.C. Banerjee, *The Eastern Frontier of British India* (Calcutta, 1946), pp. 22-23.
30. *Bengal & Assam, Bihar & Orissa,* ed. by A. Wright (London, 1917) p. 463; see also E.F. Sandys, *History of Tripura* (compiled from authentic sources), Calcutta, 1915, rept. Agartala, 1997, p. 10.
31. JARS, Vol. VII, No. 2, July 1939, p. 38.
32. *Descriptive Ethnology of Bengal* (Calcutta, 1872, reptd. Calcutta, 1960) p. 110.
33. *Op. cit.* p. 136 f.
34. *North-Eastern Affairs,* Vol. I, Jan.-March 1973, p. 11; W.W. Hunter, *The Statistical Account of Bengal* (London, 1876), Vol. VI, p. 45.
35. JARS, Vol. XVI, 1962 (pub. 1964), pp. 22-23.

36. JARS, Vol. VII, No. 2, July 1939, p. 38.
37. *Kāmārupā Sāsanāvali,* introd. P. 27, ref to JARS, Vol. VII, No.2, 1939, p. 60.
38. JARS, Vol. XX, 1972-73, p. 52.
39. *Early History of Kāmārupā,* pp. 108, 115.
40. *Report of the Archaeological Tour in Assam,* 1905, Home "B" Progs, Nos-702-708, File No. V.A. 8.
41. JARS, Vol. XIV, 1978, p. 1.
42. JARS, Vol. Ill, No. 2, July 1935, p. 45.
43. Ref. to JARS, Vol. Ill, No. 2, July 1935, p. 46.
44. JARS, Vol. VI, No. I, April, 1938, pp. 8-9.
45. *Sadhana Mala,* II (Oriental Institute, Baroda 1928), p. 455, ref. to JARS, Vol. XVI, 1962 (pub. 1864), p. 56.
46. JPASB (new series), Vol. X, 1914, p. 346.
47. *Op. cit.* p. 15.
48. *Op. cit.* pp. VU-V1II.
49. *Op. cit.* p. 58.
50. Hoernle, JASB, Vol, LXVI, Pt. I, 1897, p. 129, First plate, verse 13.
51. IGI, Vol. VI, p. 36.
52. *B.K. Kakati, op. cit.* pp. 60-64.
53. *Op. cit.,* p. 268.
54. Letters Received from Govt., 1832, Vol. 8, pp. 129-130.
55. S.K. Chatterjee, *Kirāta-jana-Krti,* pp. 19ff, 122.
56. *Calcutta Review,* Vol. XXXVIII, 1863, p. 283.
57. S.K. Bhuyan, *Deodhai Assam Buranji* (DHAS, Gauhati, 1932), pp. xxiii, 169-175.
58. *Op. cit.* pp. 264-65.
59. *Where India, China and Burma* Meet (Calcutta, 1933), p. 26.
60. BPP, Vol. XLVIII, Nos. 95-96, July-Dec. 1934, p. 38.
61. JARS, Vol. VI. No.I, April, 1938, pp. 7-8.
62. *Indian Culture,* Vol. VI, p. 288, quoted by K.L. Barua, JARS, Vol. VI, April 1938, pp. 10-11.

63. JARS, Vol. VI, No. 2, July 1938, pp. 55f.
64. MI, Vol. II, No. 3, 1922, p. 150.
65. IHQ, Vol. X, No. I, 1934, pp. 14-20.
66. *Op. cit.* Vol. II, pp. 278-79.
67. *The Outlook on NEFA* (Assam Sahitya Sabha, Jorhat, 1958), p. 45.
68. *Op. cit.* pp. 122, 169.
69. JARS, Vol. XX, 1972 (pub. 1972-73), p. 62.
70. *Extract from the Proceedings of the Govt. of India* (Home Deptt.), 1902, April, Shillong, 4th Feb., 1901, No. 175/433.
71. DEB, p. 77; DAB, pp. xxvif.
72. JASB, Vol. XXXVIII,1868, pp. 194-97.
73. JASB, Vol. LXIX, Pt. Ill, 1900, p. 59.
74. *Op. cit.* p. 46.
75. DEB, p. 82.
76. *Op. cit.* pp. 109, 113.
77. My Experiences in Manipur and the Naga Hills (London, 1896, reptd. Delhi, 1971), pp. 83-84.
78. *Naga Path* (London, 1952), p. 41. The statement runs contrary to the truth. Jadonang and his follower Rani Gaidinliu Vehemently opposed Christianity and strongly supported Hinduism (during 1927-31 and 1931-32 respectively) as the latter herself revealed to me in the course of my interviewing her in August 1984 at her official residence at Kohima. The former had faith in the worship of Vishnu.
79. *Demographic and Socio-Econimic Profiles of the Hill Areas of North East India,* (Delhi, 1970), pp. 105, 107.
80. Annual Report of Mr. Coxhead, cf. Foreign Dept. Political Consultation, Octob. 1877, Nos. 271-273.
81. *Report on the Census of Assam* for 1881 (Calcutta, 1883), Report by C.J. Lyall, pp. 34-37, 75 f; *Census of India* 1891, Assam (Shillong, 1892), Reports by E.A. Gait, Vol. I, pp. 80-84, 225, 233, Vol. II, Table VII, Vol. Ill, pp. Ixxii-lxxxi; *Census of India* 1901, Vol. IV, Assam, pt. I. (Shillong, 1902), Report by B.C. Alien, pp. 39-50; *Census of India*

1911, Vol. Ill, Assam, pt. I (Shillong, 1912), Report by J. McSwiney, pp. 39ff, 133.

82. *Census of India* 1891, Assam, Vol. I, pt. II, p. 51.
83. *Ibid.,* pp. 51, 80-84.
84. *Census of India,* 1931, Vol. Ill, Assam, pt. I, pp. 188-91.
85. *Gazetteer of Bengal and North East India,* by B.C. Alien, E.A. Gait, C.G.H. Alien and H.F. Howard (Delhi, 1979), pp. 434, 454, 564, 571, 603.
86. Shihab-ud-din Talish, *Fattiya-i-Ibriya,* Eng. trans. by Sir, J.N. Sarkar, JBORS, Vol. I, Pt. II, 1915, pp. 179-195.
87. *Op. cit.* pp. 206-7.
88. *Op. cit.* pp. 206-7, 220.
89. *Op. cit.* pp. 220-21.
90. IGI, Vol. VI, p. 24.
91. *Indo-Aryan and Hindi* (Calcutta, 1969), pp. 32-34.
92. *Ibid.,* p. 50.
93. Atkinson, *The Himalayan Gazetteer,* Vol. II, Pt. II, p. 734f.
94. *History of Upper Assam, Upper Burma and North Eastern Frontier* (London, 1914), p. 7If.
95. For details see N. Sarkar, "Historical Account of the Introduction of Buddhism among the Monpas and Sherdukpens", *Arunachal News* (a monthly Journal, pub. by the Arunachal Pradesh Administration, Shillong), Vol. 4, No. 7, Octob, 1975, pp. 11-15; Vol. 4, No. 8, Nov. 1975, pp. 14-17.
96. See Sarkar, *op. cit., Arunachal News,* Vol. 4, No. 8, Nov. 1975, pp. 14-17; "A Historical Account of Tawang Monastery", *Resarun* (Journal of the Research Department, Directorate of Research, Govt. of Arunachal Pradesh, Shillong), Vol. IV, No. 2, 1978, pp. 17-24.
97. See also J.N. Chowdhury, *Arunachal Panorama* (Shillong, 1973), pp. 47-8.
98. *As. Res.,* Vol. XVI, 1828, pp. 337, 345-48.
99. "Buddhism in Assam", JARS, Vol. III. No. 4, 1936, p. 117.
100. *A Sketch of Assam,* pp. 80-81.
101. DEB, p. 5.

102. *Report on the Census of Assam for 1881,* Report by C.J. Lyall, p. 39; *Census of India 1891, Assam,* Vol. I, Report by E.A. Gait, p. 91.
103. S. Dutta and B. Tripathy have dwelt at length upon the subject in their jointly written article "Buddhist Monuments of the Khamtis-A Preliminary Survey" pub. in PNEIHA, 24th Session, Guwahati, 2003, pp. 146-56.
104. See Y.A. Raikar, *Vijaynagar - The Forgotten Khomong,* Shillong, 1977; "Khomong in the History of the Khamptis", *Research in Arunachal* 1951-1976, Shillong, 1978, pp. 11-26.
105. A.K. Das, "Archaeological sites and Historical Monuments of Arunachal", *Arunachal News,* Vol. 2, No. 2, May 1973. p. 16.
106. *Ethnological Report on the Akas, Khoas, Mijis and the Monbas (Monpas) of Tawang* (Shillong, 1914), p.8; also V. Elwin, *India's North-East Frontier in the Nineteenth century* (Calcutta, 1959), p. 442.
107. PASB, No. XI, 1884, pp. 198-99.
108. SAB, Vol. VI *(Chittagong Hill Tracts, Chittagong, Naokhali, Tipperah, Hill Tipperah),* London, 1876, p. 45.
109. *Alamgirnamah,* p. 940.
110. "Buddhism in Kamarupa and Sylhet", JARS, Vol. IV, No. 2, 1936, p. 47.
111. Sipra Sen, *Tribes of Tripura* (Delhi, 1993), p. 46.
112. *Ibid., pp.* 60, 62.
113. R.M. Nath, *op. cit.* p. 100.
114. See also Nath, *op. cit.* pp. 80-81; JARS, Vol. IV, No. 2, 1936, p. 36, note 13.
115. S. Beal, *The Life of Hiuen Tsiang* (London, 1884, rept. Delhi, 1973), Preface, xf.

6

The Evolution of Vaishnavism in Assam with Reference to its Impact on Literature

The roots of Vaishnavism, one of the four important sects of Hinduism, which flourished in different parts of Eastern India during the period concerned, were deeply embedded in the tenets of Vishṇu-Vasūsdeva-Krishṇa cult and the Bhāgavata Purāṇa. There were two different phases of the growth of Vaishnavism in Assam. In the early phase (from the Epic Age to the 12th century A.D.) it was more or less a queer mixture of the Purānic and Tantric faiths, and in the later (15th-16th centuries) it was principally based on the doctrine of Bhakti or monotheism as propounded by Shankaradeva, a great social and religious reformer, philosopher, artist, musician, poet, dramatist and linguist, all combined into one. The Bhāgavata tradition in Vaishnavism which virtually emerged in the early centuries of the Christian era with emphasis on devotion or Bhakti of the worshipper for an individual deity and gained ground in the post-Gupta period attained greater popularity in Medieval Assam, Bengal and Orissa. Bhagavatism, in fact, constituted the corner-stone of the Vaishnava cult of Hinduism prevalent in these three different states during the Medieval period. A substantial part of Hinduism itself had undergone transformation with the popularity of the Bhagavata cult in Eastern India. By the Medieval period this Cult had been absorbed into Classical Hiṇduism. There were successive stages through which Vaishnavism evolved in Eastern India. The ancient literature, foreign accounts, epigraphic records, particularly the inscriptions of Assam, and other archaeological evidence testify to the prevalence of Vaishnavism in Assam in the early period in the form of the worship of Vishnu and his incarnations, i.e. Hayagriva, Mādhava, Vāsudeva-Krishṇa, Varāha and Nārāyana.

The antiquity of the worship of Vishṇu and Vāsudeva-Krishna in the Indian perspective can be traced back to the early Vedic age and the later Vedic age respectively. Vishnu was known in the Rigvedic period. Later on, he became the object of worship and devotion as the supreme God.

The earliest reference to Vāsudeva-Krishṇa cult occurs in the *Chhāndogya Upanishad*. This cult was in a flourishing stage in the 5th century B.C. as evidenced by the statements of *Pāṇini*. In course of time, Vāsudeva-Krishna of the Vāsudeva-Bhāgavata cult was identified with the Vedic deity Vishnu and thereafter the Bhāgavata religion came to be popularly known as Vaishnava Dharrna. The Brāhmaṇs encouraged this identification and brought this new and powerful religious sect within the pale of the orthodox Vedic faith. The Vāsudeva cult also emerged in the form of a religious movement. It also developed along the same lines which the followers of Buddhism and Jainism followed. The followers of this cult denounced the elaborate sacrificial ritual, repudiated the slaughter of animals and advocated the path of devotion as the way of salvation. Vāsudeva-Krishṇa-Vishnu also got identified with a sage (personified as god) named Nārāyan. The earliest evidence of the identification of Naiayan with Vishnu has been furnished in the *Baudhayana Dharma Śūtra*. The *Śatapatha Brāhmaṇa* refers to a Purusha Nārāyana performing a *Pancharātra Satra* (sacrifice that continued for five days). The name Pancharātras was applied to the followers of one of the schools of Vaishnavism, who strictly adhered to this five day Satra of Narayana in contradistinction to another school of Bhāgavatas. The emergence of the Vāsudeva-Krishna-Vishnu-Nārāyan cult proved to be a powerful religious force in ancient India. However the followers of the Bhāgavata sect confined themselves to the worship of Vasudeva-

Krishṇa. Vishṇu-Vāsudeva was deified and His worship in anthropomorphic form began in the earty centuries of the Christian era and continued onwards.

From an analysis of the data presented above one can find that in the early period different cults were absorbed into Vaishnavism. And Assam was no exception to this. We find that Bhagadatta, a king of Assam in the epic age, was a devotee of Krishna which can be amply substantiated by the Tezpur grant of Vanamala Varmadeva (835—65 A.D.). The *Kālika Purāna* (composed in the 10th cent. A.D. in Assam itself) provides a positive evidence of the worship of five incarnations of the deity Vishnu in the form of Hayagriva in Manikuta (Hajo), Mādhava (or Bhairava) in Rakshakuta, Vasudeva-Krishna in the Dikkaravasini region (modern Sadiya), etc. The mode of worship of Vāsudeva-Krishna as stated in the *Kālika Purāna* bears close resemblance to the rules laid down in the *Pancharātra Saṁhitās*. The faith of the people of Manikuta in Vishnu worship can also be confirmed by a very popular Tantric text—*Yogini Tantra*. From the Purāṇic literature it is quite evident that the worship of Hayagriva- Mādhava represents a synthesis of both Purāṇic and Tantrik elements.

The most reliable information with regard to Vishnu worship in the 6th century A.D. is found in the Badaganga inscription ascribed to Bhutivarman (553-54 A.D.). From this rock inscription found near Davaka in modern Nowgong it distinctly appears that the king was a follower of the Bhagavata tradition. The extensive archaeological remains of temples dedicated to Vishnu and his incarnations and icons of the deity concerned in different parts of Assam constitute the monumental evidence to the spread of Vaishnavism in general, and the popularity of Vishnu worship in the iconographic form, in particular, in the 5th-6th century A.D.

The *Harshacharita* of Bāṇabhatta (7th century A.D.), the account of Hiuen-Tsang (629-45 A.D.) and the Nidhanpur grant bear an eloquent testimony to the fact that Bhaskaravarman (A.D. 594-650), the illustrious monarch of Eastern India and a contemporary of Harsha, belonged to the Vaishnava family and popularised Vishnu (Nārāyanadeva) cult before he embraced Buddhism.

Vaishnavism in the early period received a great impetus at the hands of the rulers of Pāla dynasty. The Bargaon grant of Ratnapāla (A.D. 1010-1050) and the Gauhati Grant of Indrapāla (A.D, 1050-1075) bear witness to the fact that Ratnapāla had abiding faith in the worship of Krishna. The inscriptions of his period bear the words "Krishna". "Purushottama", "Janardana", etc. The Gauhati grant of the king concerned, Khonamukhi grant and Pushpabhadra grant of Dharmapāla (1095-1120 A.D.) and other grants of the Pala period and the Tezpur grant prove that the rulers were great devotees of Vishnu, Hari, Narayana, Krishna, etc..

The appearance of Shankaradeva on the scene in the latter half of the 15th century heralded the dawn of a new age in the socio-religious history of Medieval Assam. His period marked a fundamental departure from the earlier tradition based on Tantrik rites. The earlier Tantrik-Buddhist system, which started gaining popularity after the extinction of Pāla rule in the 12th century, was put under check to a certain extent. The absorption of Tantrik Buddhist rites into the Neo-Vaishnavism of later period to some extent cannot be denied. However, it may be admitted that Vaishnavism in his times entered upon a new phase of orientation.

Shankaradeva preached basically the Bhakti cult of Vaishnavism. He was greatly inspired by the ideals embodied in the *Bhāgavata* and the *Upanishadas*. He revived the monotheistic doctrine, which is the core of the religio-philosophical system of India. He raised the banner of revolt against the prevailing Shakta and Tantrik practices in Assam. He also raised a voice of protest against the elaborate and excessive rituals, other superficial paraphernalia of religion and the domination of the priestly class. The religion that he preached was fundamentally based on the theory of "Ekasharaniya worship" i.e. surrender to and worship of one God only. It is commonly believed that his theory of worship of one God to the total exclusion of the others was propounded by him after deriving an inspiration from the Jagannatha temple in Puri (which he visited first in 1491), where the individual personality of all the Hindu gods and goddesses losses its identity in the body of Jagannatha. Here it may be pointed out that even though Jagannathism emphasises the worship of all the gods and goddesses in the form of Jagannatha, still it recognises the offer of worship to the other gods and goddesses individually and separately. In the course of his second visit to Puri at the age of 97 he was profoundly influenced by the Oriya translation of the Bhagavata by Jagannatha Das. Like most of the Vaishnava reformers of his time he also preached the fundamental equality of all religious and the unity of Godhead. But the patterns of Tantrik worship prevalent in Assam in those days might have presented hurdles in the way of the worship of the presiding deities of the other cults. However, the new path of devotion popularised by him came to be known as Bhagavata Nama Dharma, which exercised a tremendous impact on the Assamese community. He not only preached the doctrine of Bhakti through his Nama ' Dharma, but also remoulded the fabric of the socio - cultural life of the Assamese people. He achieved remarkable success in his attempt by setting up Satraa and Namghars; the former was developed as the socio-religious centre while the latter was founded in every village to serve as a prayer hall, cultural 'centre, etc. These two socio-religious institutions became not only the media for propagating his views, but also fostered the spirit of oneness among the people concerned. Thus, he became an aposte of socio-cultural renaissance in Eastern India.

Vaiahnavism also paved the way for the efflorescence of Assamese literature. Shankaradeva's monumental literary works, permeated with great devotional fervour, include the Assamese translation of the *Bhāgavata*, and *Kirtan, Dasham, Bhakti Pradip* and *Gunamala.* Vaishnavism had left its marks on the pages of the devotional literature of his times. The contribution of this great Vaishnava saint to the richness of Assamese language and literature will always be remembered in the history of Assam.

The literature also became the fountain head for the further progress of Vaishnavipm among the masses. Shankaradeva's creed was Qualified Monism as expounded by Rāmānuja and it differed from the Absolute Monism of Shankaracharya. His philosophy of Vaishnavism brought multitudes of people under his influence even during his own life time, and some of these ultimately became his disciples and great Vaishnava preachers. Actually, it was due to the influence of his Vaishnava movement in the 15th century that some sections of the tribal people of the hills and plains of Assam came unhesitatingly within the fold of Vaishnavism. Some of them were the Nagas, Garos, Mikirs, Miris, Akas and Kacharis. Venerable preachers were Narottam of the Nagas, Govinda of the Garos, Balai of the Mikirs, Paramananda of the Miris, Ramai of the Kacharis, Damodar of the Bhutias and Aghora Chandrama Gama Dafla. They went in every nook and corner of the hills as ambassadors of the unity of the hills and the plains, and preached the religious philosophy of Shankaradeva. The Noctes and Wanchoos (of present Arunachal Pradeah) became, by and large, Vaishnavites and accepted the Goswami of Baraghar Sattra near Nazira as their religious teacher. The devotional songs pertaining to Lord Krishna and dances depicting various episodes connected with his life and Radha also became popular particularly among the Noctes-frontier tribes. The Aka tribes also started worshipping the "God Hari" or "Hari-Deo".

7

The Paurāṇic Account of Naraka's Conquest of Ancient Kingdom of Prāgjyotisha and the Kirātas in North-East India with Reference to Its Consequential Politico-Cultural Changes

The present paper aims at portraying a vivid picture of Naraka's conquest of the ancient kingdom of Prāgjyotisha, situated on the extreme eastern fringe of Bhāratavarsha, and its earliest inhabitants popularly known as the Kirātas as depicted in the paurāṇic texts with new interpretation of facts. This interesting episode occurred in Pre-Yudhisthira period. The subject under review still stands as one of the most obscure aspects of the political history of ancient Assam.

Naraka[1], generally known as mytho-historical figure, (the ancestor of Bhagadatta) came from Videha to Prāgjyotisha as a political adventurer in pre-Bhārata war period (roughly ascribed to 3100 B.C.) before the commencement of Kali-Yuga or Iron Age and after having inflicted a crushing defeat on the Kirātas[2] in a fierce battle conquered the land, installed himself on the throne of Prāgjyotisha (later known as Kāmarūpa), proclaimed his political supremacy, laid the foundation of first Āryan kingdom and paved the way for the spread of Āryan culture which gradually led to the evolution of synthesis of the Āryan and non-Āryan culture in North East India.

According to *Kālika Purāna*[3], before the advent of Naraka the Prāgjyotisha was under the political sway of the famous Kirāta Chief named Ghataka. Lord Vishṇu found him very majestic ruler and famous for his glory and splendour. After having got firmly convinced that Naraka's purpose is to usurp his throne, Ghataka marched with his army and started showering arrows after arrows on his political adversary. The war started between the Kirāta king and Naraka. Naraka, being redoubtable warrior fought gallantly with arrows, bows and other weapons. In this war all the chiefs of the Kirātas, their commander-in-chief and other prominent soldiers were killed. Their most beloved king Ghataka was beheaded. Naraka captured twenty five hundred elephants of Ghataka and also cavalry, jewels, ornaments of women, costumes, state banner etc. After overthrowing the Mleccha King, Naraka unfurled the banner of victory over newly besieged kingdom of Prāgjyotisha. After the death of Ghataka many of his Kirāta subjects deserted the country and fled away eastwards to the sea-shore. Those who survived the massacre submitted to the invaders or surrendered at the feet of triumphant Naraka. After this historic war, which constituted a landmark in ancient history of North-East India, the Kirātas were pushed back to the hills from the plains. Naraka provided shelter to those who surrendered at his feet. Actually it was Lord Vishnu who asked Naraka to exterminate the Kiratas running away towards Dikkaravasini Devi and to protect those who have taken shelter. Naraka is stated to have pushed the Kiratas towards Dikkaravasini. Many Kirātas were driven towards the Sea or marshy region. The *Kālika Purāṇa*[4] also furnishes clear evidence that the Kirātas were driven back in the eastern side lying at the end of marshy region.

After the annihilation of the Kirātas who did not recognise the authority of the Vedas and Śāstras, the Dvija or twice born people-followers of Sanatana Dharma were allowed to settle. The Vedic rites and rituals were revived. Naraka adopted Maya, daughter of the Raja of Vidarbha as his queen and thereafter his Coronation Ceremony took place[5]. This ceremony was attended by his God-father and God-mother who came from Mithilā to Prāgjyotisha. Janaka, the Lord of Videha came with his queen and retinue, visited the conquered kingdom of Prāgjyotisha, enjoyed his hospitality, blessed his enterprising foster child and left for Videha after some time. Janaka had certainly some affection for him otherwise he would not have visited the new kingdom. Actually, the visit of Janaka to Prāgjyotisha constituted a milestone towards the beginning and growth of politico-cultural relations between Kāmarūpa and Videha[6]. The credibility of this ancient historical tradition has been fairly attested by one of the local scholars, R. M. Nath[7] who observes that "In imitation of the custom of the family of the God father, new king assumed the title Nara-Ka (protector of men) as Jana-Ka (protector of men) was the title of the royal family of Mithila. The capital was established near the present Gauhati town and its old name Prag-Zuh-this was rejoined as Pragjyotishpur." Prāgjyotishpur looking like Indrapuri was regarded by Naraka as Amaravati.

After Naraka came to power and rose to prominence, the name of the kingdom was changed from Prāgjyotisha to Kāmarūpa, "Pragjyotisha and Kamaiupa, though very closely associated at one time, formed two distinct Janapads. Kāmarūpa in later time came to be regarded as the name of the kingdom or Janapad of which the Pura or headquarter had the name of Prāgjyotisha". The Āryans or Brāhmins coming from Mithila and other parts of the Aryavarta to Pragjyotish were granted the royal patronage, which marked the beginning of the process of Aryanisation in North East India. R. M. Nath[8] has correctly stated that the "new kingdom was gradually extended and the people from Mithila were brought to man and administer the country". This paved the way for the spread of Maithili language and culture in ancient Assam. Naraka is also believed to have introduced and popularised the cult of Saktism, which was very much associated with Austric elements. While supporting R. M. Nath and the pauranic evidence K. L. Barua[9] also states that Kāmarūpa known in ancient times as Prāgyotisha is very much associated with Naraka which goes back to the epoch of Mahābhārata war. The Āryan name was "extended to the regions directly from Videha and Magadha long before central or lower Bengal became either habited or Aryanised." In other source[10] also he mentions that after having killed the Kirāta king Ghatak and conquered the Prāgjyotisha, Naraka allowed the Aryans to settle in his new kingdom before the Bharat War. This fact has been also substantiated by E. Gait[11]. Naraka's period is marked by the genesis of a synthetic culture-the Āryan and non-Āryan, Alpine Āryans, the Austric, the Bodos and the other Kirātas.

According to Robinson[12] the earliest tradition connecting history of Kamarupa is that it was given by Lord Krishna to Naraka. Lord Krishna appointed him guardian of the temple of Kāmākhyā. Being a great oppressor and worshipper of rival God Siva, he was put to death by Krishna. About the death of Naraka the pauranic tradition relates that Lord Krishna in one fierce battle fought in Pragjyotisha cut Naraka to pieces with his discus, a Celestial Missile.

It is of course very difficult to determine the antiquity of this historic event in the classical history of Assam. B. K. Kakati'[13] suggests that the forward limit of Naraka's time could not be later than the end of 4th century and backward limit can't be earlier than the 3rd Century. Further he suggests that Naraka of Mithila established himself sometimes between 200-500 A.D. This is not a reasonable postulation. Hence forward we can't find ourselves in agreement with this chronology. Naraka's episode in Prāgjyotisha can be tentatively fixed about 3100 B.C. before which he had undoubtedly flourished and founded the kingdom.

Notes and References

1. About Naraka's early life, genealogy, antiquity and migration from Videha or Mithilā to Prāgjyotisha, several

traditional, mythological and historical accounts are available. According to *Kālika Purāṇa* (herein after abbrev. as K. P. Barailley, 1973, Vol. I, Vs. 1-60, pp. 470-80, Vs. 1-98, pp. 481-497) this orphan boy was brought up in the court or family of Janaka, the king of Videha alongwith the royal princes till he attained sixteen years of age. We also can't preclude the possibility of Naraka being the son of king Janaka himself through maiden or midwife named Katyayani which can be clearly substantiated by the fact as stated in this Pauranic text that Naraka himself regarded Janaka his father and his wife Sumati his mother and Sita as his sister. Whatever may be the fact, Naraka was no doubt adopted or foster child of King Janaka. Upto the age of sixteen he was imparted training with other royal princes in the art of polity and war. As he grew up he was found to be surpassing and excelling all royal princes in valour, intelligence, prudence and so on. He gradually became ambitious and powerful. Consequently both King and Queen became perturbed to think that this helpless orphan would one day usurp the throne or wrest the whole kingdom of Mithila. Ultimately this Kshatriya prince was removed or banished from the Court of Videha by his god father and god mother. He came accompanied by Lord Vishnu to Pragjyotishpur. Here it must be made clear that he was the first Aryan Chief of Pragjyotisha completely different from other Naraka having the ephithet of 'Sura' belonging to Asura or Danava dynesty. In the *Kālika Purāṇa* Naraka has nowhere been described as Naraka Sur. Some other *Purāṇas* like *Vishṇu Purāṇa* (Hindi Edn; Gorakhpur, Magh, Vs. 2010, Jan. 1954, p. 767; H. H. Wilson, *Vishṇu Purana,* English trans., Calcutta, 1961, Ch. XXIX, p. 459) and *Brahma Purana* (Hindi Edn., Gorakhpur, Magh. Vs. 2003, Jan 1947, pp. 518-19) also state that Naraka, adopted son of King Janaka, later became ruler of Pragjyotisha (stretching upto 100 *yojana* properly fenced round with iron palisades) after exterminating the Kiratas living near sites or shrines of *Devi-Dikkarvasini* and *Kāmākhyā.* The historicity of this pauranic account is beyond doubt. This pauranic evidence has been strongly supported by some local popular authorities, notably, B. K. Kakati *(The Mother Goddess Kamakhya,*

Gauahati, 1967, pp. 26 f.X), R. M. Nath *(The Background of Assamese Culture,* Shillong, 1948, pp. 26 f), and E. Gait *(History of Assam,* Calcutta, 1926, p. 13). Dr. P. Gogoi *(Journal of the Assam Research Society,* Vol. XVI, 1964, pp. 54-55) has also correctly stated that Naraka of *Kalika Purana* was 'a historical figure.' In the *Kishkindha Kanda* of *Valmiki Ramayana* (Edtd. by Pt. Akhilananda, Amritsar, 1st edn., Samvat, 2021, Vs. 30-31, p. 915) also it is clearly stated that in the sea-coast, 64 *yojana* in length and breadth there was a Varaha Mountain near which golden coloured Pragjyotisha was ruled by Naraka. Epigraphy also confirms this truth. See, A. F. Rudolf Hooernle, "*Gauhati* Copper Plate Grant of Indrapala of Pragjyotisha in Assam and the Nowgong Grant", J. A. S. B., 1897, Vol. XVI, Nos. 1 to IV, pt. 1, pp. 117-20; "Two Copper Plate Grants of Ratnopala of Pragjyotisha and Bergaon Grant," J. A. S. B., 1898, Vol. LXVII, pt. 1 Nos. 1 to 4 Text 1, 1st plate, Line, L. Vs. 3 pp. 113, 114, 163. These epigraphical records also testify to the truth that this Mleccha king conquered the ancient country of Kamarupa and took his residence in the town (Pura) of Pragjyotisha and was ultimately slain by Lord Krishna. However, the theory of his divine origin can be outrightly rejected. The other theories connected with the probabilities of the Dravidian or Phoenician origin as profounded by K.L. Barua *[Early History of Kamarupa* (E. H. K.), Shillong, 1933, pp. 20-21] and N. N. Vasu *(Social History of Kamarupa,* Calcutta, 1926, Vol. I pp. 211-22) and the Alpine origin as indicated by P. C. Choudhury *(The History of civilisation of the people of Assam,* Gauhati 1959, pp. 107,113,121,123) also do not appear tenable or very much convincing as the suggested facts have neither been widely accepted nor do we have any corroborative evidence to uphold this contention. P. C. Choudhury (op. cit. p. 123) seems to be correct to a considerable extent in suggesting that Naraka might have taken his birth in some hilly region to the north of Videha or Assam and he probably flourished during the Epic Age. In the *Imperial Gazetteer of India* (Vol. VI. p. 24) also Naraka has been mentioned as a reputed founder of the ancient and famous city of Pragjyotishpur (modern Gauhati). According to popular tradition he ruled from the Karatoya river to the extreme east of the Brahmaputra. "The *Kālika Purāna* and *Yogini Tantra* present the name of several kings whose titles Danava or Asura betray their aboriginal descent."

2. The appellation 'Kirāta' has been profusely referred to in numerous sources mainly the literary and classical, but the problem relating to their identification with special reference to the tribes of North East India still remain unsolved. Here we are faced with one baffling question as to who were the Kirāta people who fought with Naraka? The earlier recorded allusion to the appellation Kirāta occur in the Vedic literature *(Atharva Veda,* Brailley, 1975, Vol. I Ch. X, Sukta— 4 Vs. 14, pp. 530 f; *Yajurveda,* Brailley, 1974, Vs. 16 pp. 481 f), but nothing is explicitly expounded. It is true that sometimes no clear picture emerges from the twilight of early history. But, however, on the basis of some faithful records *Kiṣkindhā Kāṇḍa of Vālmiki Rāmāyana.* ch. 40, Vs. 27, 28 p. 906; *Mahābhārata, Sabhā Parva,* Hindi edn. ch. 26 Vs. 8-10. p. 743, ch. 30, Vs. 1, 4, 23 27, p. 753; *Bhiṣma Parva,* ch. IX. Vs. 51, 57, 69 pp. 2565-66; H. H. Wilson, *Vishnu Purāṇa,* BK III. ch. Ill, pp. 156-58, 162; Pargiter, *Mārkandeya Purāna,* Eng. trans. *Bibliotheca Indica,* Vol. II pt. II. Canto LVII, pp. 282-84, 322; *Vishnu Purāṇa,* Hindi edn. p. 671; *Mārkaṇḍeya Purana,* Hindi edn. pp. 154-55; *Brahma Purāna,* Hindi edn. pp. 308 f; Pargiter, J. A. S. B., 1897, Vol. LXVI, Pt, I, pp. 85, 105, 108-10; S. N. Majumdar Sastri, J. B. O. R. S. 1922, Vol. VIII, pp. 41-42 ; E. T. Atkinson, *The Himalayan Gazetter,* Vol. II pt. I. P. 357 ff; H. C. Chakadar. *The Geography of Kālidāsa,* Calcutta, 1965, pp. 23-24; D. C. Sircar, *The Geography of Ancient and Medieval India,* pp. 160-61) we can safely presume that the Kiratas were the dwellers of Eastern Himalayas in the marshy region near the sea-coast known as Sagararupa-Vasin which in all its probabilities comprised whole of North and South-East Bengal and the hills of Assam. They have been also described as the Himalayan

tribes inhabiting the Eastern extremity of the Bhāratavarsha that was Prāgjyojyotisha. Pargiter opines that the centre of the country of Kāmākhyā were inhabited by the Kiratas. However, in none of the above mentioned sources, the Kiratas have been properly identified with the tribes of Assam or the people of Pragjyotisha. Suniti Kumar Chatterjee *(KirataJana-krti,* Calcutta, 1974, pp. 26-38) has also frequently referred to the Kiratas of Assam as Indo-Mongoloids or Tibeto-Burmans but no clear identification has been given. Moreover his findings is not based on the dispassionate investigations of all the relevant sources. Most of the views established by him can be fairly disputed and disposed off. Hence, for the purpose of identification we shall have to place our exclusive reliance on the trustworthy accounts of the classical authors. On the basis of some valuable classical treatises (W. H. Schoff. *The periplus of the Erythraean sea,* London, 1912, pp. 253 ff; McCrindle's *Ancient India as described by Megasthenes and Arrian,* edtdo by R. C. Jain, Delhi, 1972, pp. 80, 177-78, App. 4, pp. 230-33; MC Crindle, *Ancient India as described by Plolemy,* Calcutta, 1927, pp. 191-94; Gerini. *Researches on Ptolemy's Geography,* London, 1909 pp. 28 ff; Lessen, *Zeitschr Kundel Morgini,* II, 40 ; Accounts of St. Martin) the Scyritae or Airrhadoi or Kirrhadia (Kiratas) have been identified with the Khasis, the Jaintias, the Garos, the Nagas, the people who settled in the neighbourhood of the Lauhitya or Brahmaputra and the people of Kachar, Tipperah, Sylhet, Burma and Arakan. The accounts of the early Greek and Roman geographers, particularly, Ptolemy, Arrian and Pliny have been strongly supported by E. T. Atkinson, (op. cit. pp. 357, 361, 363-66).

However, depending on the combined testimony of all the sources in general and classical in particular we can reasonably suggest that the Kiratas of Pragjyotisha can be identified with the Khasis, the Jaintias, the Garos, the Kacharis, the Chutias, the Tipperahs, the Nagas and other neighbouring tribes of North East India living during the time of Naraka. This finding will carry some weight, if we quote R. M. Nath (op. cit, pp. 20-21) who puts forth that the Austrics (the Khasis and the Jaintias) and the Bodos (the Garos, the Kacharis, the Chutias and Hill-Tipperahes) were termed as Nishadas, Kiratas and Dasyus in the same way as the Dravidians were termed as the Danavas and Daityas and Negroids as the Vanaras. Another local authority of great iminence and distinction K. L. Barua (op. cit. p. 8) has also identified them more or less in the same manner. Thus here we can prove that the above stated Kirāta people living in and around Prāgjyotisha after being subjugated by Naraka in this war deserted the country, got dispersed in different groups and settled in different Himalayan and sub-Himalayan regions as autochthones or aboriginals.

3. K. P., pp. 497-504.
4. K. P. Vs., 100-116, 125-26, pp. 497-501.
5. K. P. Vs., 128-133, p. 502.
6. For details see G.P. Singh's article in Proceedings of the N.E.I. History Association, Dibrugarh, 1981, pp. 63 ff.
7. *Op. cit.,* p. 26
8. *Op. cit.,* p. 27
9. J.I.H. 1933, Vol. XII. pt. I to II p. 303.
10. E.I.H. pp. 20-21, 27-30.
11. *A Descriptive Account of Assam* (Delhi 1975), pp. 146-48.
13. *Op. cit.,* p. 29; see also Farquhar, *Outline of the Religious Literature of India,* 1920, pp. 122 ff.

8

Some Aspects of Politico-Cultural Contacts Between Assam and Bihar and its Impact from the Later Vedic Age to the Late Medieval Period

The present paper aims at making an attempt to trace the history of politico-cultural contacts between Assam and Bihar—the two ancient kingdoms of the Prāchya Desha—and its impact during the period under review. The archaeology, palaeography, epigraphy and numismatics help us, professedly, very little in recasting the history of the obscure period in correct perspective, but, however, on the basis of slender thread of evidence at our disposal we can unfold some truths bearing upon the history and culture of North-East India which will certainly inspire the interested scholars to undertake further historical research and investigation. The treatment of the subject concerned is based on the literary, chinese, epigraphic, numismatic, archaeological and other contemporary sources.

The history of the politico-cultural contacts between these two ancient kingdoms can be traced back to the later Vedic Age (i.e. the age of the *Brāhmanas*). During that age, Mathava, king of Videha or Mithila, accompanied by his priest, Gautama, and large number of Brāhmins settled in Kāmarūpa and spread the light of Vedic culture and religion as evidenced by some of the passages occurring in one of the *Brāhmana* text.[1] This literary evidence can be further confirmed by another source.[2] This was perhaps the first Āryanisation of Assam.

According to some reliable sourcess, this contact became more close and intimate sometime before the Bhārata War when Naraka, a foster child of Janaka of Kshatriya origin, came to Prāgjyotisha as a political adventurer at the age of sixteen and after having inflicted the crushing defeat on the Kirātas in a fierce battle, conquered the land and installed himself on the throne, proclaimed his political supremacy, laid the foundation of the first Āryan kingdom and paved th way for the infiltration of the Āryan ideas and culture. His coronation ceremony was attended by his God Father—Janaka who came from Mithilā to Prāgjyotishapura along with his queen and retinue to establish his son as a feudatory chief of the new kindom. Actually the visit of the king Janaka to Prāgjyotisha constituted a milestone towards the real begining and growth of the politico-cultural contacts between these two kingdoms. The name of the kingdom was changed from Prāgjyotisha to Kāmarūpa which became the part of the Āryavarta and came within the pale of Āryandom. The frontier of the new-kingdom was extended and people from Mithilā were invited to settle and undertake the administration of the country. The Brāhmins came from Mithilā in successive waves and settled in different parts of Kāmarūpa and further enjoyed the royal patronage. The process continued upto the first half of the first millennium B.C. Naraka introduced and popularised the cult of Saktism associated with Austric elements. Naraka period withnessed the evolution of synthesis of different cultures—the Āryans, non-Āryans, Alpine, Austric, Bodo and Mongoloid. As a result of this contact the language, religion and culture of Kāmarūpa entered upon the new phase of orientation. Maithli language and culture spread in kamarupa which gradually influenced the Austric and Bodo culture. Maithli language mixed with Austric and Bodo words became the dialect of common people. Various Hindu and Puranic tradition and institutions developed. The process of Āryanisation, Brahmanisation and Sanskritization was accelerated.

The period 350-654 A.D., marked the opening of a new chapter in the direct contact of the Varman rulers of

Kāmarūpa with the Imperial Guptas of Magadha. During this period a large number of Brāhmins and other educated and highly talented persons were recruited from Magadha for general, educational, administrative and socio-cultural improvements of Kāmarūpa. The Brahmins of pure vedic knowledge coming from both Magadha and Mithilā settled in different parts of Kāmarūpa and they enjoyed the royal patronage and received the land grants from the Varman rulers. The Gupta era was introduced in Kāmarūpa; pure Sanskrit was adopted as the court language and Magadhi Prakrit influenced by Austric and Bodo intonations became the dialect of the common people. The upper hierarchy of the Hindu administrators of Kāmarūpa belonged both to the courts of Mithilā and Magadha. By the end of first millennium A.D. the Kāmarūpi language went deeply under the influence of Maithli, Magadhi, Prākrit and Sanskrit.[4] Judging from the trends of Āryanisation in Bengal we can safely presume that it was the Gupta period which saw the progressive and intensive Hinduization of Assam.

Placing our reliance on the narratives of the Chinese pilgrim Hiuen Tsang[5] we can affirm that the Varman rulers of the Kāmarūpa used to maintain some sort of direct connection, with the famous Buddhist University of Nālandā. This University got regular contributions from Varman rulers of Kāmarūpa, The learned Pandits of Kāmarūpa used to visit the University to take part in the scholary disputation with the Buddhist Scholars and other professors assembled there. This contact became very close during the time of Bhāṣkarvarman (A.D. 594-650), popularly known as Kumararaja. Hiuen-Tsang (A-D. 630-644) during his stay at Nālandā found various Brahmin scholars and messengers from Kāmarūpa or Eastern India, who were received by Silabhadra, the head of the Nālandā Mahāvihāra. The Chinese account may further be confirmed by the epigraphic evidence. The terracotta seals of Bhāṣkarvarman discovered by Dr. Spooner during the excavation of the ruins of Nalanda in the year 1917-18 and later on deciphered by R.D. Banerjee clearly testify to the direct political and cultural contacts of Varman rulers with Nalanda University in South Bihar. The Nalanda seal of Bhaskrvarman is supposed to have been left there to commemorate his visit to this University in 643 A.D. in company with Shri Harsha. Some more fragmentary seals of Varman dynasty were discovered from Nalanda Monastry in 1927-28. The corrected reading of the text of the seal as subsequently given by Mr. K.N. Dikshit is as follows:— (1), "Sri Ganpati Varma Sri yajna (Na) vatya- (M) Sri (2) Mahendra Varma Sri Suvra-ta yam Sri-Narayanavarma (3) Sri-Devavatyam Sri Mahabhuta (or Bhuti) varma Sri- Vijnavatyam Sri Chandramukhavarma (4) Sri Bhoga vatyam Sri Sthitavarma-tena Sri Nayanasobhayam (5) Sri Susthitavarma Sri-Syamalak-Shyam-Sri Supratisthitavarma (6) Sri Bhoskaravarmeti."[6]

The nature of contact between Kamarupa and South Bihar is exactly not known and only the further historical enquiry can reveal something more substantial. However on the basis of the available evidence it can be surmised that culturally the relationship was undoubtedly very cordial but politically it was strained being actuated by the rival political ambitions of the monarchs of Kāmarupa and Magadha. On the basis of some stray references[7] we can further add that the kingdom of Magadha and Kāmarūpa maintained hostile political relationship for some time. Mahasena Gupta of Magadha attained a glorious victory in a war fought with Susthitavarma (A.D. 585-93) of Kāmarūpa. The Apshad stone inscription of Adityasen also refers to the hostilities which prevailed between the later Guptas of Magadha and the Varman rulers of Kāmarūpa. Bhaskarvarman is also said to have extended his conquest upto Nalanda. One of the facts of greater importance than hither to supposed is that greater part of the Magadha came into possession of Bhaskarvarman— the king of Eastern India. K,L. Barua[8] has correctly stated that "before the rise of Pala power the kingdom of Kāmarūpa had absorbed the greater part of modern Bengal, Bihar and Orissa. These kingdoms were always at war with each other." Even a Buddhist scholar Taranath[9] has made some references to the political contact between Magadha and Kāmarūpa in post-kanishka period.

During the times of some of the rulers of the Pala dynasty of Magadha and Kāmarūpa the politico-cultural contacts between these two kingdoms took a different turn. Dharmapale, placed roughly between 1057-1120 A.D. consolidated his power over the greater part of Magadha. He also invited some Brahmins from Tirhut or Mithila and other places.[10] Babu Nanda Lal Dey" has gone to the extent of warranting the belief that Tranticism as an off shoot of Buddhism of the Mahayana school, which developed about the Nineth Century under the Pala rulers of Magadha probably spread in Kamarupa from the Buddhist University of Vikramsila in Bihar, founded by Dharma Pala. The Pala rulers after having conquered Magadha reigned from the time of Gopala to the end of the 12th century (1173 A.D.). maintaining the occasional supremacy over Kamarupa. According to Archaeological evidence[12] we find that Devapala of Magadha conquered Kamarupa, which is further supported by the Monghyer copper plate inscription translated by Wil kins.[13] On the basis of some epigraphic records[14] we come to know that Ramapala (1084-1130 A.D.) conquered the country of Janaka, popularly known as Mithila. Vaidyadeva, the Prime Minister of king Kumārapāla (1130-1142 A.D,) of the great Bihar dynasty was made the tributary ruler of Kamarupa in the place of the original ruler who had rebelled. Vaidyadeva began to rule over Kamarupa probably from 1138 A.D.— the year which marked the extinction of the Pala dynasty of Kamarupa.

It will not be out of place to mention that after the destruction of the Buddhist kingdom of Magadha and the universities of Nalanda, Odantapuri and Vikramsila by Bakhtiyar Khilji towards the closing years of the 12th century A.D., a large number of Budddists migrated from there, dispersed in plains and hills of Assam including Cachar, Sylhet and Tripura and propagated Buddhism.[15]

One of the important aspects of cultural intercourse between these two kingdoms is that the team of Sanskrit scholars of Kamarupa and Mithila used to visit each other's place to have exchange of ideas and knowledge on vedas, sastras, puranas, vayakaranas, yogas, tantras and the Indian School of Philosophy. Some of the books on Sanskrit written by the scholars of Kamarupa were taught in Mithila upto 1808 A.D. Ancient Mithila or Tirhut maintained the glorious tradition of holding the learned debate joined by the prominent philosophers and Brahmin scholars right from the time of Janaka. About 1600 years ago in the Upanishadic Age Tirhut bacame the centre of learning and enlightenment. According to S.K. Chatterji the Assamese students of Sanskrit used to go to mithila for advanced studies in the Medieval period. "Assam kept her connection with heart and brain of India as a whole during the entire medieval period of her history...."[16] James Longt[17] has also observed that Kamarupa and Tripura like Nadiya derived its learning from Tirhut or ancient Mithila which has always been "Point de appui" for the Brahmin influence. A colony of Brahmins from Mithila, Nadiya, Kashmir and other places effected the work of proselytism in both Assam and Tripura. The strongest current was always from north Bihar. The streams of this influence moulded the culture of Assam and various Hindu institutions and Sanskrit language flourised there. According to Mr. K.N. Dikshit[18] the artistic affinities of Assam with the contemporary schools of Bihar and Orissa affords a distinct illustration of the inter cultural contacts among these kingdoms.

The period, 14th to 16th century constitutes a bright chapter in the history of the cultural contacts between these two kingdoms. During the period concerned the Ahom monarchs invited various craftsmen, artists, musicians and dramatists from Mithila and Bengal, as a result of which the arts, crafts, music, drama, architchture. sculpture, painting and textile of Assam were greatly moulded. It was through North and East Bengal and Bihar that close connection was maintained between these two kingdoms. Equally close was the connection between Assam and Mithila in the literary field. The influence of Maithli on the Assamese literature was profound during this period. Practically from the beginning of 14th century the Maithli literature started attaining great perfection. The oldest Maithli work is "Varnaratna Kara" of Jyotirisvara Thakura (*c.* 1325) in prose style. The Maithli tradition of composing the lyrics from the time of poet Vidyapati (*c.* 1350-1450) had their impact on the development of the Vaishnava devotional as well as romantic and religious lyrics of both Assam and Bengal. The Caryapadas of Vidyapati of Mithila profoundly influenced the Assamese, Bengali and Oriya language. The possibility of Maithli influence on Brajbali a poetic language flourishing in Assam from the 14th century onwards can't be precluded. The Brajbali dialect mixed with Maithli and earlier form of Apabhramsa became very popular in Assam during the 15th and 16th centuries.[19] The geographical proximity rendered it more possible for the cultural exchanges among the linguistic groups of Eastern India. According to S.K. Chatterji[20] Sankaradeva (1449-1569 A.D.) of Assam, while undertaking the tour of the holy places of northern India for twelve years in 1483 visited Gaya and Sitakunda near Monghyer town in Bihar.

In the late Medieval period also during the time of Rudra Singh (1695-1714) the politico-cultural contacts between Assam and Bihar was revived for a brief interlude. While making a historic attempt for building up a sort of confederacy of the princes of Bengal and Bihar for defending the Hindu religion against the onslaughts of Islam and ousting the Mughals from North-East India, he came in contacts with some rulers of Modern Bihar also, the details of which is not known. In order to perform the obsequies of his father he had sent a Brahmin priest and scholar with attendants to Gaya or Magadha.[21] The reminissences of past became an inspiring factor for the Ahom rulers to weave some more threads in the fabric of the close politico-cultural contacts between these two kingdoms.

Notes and References

1. *Śatapatha Brāhmaṇa*, XIV, 1-17 vide, Eggeling's translation, pp. 105-6.
2. V.R. Ramachndra Dikshitar, "Aryanisation of East India-Assam," I.H.O. 1945, Vol. XXI, pp. 29-33; See also H.C. Chakladar, *The Aryuan occupation of Eastern India*, (Calcutta 1962), pp. 188.
3. *Kālika Purāna* (ed. Chamanlal Gautam Bareilley, 1973) Vol. I, pp. 470-497; Dr. Hoernle: J.A.S.B., 1897, Vol. LXVI, pp.117, 120; K.L. Baruah: J.I.H. 1933, Vol. XII, pt. I to III, p. 303; K.L. Baruah: E.H.K. (Shillong-1933) pp. XIV, 20-23, 27, 29, 31, 39, 92-93; E. Gait, *History of Assam* (Calcutta, 1926), p. 13; B.K. Kakati, *The Mother Goddess Kamakhya*, (Gauhati, 1967) pp. 26-27; R.M. Nath, *The Background of Assamese Culture*, (Shillong, 1948). pp. 26-30; P.C. Choudhury. H.C.P.A. (Gauhati, 1959), pp. 121, 140; S.K. Chatterji, P.A.H.C.I. (Gauhati, 1955) p. 13; Dr. Maheswar Neog, A.O. 1967, Vol. 4, p. 13.
4. R.M. Nath, op. cit. pp. 32-38; See also J.A.R.S,. Octob. 1935. Vol. III. N. 4, pp. 96-97; J.A.R.S. Jan. 1936, Vol. HI, N. 4, pp. 131 32; G. Bertrand, *Secret Lands Where Women Reign*, (London-1958) p. 33; N.N. Basu. S.H.K. (Calcutta. 1922). Vol. I. p. 7, S.K. Chatterji. op. cit, p. 34; W. Robinson. *A Descriptive Account of Assam* (Delhi, 1975), pp. 150-52.
5. S. Beal. *The Life of Hiuen Tsiang* (London-1884) pp. 166-171, 257-258; See also Watters, *Life of Yuan Chwang*, Vol. I. pp. 165 f. 348; A Cunnigham, *Ancient Geog. of India* (Varanasi, 1975), pp. 422-23 ; K.L. Baruah, E.H.K., pp. 73-75, 162; P.C. Choudhurv, op. cit., pp. 195 ff.
6. J.B.O.R.S. March, 1920, 1933. Vol. VI. pp. 151-52; J.I.H., 1933, Vol. Xll, pt. I to HI. pp. 305 f; KL. Baruah. E.H.K. pp. 96-98; H.N. Sastri. "Nalanda and its epigraphic Material", cf. M.A.S. I. 1942 ; K.L. Baruah, J.A.R.S. July, 1935, Vol. Ill, N. 2. p. 62.
7. R.G. Basak, *The History of North-Eastem India* (Calcutta 1967). pp.146-47, 159. 264. 270-71; K.L. Baruah, E.H.K. pp. 57, 71, 72; See also, N.N. Das Gupta, "The Occupation of Bengal by the King of Kamrupa" *Indian*

Culture Vol. II. N. I, pp. 37-45 cf, J.A.R.S. July 1935, Vol. iii, N. 2. pp. 69-74.

8. J.A.R.S. July 1935, Vol. III, N. 2, p. 49.
9. l.A. 1875, Vol. IV. p. 365.
10. K.L. Baruah, E.H.K. pp. 119. 136 ; E.l. Vol. Xll, pp. 37; S.K. Bhuyan, *Annals of the Delhi Badshahate* (D.H.A.S. Gauhati, 1947) p. 180.
11. J.P.A.S.B. (New Series) 1914. Vol. X p. 346.
12. A. Cunningham, A.R.A.S.I. (Calcutta 1882) Vol. XV, pp. 148-51.
13. A.R. Vol. I, p. 123.
14. *A Collection of Inscriptions Supplementary to the Corpus Inscriptionum Indicarum of the A.S.I*, trans. by Oriental scholars edited by JAS. Burgess and Assisted by A Fuher and copper plate grant of Vaidyadeva, King of Kāmrūpa by A. Venis (Principal, Sanskrit College Varanasi)-Ref. to E.J. 1894, Vol. II, p. 1, verse-4, pp. 348-55; Dr. A.F. Rudolf Hoernle, "The Gauhati Copper Plate Grant of Indrapala," J.A.S.B. 1897, Vol. LXVI, pt-I, pp. 121 f. See also, pt. Udayavira Sastri, *Sānkhya Darshan kā Itihās* (Delhi, V.S. 2006) pp. 343-44.
15. J.A.R.S. July, 1936, Vol. IV. N. 2, pp. 33 ff.
16. P.A.H.C.I. pp. 73-74; See also J.B.R.S. 1962, Vol. XLVIII, pt. I to IV, sec. III, pp. 79 f.
17. J.A.S.B. 1850, Vol. XIX, pp. 544-56.
18. A.R.A.S.I. 1927-28, pp. 112-13.
19. S.K. Chatterji, *op. cit.,* pp. 54-63; See also Dr. Maheswar Neog, A.O. Vol. 4, N. 1, p. 61.
20. *Op. cit.,* p. 66.
21. S.K. Chatterji, *op. cit.,* pp. 49-51.

9

Early Political and Cultural Relations of Kāmarūpa with Bihar, Bengal and Orissa

The literary and archaeological evidence, the Chinese account, the contemporary records and other collateral sources bear testimony to the fact that some sort of political and cultural relations were maintained between Prāgjyotiṣa (also called Kāmarūpa) and three eastern kingdoms, viz. Bihar, Bengal and Orissa in ancient times down to the twelfth century A.D.

The antiquity of relationship between Prāgjyotiṣa and Bihar can be traced back to the pre-Bhārata war period, when Naraka, a foster child of king Janaka of Mithilā of Kṣatriya origin, came to Prāgjyotiṣa as a political adventurer at the age of sixteen and after having inflicted a crushing defeat on the Kirātas and their chief, Ghataka, in a fierce battle conquered the kingdom and installed himself on the throne, proclaimed his political supremacy, laid the foundation of the first Āryan kingdom and paved the way for the slow infiltration of the Āryan ideas and culture. His coronation ceremony was attended by his God-like father, Janaka, who came from Mithilā to Prāgjyotiṣapur along with his queen and retinue to establish his son as a feudatory chief of the new kingdom. This episode actually constituted a milestone towards a real beginning of the politico-cultural contacts between these two kingdoms. The kingdom of Prāgjyotiṣa or Kāmarūpa formed a part of Āryāvarta and came within the pale of Aryandom. The frontiers of the new kingdom were extended and the people from Mithilā were invited to settle and undertake the administration of the country. The Brāhmaṇas came from Mithilā in successive waves, settled in different parts of Kāmarūpa and further enjoyed the royal patronage. The process actually began in the first half of the first millennium B.C. and continued down to the 12th century A.D. Naraka is credited with having introduced abnd popularised the Śakti cult associated with Austric elements. Naraka's period witnessed the evolution of synthesis of different cultures the Āryan, non-Āryan, Alpine, Austric, Bodo and Mongoloid. As a result of this contact, the language, religion and culture of Kāmarūpa entered upon a new phase of orientation. Maithili language and culture spread in Kāmarūpa which gradually influenced the Austric and Bodo culture. Maithili language, mixed with Austric and Bodo words, became the dialect of the common people. Various Hindu and Puraṇic traditions and institutions developed. The process of Aryanisation, Brahmanisation and Sanskritization was accelerated.[1]

The period: A.D. 350-654 marked the opening of a new chapter in the history of politico-cultural contacts of the Varman rulers of Kāmarūpa with the imperial Guptas of Magadha in South Bihar. During this period a large number of Brahmanas and other educated and highly talented persons were recruited from Magadha for general, educational, administrative and socio-cultural uplift of Kāmarūpa. The Brāhmaṇas of pure Vedic knowledge coming from both Magadha and Mithilā settled in different part of Kāmarūpa, received the land grants from the Varman rulers and enjoyed their royal patronage. The Gupta era was introduced in Kāmarūpa, pure Sanskṛt was adopted as the court language and Māgadh Prākṛt, influenced by Austric and Bodo intonations, became the dialect of the common people of Kāmarūpa. The upper hierarchy of Hindu administrators of Kāmarūpa belonged to Mithilā and Magadha. By the end of the first millennium A.D., the Kāmarūpi languages were deeply under the influence of Maithili, Māgadh, Prākṛt and Sanskṛt.[2] Judging by the trends of Āryanisation in Bengal, we can safely presume that it was the Gupta period which saw the progressive and intensive Hinduization of Kāmarūpa.

Here mention may be made of the grant of whole Pāncakhaṇḍa to Brāhmaṇas from Mithila in the 7th century A.D. which is fairly attested by the copper-plate grant issued in A.D. 641.[3] The lands donated to five Brāhmaṇas were in the Surma valley. One of the important aspects of cultural intercourse between Kāmarūpa and Mithilā in ancient times is that the team of Sanskṛt scholars from these two oriental kingdoms used to visit each other's place to exchange ideas and knowledge on the Vedas, Śāstras, Puranas, Vyākaranas, Yogas, Trantras and the Indian school of philosophy. Some of the books on Sanskrt written by the scholars of Kāmārupā were taught in Mithilā up to A. D. 1808. Ancient Mithilā or Tirhut maintained the glorious tradition of holding the learned debate joined by the prominent philosophers and Brāhman scholars right from the time of Janaka. In the Upanisadic age Tirhut became the centre of learning and enlightenment.[4] James Long has correctly observed that "Kāmarūpa and Tripura like Nadiya derived its learning from Tirhut or ancient Mithilā, which has always been "point de appui" for the Brāhmin influence".[5] A colony of Brahmins from Mithilā, Nadiyā (West Bengal) and other places effected the work of proselytisation in both Kāmarūpa and Tripura. But the strongest current was always from North Bihar. The streams of this influence moulded the culture of Kāmārupā and various Hindu institutions and Sanskrt language flourished there. During the period concerned, various craftsmen artists were also invited from Mithilā and Bengāl, as a result of which the arts and crafts of Kāmarūpa, were greatly moulded. Mr. K.N. Dikshit[6] has rightly pointed out that the artistic affinities of Assam with the contemporary schools of Bihar, Bengal and Orissa affords a distinct illustration of the inter-cultural contacts among these kingdoms.

The eye-witness account of the Chinese pilgrim, Hiuen Tsang (A.D. 630-644) enables us to establish that the Varman rulers of Kāmarūpa used to maintain their direct politico-cultural links with the famous Buddhist university of Nalanda. The said university used to receive regular contributions from the Varman rulers of Kāmarūpa. The learned *pandits* of Kāmarūpa used to visit the nuniversity regularly to take part in the scholarly disputation with the Buddhist scholars and other professors assembled there. This contact became very close during the time of Bhāṣkaravarman (A.D. 594-650). Hiuen-Tsang during his stay at Nālandā found various Brāhmin scholars and messengers from Kāmarūpa who were received by Silabhadra, the head of the Nalanda Mahāvihāra.[7] The Chinese account finds confirmation in the contemporary epigraphic evidence. The archaeological discovery of the terracotta seals of Bhāskaravarman by Dr. Spooner during the excavation of the ruins of Nālandā in the the yearss 1917-18 and deciphered by R.D. Banerjee clearly testify to the direct political and cultural contacts of Varman rulers with Nālandā university in South Bihār. The Nālandā seal of Bhāskarvarman is supported to have been left there to commemorate his visit to this university in A.D. 643 in company with Sri Harsa, some more fragmentary seals (all inscribed) of the rulers of Varmana dynmasty including thatt of Bhāṣkaravarman were discovered from Nālandā Monastry in 1927-28, and deciphered by K.N. Dikshit,[8] which further confirm the truth as stated above.

Culturally, the relationship between Kamarupa and Magadha was, undoubtedly, very cordial, but politically it was strained because of the conflict of ambitions of the two rival monarchs of two different mighty kingdoms. Mahāsena Gupta, the later Gupta ruler of Magadha, invaded Kāmārupā and attained a glorious victory in the battle fought with Susthitavarman (A.D. 585-93) the father of Bhaskaravarman on the bank of the Brahmaputra sometime between C.A.D. 590 and 593 which can be confirmed by the Aphsad stone inscription of Aditya Sena (C. 660-750 A.D.). The Varman ruler concerned became his subordinate ally.

But Bhāṣkarvarman extended his conquest upto Nālandā in the early part of the 7th century A. D. Greater part of Magadha came into his possession.[9] As the vicissitude of fortune of the Varman rulers of Kāmarūpa was always linked up with that of the Guptas, he stemmed the tide of their rising power in North Bengal. He defeated the kings of northern and eastern Bengal and got his kingship over the paternal kingdom. K. L. Barua has rightly stated that before the rise of Pala power, the kingdom of Kāmārupā had absorbed the greater part of modern Bengal, Bihar and Orissa. These kingdoms were always at war with each other."[10] Even a Buddhist scholar, Taranath, has referred to the political contact between Magadha and Kāmārupā in the post Kaniska period.

The political and cultural relations between the rulers of the Pāla dynasty of Magadha and Kāmarūpa took a different turn in the 11th and 12th centuries A.D. The contest for supremacy over each other's kingdom continued till the extinction of the Pālā dynasty of Kāmarūpa. Dharmapāla, placed roughly between, A. D. 1057 and 1120, consolidated his power over the greater part of Magadha. He also invited some Brāhmaṇas from Mithilā and other places.[12] The Pāla rulers, after having conquered Magadha, reigned from the time of Gopāla to the end of the 12th century A.D. or 1178 A.D. maintaining the occasional supremacy over Kamarupa.

According to an archaeological evidence,[13] we find that Devapāla of Magadha conquered Kāmarūpa, which is further supported by the Monghyr copper-plate inscription deciphered by Wilkings.[14] Some of the epigraphic records confirm the truth that Rāmapāla (1084-1180) A.D. conquered the country of Janaka, popularly known as Mithilā. Vaidyadeva, the Prima Minister of king Kumārapāla (1142 A.D.) of the great Bihar dynasty, was made the tributarty ruler of Kāmarūpa in place of the original ruler, who had rebelled. Vidyadeva began to rule over Kāmarūpa probably from A.D.1138 onwards.[15]

N.L. Dey has gone to the extent of warranting the belief that Tantricisma as an offshoot of Buddhism of the Mahāyāna school, which developed about the ninth century under the Pāla rulers of Magadha, probably spread, in Kāmāprupā from the Buddhist university of Vikramaśila in Bihar, founded by Dharmapāla.[16]

It will not be out of place to mention here that after the destruction of the Buddhist kingdom of Magadha and the unviersities of Nālandā, Odantapuri and Vikramaśila at the hands of Bakhtiyar Khilji towards the closing years of the 12th century A.D., a large number of Buddhists migratd from there and dispersed in the plains and hills of Assam including Cachar, Sylhet and Tripurā and propagated Buddhism.[17]

The nature of relations between Kāmarūpa and Orisa is not exactly known. However, on the basis of inferential evidence, it has been suggested that "the people of Orissa, with the now-forgotten Buddhist university of Puspagiri (Cutack dist.) as their centre of scholarship, must have established living links with the Kamakhya Pitha in Assam."[18] No evidenc has been produced in support of this hypothesis. Only furtner historical enquiry can reveal something more substantial in this regard.

Notes and References

1. For details see *Kālikā Purāṇa,* ed. Chamanlal Gautam (Bareilly, 1973). Vol. 1, vv. 1 60. pp. 470-80; vv. 1 - 147, pp. 481-504; Hoernle, JASB; vol. Lxvi, 1897. pp. 117, 120; K. L. Baruah, JIH; Vol. xii, pts. 1-111, 1933, p. 303; EHK (Shillong, 1933), pp. xiv, 20-23, 27, 29, 31, 38-39, 92-93; E. Gait, *History of Assam* (Calcutta, 1926), p. 13; B.K. Kakati, *The Mother Goddess Kāmākhyā* (Gauhati, 1967). pp. 26-27; R. M. Nath, *The Background of Assamese Culture* (Shillong, 1948), pp. 26-30; P. C. Choudhury, HCPA. (Gauhati, 1959) pp. 121,140; S. K. Chatterji, PAHCI. (Gauhati, 1955), p. 13; Maheswar Neog, AQ; Vol. iv, 1967, p. 13. For antiquity, identification and historicity of Naraka, see G.P. Singh *'The Pauranic*

Account of Naraka's conquest of Ancient kingdom of Pragjyotisha and the Kirātas in North East India' in procds. of N. E. India History Assocn; Barapani session, 1983, P. P. 19-20, Ref. No. 1.

For details about the Kirātas see G.P. Singh, op. cit. pp. 21-22, Ref. No. 2; *The Kirātas in Ancient India* (Delhi, 1990), pp. 349, 355-60.

2. R. M. Nath, op. cit. pp. 32-38; JARS; Vol. iii, No. 4, Octob. 1935, pp. 96-97; JARS; Vol. iii, No. 4, Jan. 1936, pp. 131-32; G. Bertrand, Secret Lands where women Reign (London, 1958), p. 33; N. N. Basu, SHK (Calcutta, 1922), Vol. i. p. 6; S. K. Chatterji, op. cit; p. 34; W. Robinson, *A. Descriptive Account of Assam* (Delhi, 1975), pp. 150-52.
3. See JARS; Vol. iii. No. 3, Octob. 1935, pp. 96-97.
4. S. K. Chatterji, PAHCI; pp. 73-74; see also JBRS; Vol. XLVItl, pts. I-IV, see, III, 1962, pp. 79 f.
5. JASB; Vol. XIX, 1850, pp. 544-56
6. ARASI; 1927-28, pp. 112-13.
7. S. Beal, *The Life of Hiuen Tsang* (London, 1884), pp. 166-171, 257-58; see also Thomas Waters, *On Yuan Chwang's Travels in India* (Delhi, 1977), vol. I, p. 348; A. Cunningham, Anc. Geog. of India (Varanasi, 1975), pp. 422-23; K. L. Baruah, EHK; pp. 73-75,162; P. C. Choudhury, op. cit; pp. 195 ff.
8. For details see JBORS, Vol. VI pt. 1, March, 1920, pp. 151-52; JIH Vol. XII, 1933, pp. 305 f; K. L. Baruah, EHK; pp. 96-98; H. N. Sastri, *'Nalanda and its epigraphic Material',* MASI; 1942; K. L. Baruah, JARS; Vol. Ill, No. 2, July 1935, p. 62; Kāmārupās'asanāvali, ed. D. Sarma (Gauhati, 1981), pt. 11, pp. 5-6, pt. 111, p. 151.
9. R. G. Basak, *The History of North-Eastern India* (Calcutta, 1967), pp. 146-47. 159, 264, 270-71; K. L. Baruah, EHK; pp. 57, 71-72; N. N. Das Gupta, "The occupation of Bengal by the king of Kāmārupā", *Indian Culture,* Vol. 11, No. 1, pp. 37-45; JARS; Vol. 111, No. 2, July 1935, pp. 69-74; Cll; 111, No. 42, pp. 203, 206, 11, 10-11; No. 43, pp. 209-10.

10. JARS; Vol. 111, No. 2, 1935, p. 49.
11. Ind. Ant; Vol. IV, 1875, p. 365.
12. EHK; pp. 119, 136; El, Vol. XII, pp. 375; S. K. Bhuyan, *Annals of the Delhi Badshahte* (DHAS; Guahati, 1947), p. 180.
13. A. Cunningham, ARASI; Vol. XV (Calcutta, 1882), pp. 148-51.
14. AR, Vol. I, p. 123.
15. A. Venis, "Copper-Plate grant of Vaidyadeva, king of Kāmārupā", El; Vol. II, 1894, P. I. verse-4, pp. 348-55; A. F. Rudilf Hoernle, "The Gauhati Copper plate grant of Indrapāla", JASB; Vol. LXVI, pt. 1, 1897, pp. 121f.
16. JPASB; Vol. X, 1914 (new series), p. 346
17. JARS; Vol. IV, No. 2, 1936, pp. 33f.
18. See A. N. Tiwari, "Cultural Relations Between Assam and Orissa", *Souvenir Purba Baharat Sanskrtik Sammelan,* Jan. 6 to 15, Gauhati, 1975, pp. 101f.

10

The History and Culture of Ancient Tripura : A Re-Appraisement

The early history of Tripura is still shrouded in mystery and wrapped into great degree of obscurity All the statements made so far alluding to the subject under review are not only confused and meagre but rather unsystematic, incomplate, vague, conflicting and contradictory. In this paper, a sincere and concerted attempt has been made to present as far as possible the systematic, descriptive, critical and graphic account of subject on the basis of tradition—both recorded and unrecorded—literary evidence, Persian sources, epigraphic records, Royal chronicles, standard historical texts, contemporary writtings and other collateral evidences.

Various conflicting theories have been propounded by multitude of authorities regarding the origin of the appellation Tripura and its royal family as well as its identification and antiquity. Some theories, of course, contain substratum of historical truth but some are certainly unworthy of credence. It is undeniable fact to be reckoned with that in ancient time Tripura was known as Kirāta-Desha. The view of Reved J. Long[1] that Kirāta was a person of that name meaning "the hunter of the Lunar Race the brother of Puru" can be outrightly rejected. On the testimony of classical sources[2] it can be amply substantiated that the "Kirrahadia' or the Kirāta was the first name of the country of Tripura. Nowhere Kirāta has been discussed as an individual's name. In the genealogical list furnished in the Royal chronicle[3] of Tripura, nowhere Kirāta has been shown as a person. Both D.C Sircar[4] and S.K. Chatterjee[5] hold the view that the name Tripura is undoubtedly the sanskritized of Tribal name Tipra borne by the aboriginal people inhabiting the eastern fringe of south east Bengal to which the royal family of Tripura belonged. This is further corroborated by K.C. Sinha[6] and R C . Mazumder[7]. Just contrary to this W.W. Hunter[8] suggests that the name Tripura is given by Āryan speaking immigrants. He further states that the name was probably given to country in honour of the temple of Udaipur which ranks as second Tirtha or sacred shrine in this part of Bengal, dedicated either to 'Tripura Dana' or the Sun god or Tripure - shwari— the "mistress of the three world". All these views contain some elements of truth. As a matter of fact, the country was known Tripura, after the name of its founder Tripur the contemporary or your Yudhisthira (2380 before Vikram—in Vikram Era). The Purānic evidence[9] lead us to warrant the belief that Bali of Titikshu line above sixteenth is descent from Pururavas pedegree gave birth to five sons. Anga, Banga, Kalinga, Sunha and Pundra from whom five kingdoms in the East, East Bihar, East Bengal, Orissa, Tripura and North Bengal are name respectively. This theory has no doubt, got historical colour and as the most relaiable account still forms the basis of our ancient historical knowledge Hera it must be made clear that Tripura as mentioned by E. J. Rapson[10] Kalhan[11] and Shih-Li-Cha ta-Lo or Srikshetra of Yuan Chwang[12] corresponding to Samatata and Tipperah District should not be mistaken as present Tripura under discussion. Kālidāsa in his *Meghadutta*[13] the crest-jewel of Khaṇḍakāvyas, composed before A.D. 413, refers to natural beauties of present Tripura. The Tripura Raj is also mentioned in the list of kingdoms in the third paragraph of the inscription of Emperor Asoka's pillar installed in the fort of Allahabad, built by Mughal Emperor Akbar in 1557, as frontier kingdom.

Equally great and interesting is the divergence of opinions revolving round the pivot of the origin of the royal family. Sometimes the prevailing confusion is made worse confounded by advancing number of contradictory arguments. The views put forth by R M. Nath[14] S. P. Gupta[15] and Persian Chronicler Ghulam Hussain Salimls[16] that Tipperahs came originally from the Bodo Hone in central Asia and belong to Tibeto-Burman stock or are of Mongolian origin seem to be untenable in view of the fact that they are of mixed origin and none of them came from outside. This theory can no more be recognized either as authentic or convincing. Number of valuable new facts as counnter arguments have already been discovered and brought to light. Many unfounded facts have been invented without having deeper insight into the matter D C Sircar[17] seems to be perfectly right in suggesting that "the early members of the family were leaders of some aboriginal tribes of neighouring hilly region... It is not, however possible to think that they were outsider like the Mongoloid". Major Fisher in his "Memorial of sulhet,, Kecher & C-"[18] tells us that the similarity of religion custom and appearance makes this probable that the people of Tipperah or Tripura and Kacharis are of same origin 'The Tipperah family are described as a younger branch of the ancient royal family who on the explusion of the latter from Kamarupa established themselves independently in the country which they formerly held as province". According to extracts from the General Report of the Tipperah District by J.F. Browne.[19] The Tipperahs or inhabitant of the Tipperah hill ranges are said by some to be colonsists from Manipur from which place they were driven by Burmese invasion. But there can be little doubt that the opinion of those who assert them to have inhabited this part of the country from time immemorial, is equally well founded. Nothing is known out the ancient history of these people, but tradition names as their first King Asango, the ancestor of Trilochan". Actually nowhere Asango has bean mentioned as Tipperah king. K C. Singh[20] observes that one branch of the shan dynasty of upper Burman established an independent kingdom on the eastern side of Kāmrūpa whose desendants were driven away by another tribe of that area and after being defeated by another tribes people of that area the youngest son of the King of Kāmrūpa migrated to the northern side of Cachar where the ancient Tripura kingdom was set up. All these theories,, being very much paradoxical lack general support S.K. Chatterjee reasonably[21] suggests that the rulling house of Tipperah are of North Indian Kshatriya origin claiming kinship with the Pandava as "scions" of the Lunnr race. He further states that the early immigration of Aryan speakers from upper India among the Tipra section of southern Bods is quite in the fitness of natural event. But he seems to be wrong in concluding that the Sanskrit names of earlier Tripura kings are traditional and fictitious and Bodos or Tripra names which are plentiful up to 14th century appear to be qenuine. Here it will be more historicaly fair and convincing to expose this truth that from the genealogical list of Tripura royal house provided by Rājmālā it is evident that two different dynasties ones having the Sanskrit names up to the time of Niladhwaja and another with Bodo names ending with pha or fa" flourished here. It is most astonishing feature of this genealogical chart that most of the rulers right from the time of Niladhwaja alias Iswar Pha down to the time of Ratna-pha appear to have assumed both the names Sanskrit as well as Bodo, *e.g.,* Harihar alias Chuchungpha, Chandrashekhar alias Machi-chang-pha and likewise. Thus in probability it seems that the Rajas of Hill-Tipperah are of Indo-Āryan stock with an admixture of Non-Āryan bloods.

According to the most popular tradition recorded in Rājmālā, Tipperah kings claim their decent from Druhyu, the youngest son of Emperor Yayāti, a kshatriya of lunat race from whom the succession is carried down in direct line including thirty eight reigns to his descendants and they have adopted the family name of Deb Barman to mark thier status as member of Kshatriya caste. This theory has been strongly corroborated and widely recognized by number of distinguished authorities. This is further confirmed by literay evedence and other reliable sources'[22] Druhyu, after being sent in exile by his father retired with companions to the south eastern part of the Empire and set up a new kingdom in the north-eastern India then known as Kirātadesha by defeating the king of Kirātas. The new kingdom founded by him was situated in between Eastern Bengal and Assam. The capital of this kingdom was Tribeg. R.M. Nath[23] is of the opinion that, according to the tradition of the Tipperahs, Druhyu, married a Bodo princes against his father's will and was disinherited after which "he preferred to live with his beloved in her hilly home amongst her relatives and his progeny became a rulling race. The ruling class of the *Tipperahs* claim lineage from the lunar dynasty from this tradition episode'. Persian chronicler[24] also affirms this popular tradition and calls this ancient kingdom of Tipperah as Hindu Kingdom K.L. Barua[25] and R.M. Nath[26] observe that it was Pratardon, twentyfifth in descent from Druhyo, who came over to Assam, conquered the Kiratas and established a new kingdom the capital of which known as Trivega was on the bank of Kopili river. Whatever, may be the truth the ancient kingdom of Tripura, known as Trivaga (the place where the three streams meet) comprised the Kopili valley the North Cachar hills and also perhaps the modern districts of Cachar to the west of Manipur. R.M. Nath places this kingdom in about 1900 B.C. which is clearly open to doubts. It appaears from Rajmala that sixteen kings from Paratardana to Dakshin ruled over the Trivega kingdom on the Kopili river (a confluence of the Brahmaputra). Approximate period of not more than 500 years may be allowed for this dynasty which probably ruled for full fourteen or sixteen generations. This Kopili valley or Trivega kingdom identified with Devaka has been mentioned in the Allahabad pillar inscription of Samudra Gupta ascribad to 4th centnry A.D. as "Pratyanta rajya".

The reign of Chitrayudha, (son of Chittra Rattra, the desendant of Pratardon) an immeasurably effulgent or Kshatriya Raja of Tripura witnessed the occurences of interest ing episodes in the ancient history of the kingdom. On the basis of literary evidence[27], we can expose this truth that during the Epic Age Tripura was a subject of constant attacks by the Epic heroes Yudhisthra sit forth to conquer the lesserkings and to compel them to pay tribute lu persuasion of ths imperial policy of conquering the Eastern Himalayan Kingdoms, first of all Arjuna came to this region and defeating Bhagadatta of Pragjyotisha and reaching Manipur decided to capture mountain or hilly countries. He defeated Chitrayudha, king of Tripura. The country of Chitrayudha as well protected but ultimately accumed to Arjun's force. Arjuna was followed by Bhima who conquered the whole Estern India including Bangal Trieura. Bihar, Kamrupa Himalayan countries and the hill people living on the sea coast in the marshy region and subjected them to pay tribute. This attack has been claborately referred to by Pargiter[28] It is further confirmed by recorded traditions.[29] Chitrayudha unquestionably attended Rajasuya (Imperial Assemblage) or coronation of Raja as samuat, which was largely attended by rajas who owed allegiance to him. The honour or Khillat bestowed on Chitrayudha by the Emperor Yudhisthira was the "Svetachatre" (Svetl = white and Chitra = umbrella) or royal white umbrells which to the day is the royal insignia of Tripura[30] This rajasuvā sacrifice or royal convention was niether attended by Trilochana as supposed by H.L. Chatterjee[31] and N.R Roychoudhury[32] nor by Chittra Radha as held R M. Nath[33].

From the foregoing account it transpires that this paramount kingdom was in existence before the Great Battle of Kurukshetra (3100 B.C.) As there is no othar raja or country to be found anywhere or at any time during the whole Hindu Domination of Aryavarta elswhere other than the Tripura under notice. On the basis of this relaible evidence we can unhesitatingly dispose of the theory of D.C. Sircar[34] which contains only partial truth. He is of the opinion that the "attempt to prove the antiquity of Tripura state from Epic and Puranic references .,,...is absolutely unwarranted..." This can never be accepted. The mention of Chittrayudha and other kings like Trilochana in both Mahabharata and native chronicle Rajmala and the continuation of the practice of unflurling the royal white umbrella at the time of accession as bestowed on Chittrayudha by Yudhisthira and other corroborative evidence bear standing testimooy to the authenticity and trustworthiness of the Epic and puranas and warrant us to prove its antiquity from all the roferences cited in ancient texts.

Chitrayudhas's successor Daity, the third and youngest son of Chitra Ratra further enlarged the frontiers of the kingdom which included the hill country to the east as far as the boarders of Burmah. Tripur, the grandson of the Chitrayudha is traditionally belived to have founded the city of "Tnbeg" on the banks of Kopili as the capital of the kingdom which became known thenceforth to this day as Tripura after its founder who lived over three thosand years ago. Tripur is said to have been a passionate tyrannical ruler who neglected the due worship of Siva. Due to his oppressive policy and mismanagement all the subjects fled in a body to Hidamba Cachar and appealed to the Raja of that country. The Raja of Hidamba could not render any assistence to the people as a result of which after a capse of five years the subjects returned to their native land caried to Siva who killed Tripura but promised them a new ruler by the widow of Tripur. In due course Tripur's widowed Rani not the widow of Trilochan as wrongly suposed by Dalton[35] gave birth to a posthumous son named Trilochan (three eyed). Trilochan was placed on throne amidst rejoicing of the people and was distinguished for his wisdom and piety at an early age. His reign inauquarated a new era in the field of politico-cultural and matrimonial relations with neighbouring states. His reign also withnessed the Reorientation of the administrative policies followed by his immediate predecessors. After recoganising the state he married the daughter of the Hidamba or Kachari king. The Brahmanical tradition also supports the connection between the two states. After having conquered many countries he died at an advanced age leaving behind twelve sons. Trilochan's eldest son Drikpati, who was adopted by hierless Kachari king eventuallay inherited that kingdom. Dakshin, the another son of Trilochan in accordance with the wishes of the people inherited his fathers state, but Drikpati challanged his claim on the legal ground, invaded his kingdom and ultimately defeated him in the war which ensued on this issue. After having been defeated, Dakshin left his Tribeg kingdom and established a new kingdom in the Barak Valley with his headquarter as Kholongma some-where east of Silchar. According to K.L. Barua[36] "the ancient Trivega. Kopili or the Deveka kingdom became abosrbed in the Hedamba kingdom and this took place about the fifth century A.D." Subsequently the Kamarupa kings absorbed th vallay within their kingdom. According to R.M. Nath[37] one of the sons of Trilochan married the daughter of the king of Manipur and ruled peace fully over many races of the Kukis... 'the Haflong, the Jaflongs, the Rungrngs, the Lungais, the Luscais etc... Taidakshin, the son of the Dakshin also married the princes of Mokhali (modern Manipur) and set up a new kingdom on the bank of the river known as Chhambulanagar.

Raja Birraj the decendant of Dakshin tentatively placed about A.D. 590, was a powerful king, He is said to have extended his conquest beyond the Ganges. During his reign Tripura Raj comprised the present districts of Chittagong, Noakhali. Tippera, Sylhet; Cachar. Garo hills, Jaintia hills; Lushai land and Chittagong hill Tracts and subsequently Samtata also formed the part of Raj. In commemoration of this event he established a new chronological era in the ancient history of Tripura dating from his victory.[38] Thus narrative of the events are available in some dependable sources.

The next king was Pratiti, whose reign saw the renewal of political and matrimonial relations with neighbouring countries. He concluded a treaty with the king of Cachar, the object of which was to prevent disputes as to the boundary between the territories of the two sovereigns. But the neighbouring chiefs however, disapproved of the alliance and tried to show the seeds of dissensions which resulted in the quarrel between Pratiti and Kachari king over a hill damsel and the former having been defeated was forced to leave the country. Pratiti shifted his headquarter ts Dharmanagar on the bank of Juri-river.[39]

Pratiti was followed by one of his eccendants known as Jajor-Fa whom R.M. Nath[40] mistakenly places in 590 A.D. Actually he appeared much later than Raja Bir-raj whose accendancy has already been fixed in 590 A.D. Due to discrepancies in chronology of the Tipperah kings no date can be accepted as trustworthy. Dates may be uncertain but there is no uncertainty about the events and occurences, as evidenced by number of sources. Jajor-Fa 'probably the 74th Raja invaded Rangamati and fought with king Nikka or Lika of the hilly tracts of Chittagong who led a disciplined army of 10,000 men. The Tipperah Raja became triumphant and his kingdom extended as far as to this area and subsequently the established his. headquarters first at Rangamati and then at Vishalgarh in the hill-Tipperah area The name of the former was afterwards ohanged to Udaipur by Raja Udai-Manik and of the latter to Tripura.[41]

According the *Vaṁśāvali* of Tipperah Rajas, Adi Dharmapha alias Dungurpha or Hari Roy (640-670 A.D.) the decendant of Jajor-Fa is nineteenth ganeration upwards of Kritidhar alias Cheng-Thun-Pha (1240 A.D.) He ascended the throne in 64 Tipperah Era corresponding to 654 A.D. According to R.M. Nath[42], during his period after the downfall of the Varman dynasty due to uprising or Miachhas or Bodo-uprising, a batch of Brahmms migrated from Kamrupa to Tipperah kingdom and settled at Pancha-khanda which can be evidenced by the fact that the "copper plate grants of Bhaskar varman to Nagar Brahimns have been found at Nidhanpur hear Pancha-khanda. This can be further corroborated by other sources. K.L. Baura[43] states that Dungrahpa, a contemporary of Bhasharavarman of Kamrupa granted the whole of Panchakhanda to certain Brahmans from Mithila in 641 A.D. by a copper plate inscription which is now lost but an extract thereform can be seen in *Vaidik Sangvadini.* N.R. Roy Choudhury[44] also exposes the truth that Dharma-Fa was previously a Budhist king but later converted to Hindu religion performed great sacrifice in 51 Tripura Era or 641 A.D. and he invited five Brahmins from Mithila, including Shri Nanda Asnanda, Shripati and Purushotham, and granted them lands in Sylhet district. He was contemporary of king Balbhadra of Mithila.

Here it is to be noted that after Adi-Dharmapha numbar of other rulers also ruled over Hill-Tipperah from the last quarter of seventh century A.D. to the end of 12th century A.D., but unfortnately no account of them is available in any source. Hereafter an interregnum accurred and the systematic history begins with the begining of 13th century which is beyond the purview of this paper.

Though it is impossible to define at any given period the limits of ancient kingdom of Tipperah but at various stages throughout the ancient period it gained conquests and possession which extended from Sundarbans in the West to the Burma in the east and Northward as far as Kamarupa[45]. The ancient kingdom of Hill-Tipperah indisputably comprised the whole of the present Cachar district, Lushai Hills, Karimganj, South-Sylhet and other adjacent petty states. At the same time the various delinquent hill, tribes living in hilly villages of neighbouring kingdoms were subdued who ultimately acknowledged Tipperah king as their supreme Lord or Sarvo Bhauma emperor. Though the limits of the kingdom have been altered enlarged and reduced through number of centuries of storm and stress of the Hindu Mohamadan and British domination in India, yet the ancient Āryan Raj still survives in its present diminished form. The capital was gradually moved from Tribeg on the

Brahmaputra on the north to Udaipur on the Gomti on the south and then back again to Agartala where the present Raj has had the seat of Government

It is worthy of remark that in ancient Tipperah the influence of Hinduism and Buddhism extended far and wide. Due to migration of the Brahmins from central India or Gangetic belt, Kamarupa and Mithila the tribal religion of the Tipras got modified by Hinduism and consequently the Hindu culture became predominant. One of the noticeable features is here the rapid spread of the cult of Savism and Tantricism associated with human sacrificed in the early period of Tipperah history. At a result of the new development a system of mixed form of worshipping fhe fourteen gods and goddesses emerged. During the time of Trilochan Saivism became the national religion. These fourteen gods and goddesses known as Siva, Durga, Vishuu, Lakshmi, Sarswati, Kartik, Ganesha, Brahma, Earth Sea, The Ganges, Fir or Angi, Kama or Cupid, and Himadri or the Himalayan mountain represented by symbols and small earthern monds were worshiped in a temple situated at Udaipur, the old capital of Tripura. according to Annual Report (1921-22) of Archaeological survey of India[46] Unokoti Tirtha situated in between Dharmanagar and Kailashar, and its neibourhood have always been sacred to worship of Siva at least from 8th to 9th centuries, if not earlier. During the Pala sena period of Bengal and especially in12th century Saivism was greatly patronized. About the influence of Buddhism R.M. Nath informs us that 'Pag-bsam-bjon' a Tibetan book of Lama Taranath states that being molested by the Turks in central and Northern India many Buddhists migrated towards the east and found a safe shelter in the land of the Kukis. A small state comprising portions of modern Cachar, Tipperah and Assam was named Nan-Gata and was inhabited by Buddhists."[47] According to N.R. Roychoudhury the discovery of a colossal stone image of Avolokitesvara (9th century A.D.), number of old stone images, terracotta temple plaques and sealings depicting the

Stupa and Buddhist creed near Pilak pathar village in southern Tripura bear witness to the prevalence of Buddhism in ancient period. The period under review also saw some considerable progress in the field of education which was imparted in tol or Sanskrit pathsala, scriptural and iconographic art.[48]

From the foregoing account it is evident that from the time of Yayati belonging to Lunar Dynasty to the 12th century A.D. the rulers of both Indo-Aryan and Non-Aryan stocks maintaining politico-cultural fellowship, establishing matrimonial relationship with neigbouring kingdoms and exevcising supremacy over the hill-tribes of adjacent petty states or principalities, ruled over Hill-Tipperah for many generations. The co-existence of both the principal schools of religion-Hinduism to a greater degree and Buddhism to a lesser degree—appears as a distinguishing hall-mark of the history and culture of ancient Tripura. This kingdom of primeval antiquity seems to be one of the oldest among all the Prachya kingdoms.

Notes and References

1. Quoted by E.T. Dalton, *Descriptive Ethnolgy of Bengal* (Calcutta 1960) p. 106.
2. J.W. Mc. Crindle, *Ancient India as described by Plolemy* (Ed. by R.C. Jain, London. 1885. Delhi, Revd. 1973-74) p. 194; G.E. Gerini, *Researches on Ptolemy's Geog of Eastern Asia* (London, 1909), pp. 51-52
3. *Rājmālā* Vol.1, (1458 A.D., compiled by Pandit Baneshwara and Sukreswara, Ed by Kaliprasanna Sen, Agartala, 1336, Tripura Era= A.D. 1926) p. 38f; Kaliprasanna Sen. Shri Rajmala, (1931) Vol. ll Ref. to N. R. Roychoudhury, *Tripura through the Ages,* (Agartala, 1977), pp. 9-12.
4. *Journal of the Asiatic Society letters*, (hereafter Abbrev, as J.A.S L.)1951. Vol. XVII, NOS-1-3, p. 80.
5. *Kirāta-Jana-Krti* (A.S B. Calcutta, 1974), pp. 130f.
6. *Rājmālā* (1892) p. 2, ct. N.R. Roychoudhury, *op. cit.*, p. 5.

7. *Bangla Deshar Itihas.* Vol II (1976) p. 480, cf. N.R. Roychudhury, *op. cit.*, p. 5.
8. *A statistical Account of Bengal* (Abbrev. as S A B.) (London) 1876) Vol. VI, pp. 357-58.
9. H.H. Wilson, *Vishnu Purāna* (Calcutta, 1961) p. 154. Ch. XVIII, p. 354, *Vishnu Purāna* (Hindi Edn.) p. 732; F.E. Pargiter *Ancient Indian Historical Tradition* (London, 1922) Ch. IX, p. 109.
10. *Indian coins* (Varanasi, 1969) N. 57, p. 14.
11. *Rajatarangini*, (Ed. by R.S. Pandit, 1st Pub. 1935, Delhi. Edn. 1968), p. 647.
12. Thomas Walters, *Yuan Chwang's Travels in India* (London, 1904-05, Delhi, 1973), pp. 188-89.
13. Trans by M.R.L. Kale (Bombay 1969) verse 59, pp. 99-100.
14. *The Back ground of Assamese Culture*, (Shillong, 1948), p. 77.
15. *The journal of the Royal Anthropological Institute of great Britain and Ireland,* Jan-June 1958, Vol. 38, pt. 1, p 109.
16. *Riyazu s-salatin* (Trans by Abdus calam, I.A.D. series, Delhi 1975), p. 12.
17. H.A.S.L., 1951; Vol. XVII, p. 80.
18. Vide, Dalton, *op. cit.,* p. 106.
19. Vide; Dalton, *op. cit.,* p. 107.
20. *Rājmālā* (1896) pt. II, ch. *non* p, 8, of N.R. Roychudhury, p. 15.
21. *Op. cit.,* p. 130f.
22. *Mahābhārata.* (Hindi Edn.) *Ādi Parva* (Anshavatarana parva) verse, 35, pp. 233, 261, 262. (*Sabhā Parva*) ch. XXXXlV, verses, 20-22; Wilson *Vishnu Purana* (Edg. Trans) Ch. X, p. 331;W.W. Hunter, S.A.B,. Vol. VI 463. *Vishnu Purāna* (Hindi Edn.) pt. 9l, p. 725; *Imperial Gazetteer of India*, 1908, (I.G.I.).p. 606; *Report of E.F. Sandys*. London, 1917; C.U. Aitchison. *A collection of Treaties engagements and sanads*, Vol. II (Calcutta, 1930) p. 193.
23. *Op. cit.,* p. 77.

24. Muhammad Quazim. Ms. *Alamgirnama*. (Calcutta. 1868) p. 940.
25. *The journal of Assam Rtasearch Society* (Abbrev. as J.A. R. S.) Vol. III., Oct. 1935, N. 3, pp. 93-95.
26. *Op. cit.,* p. 77.
27. *Mahābhārata, Sabhā Parva,* (Digvijaya Parva) Ch. 27, verse 20, p. 745, ch. 30, verses 4, 15, 16, 23, 25, 27, pp. 752-53.
28. J.A.S.B. 1897, Vol. LXVI, pt. I, pp. 108ff.
29. Vide *General Report of Tripura* by J.F. Brown, ref. to Dalton, *op. cit.,* p. 108.
30. Resort pf. E.F. Sndys, 1917.
31. *Tripura Review* (August 15, 1972) p. 6.
32. *Op. cit.,* p. 8.
33. *Op. cit.,* p. 77.
34. J.A.S.L. 1951. Vol. XVII. p. 80.
35. *Op. cit.,* p. XX 106.
36. J.A.R.S. Vol. III. Oct. 1935, p. 96.
37. *Op. cit.,* pp. 77-78.
38. Hunter S.A.B., Vol VI p. 470. I.G. 1 Vol. XXIII, p. 19, Report of E.F. Sandys, 1917.
39. Vide Report submitted to the Govt. of Bengal in 1875 by Capt. W.L. Samuells Ref. to hunter, S.A.B. Vol. Vi-p. 464.
40. *Op. cit.,* p. 78.
41. Hunter, S.A.B. Vol. VI. pp. 464f; R.M. Nath, *op. cit.,* p. 78.
42. *Op. cit.,* p. 79
43. J.A.R.S. Vol. III. 1935, pp. 96-97. D.R. Bhandarkar's statement, that it was from Mithila and Kāmarūpa that mny Brahmins immigrated in Eastern India and Bengal between 5th and 6th century AD (IA, LXI, 1932, pp. 41f, 67-72), is absolutely correct.
44. *Op. cit.,* p. 9.
45. Aitchison, *op. cit.,* Vol II, p. 193, I.G.I. 1908, p. 606, Hunter S.A.B. Vol. VI, pp. 465f.
46. Quoted by N.R. Roychoudhury, *op. cit.,* p. 139-40.
47. *Op. cit.,* pp. 80-81.
48. *Op. cit.,* p. 153.

11

The Genesis and Growth of Tribal Culture and Civilization in North-East India (From Prehistoric Times to the Twelfth Century)

I

The early history of the tribal people of North-East India from the pre-historic times to the 12th Century A.D. is still wrapped in a great degree of obscurity. Some stray accounts furnished in interspersed narratives are not only meagre and scanty but also unreliable and unauthentic. The research on the origin and development of primitive culture is still in its infancy. The scientific understanding of archaic and primeval civilisation of by gone age pre-supposes the imaginative and sympathetic treatment of and sober historical investigation into those facts which laid the foundation of their thoughts, beliefs, actions, knowledge, techniques, art, religion, and mythology, etc. The transition from so called simpler culture to complex culture involves a process which took its first shape in natural surroundings. Here the primary objective is to study the change. What factors conditioned the development of their cultures? What were the distinct phases, patterns and phenomena of their general movements? And how did the early thoughts at rudimentary stage subsequently prepare the broad framework of their culture and shape their values and behavioural patterns ? These are some of the problems which have engaged our attention here.

Oswald Spengler has correctly stated that "A Civilization is born out of the primitive psychic conditions".[1] Supporting the theory of positivistic naturalism, he points out that each culture has its own characteristics which begins with primitive society and goes on to develop in various phases.[2] Social and political organisatian, art, and science etc. remain in the first stage in archaic manner and then blossom into classical period. Culture grows like a flower and it has got its childhood, youth and old age. Will Durant also observes that "It is not a great race that makes the civilisation, it is the great civilisation that makes the people. Circumstances, geographical and economic, create culture and the culture creates a type".[3] These statements can be further corroborated by A.L. Rowse.[4] Past is not to be looked with contempt and disgust like those historians who belong to the school of Enlightenment. It has to be observed with sympathy in line with those who belong to Romantic School. The past is always worthy of study, for, it is a manifestation of genuine and valuable human achievements of the primitive people. The primitive time represents the genesis of socio-religious values which the developed civilization has lost. All celebrated scholars, thinkers, philosophers and many other savants, notably B. Croce,[5] E.H. Carr,[6] J. Burckhardt[7] and R. G. Collingwood[8] have outlined the necessity of allowing history to perform the dual role which is to study the past in the light of the present and vice-versa J. Burckhardt[9] says that "History is the record of what one age finds worthy of note in another. 'Here some tribes have been selected whose origins may be traced back to primeval antiquity. The comments may be applied to all the tribes concerned in general and some in particular. Keeping in view the facts that the period under review is completely unrecorded and "in the absence of any trustworthy historical account, it will be difficult to reconstruct the past with great amount of certainty. The difficulties can be overcome by effecting maximum coordination of different theories, postalates and principles propounded by historians, anthropologists, ethnologists and social scientists which serve as general guidelines for researchers and inquirers,- addition, epigraphical records, some fragmentary references in the early literary and classical texts, native chronicles, traditional and mythological accounts, documentary evidence, discovery of archaeological remains and other collateral evidences, may help us reconstruct the history of the remote and obscure period under review.

It is true that there are different stages through which the civilization of mankind has passed which is generally reckoned as the dynamic movement of the civilization, but the way in which the different stages have been classified is questionable. The general classification of these stages known as the "Savage stage" "Barbarian stage" and "Civilized stage" is nothing but continuation of the use of conventional terminology based on hypothesis, which is neither convincing nor plausible. F. Engels' classification of epochs-savagery, barbarism and civilisation with further subdivisions of the former two into lower stage, middle stage and upper stage, may be discarded out-right.[10] The more or less similar classification of Morgan referred to in Engels' work may also unhesitatingly be disposed of. Quite contrary to the widely prevalent views and general suppositions that the primitive people were savage or barbarous in early stages, it may be stated that savagery, barbarism and civilisation have relative connotations. The primitive people were in higher stage of culture. They were the early pillars of modern civilization or fragments of progressive serles of civilization. Every age has got twin elements of savagery and civilization. All the primitive beliefs and thoughts were further systematized, perfected and modified. There are many transitional practices which are still continued by their cultured successors. A thorough examination of the available evidence leads to the conclusion that successive stages of culture are nothing more than an extension of nascent culture. Many ancient remains, which would have narrowed the gap between primeval and modern civilization, have met with destruction. Nevertheless some of the surviving records and relics of the primitive age are so impressive that we will hardly feel inclined to call them savage or barbarous. The existing classification is undoubtedly misleading. How can the primitive tribes, who handed down to posterity the marvels of art, religion and culture and provided many threads to be woven into the fabric of the composite culture be considered as savages? Will Durant writes: "In one important sense the savage too is civilised, for he carefully transmits to his children the heritage of the tribe-that complex of economic, political, mental and moral habits and institutions which it has developed in its efforts to maintain and enjoy itself on the earth. We must make sparing uss of such terms as savage and barbarism in referring to our contemporary ancestry".[11] Again "Primitive culture may be the degenerate 'remnants of higher culture". Rousseau also asserted that "Primitive savagery is superior to civilized life".[12] Taylor's classification of the various stages of development is based on "dogmatic theology".[13]

The two theories of "Progression" and "Degradation" have been contrasted in his thesis. "The advocates of progression theory are apt to look backward to trace lower original condition of mankind". The adherents of the second theory regard "higher culture as original and the savage condition is produced from it by a course of degeneration". According to one assumption, history of culture began with the appearance on the earth of a semi-civilised race of men and according to second hypothesis culture has proceeded in two ways-backward to produce savage and forward to produce civilised men".

Suniti Kumar Chatterji states, "when the Aryans came to India, the country was not a no-man's land; it was already populated by some races or peoples which had risen to a high level of civilisation...the credit for building up Indian civilization is not the Aryan alone but that of the Non-Aryans in India had a share in supplying the basis"...[14] "The Kiratas[15] or Indo-Mongloids *i. e.* mongloids of India might very well have come to India before the Aryans and they contributed a great deal in the evolution of Hindu history and culture in North East and Eastern India."

II

Genesis and Growth

J. Hawkes and Sir L. Woolley have observed that "The book of genesis is the opening section of our history of Mankind."[16] According to A. J. Toynbee's[17] interpretation, the genesis of all civilizations—the unrelated and the related class alike could be described in the phrases of General Smuts, "Mankind is once more on the move." E. B. Tylor has pointed out that "culture or civilisation taken in its wide ethno-graphhic sense is that complex whole which includes knowledge, belief, art morals, law, customs and any other capabilities and habits acquired by man as a member of the society".[18] This has been supported by other anthropologists also.[19]

This key to the investigation of primeval condition of mankind in the dimages of the past is held by prehistoric-arcbaeology The knowledge of the past which sometimes lies beyond the ken of history or tradition is attainable only by scientific interpretation of the scanty material and surviving relics of human-workmanship, such as tools, implements burial mounds,' megalithic structures', pottery and other empirical evidences. The essential features of all the four early stages - Palaeolithic Age (30,000 B.C. — 10,000 B.C.), Mesolithic Age (10,000 B.C.—7000 B.C.). Neolithic Age (7,000 B.C. — 4000 B.C.) and Chalcolithic Age or Copper, Bronze and Iron Age (4,000 B.C. — 1500 B.C.) can be fairly noticed in the early phase of the tribal civilisation of North-East India. Both the oriental and occidental scholars have given their due recognitions to this classification without any dichotomy between them. Here it must be made clear that neither the same classification and periodization nor the same chronology may be applied to all the primitive tribes, for, in the process of development, changes took place at different times in the different parts of the world. The chronology suggested here and elsewhere should be always viewed as tentative. Because in ancient history it is very difficult to preclude the possibility of anachronism. However, along with the pre-historic archaeology the three other doctrines, *i.e.*, "Evolutionism", "Diffusionism" and "Acculturation" will help tracing the origin and growth of primitive culture. From geographical, political, linguistic and cultural points of view it is found that the firm foundation of civilization is laid by commingling and contacts of various people borrowing from each other the cultural traits which have always been the chief motivating force behind the progress.

It is indeed a fact that the dawn of the Neolithic Age really marked the beginning of tribal civilization in North East India. But at the same time it can't be denied that the positive evidence of the remains of various caves in the Khasi-Jaintia Hills, the Garo Hills, the North Cachar and Mikir Hills testify to their existence or habitation anterior or much earlier to this age.

According to B.C. Alien, the caves of different shapes and sizes near Cherrapunji, the famous limestone cave of Rupasor near the village Synden, and the cave at Lakadong with mural decoration and carvings, described by Ringwood in 1876, merit our attention.[20] In the Garo Hills near the Sizu or the Someswari a large cave called by the Garos "Dobakkol" is very famous. E.D.E. Frank points out that on the hill bordering Cachar in the east known as Bhuban Parbat, 300 ft high, two caves representing the earlier patterns of tribal architecture can be noticed, but no stone implements and bone fossiles were discovered.[21] K. L. Barua observes that the Austro-Asiatic mon-khmer Khasi and Syntengs represented the earliest of the human race."[22] According to him, from the walls and roofs of Cherrapunji cave of very ancient times "quartzite chips" of which rough or polished stone implements were made, were available.

According to classical source also the ""Besatae" (The Tibeto-Burman tribes-Kuki-Chins, Naga and Garos) of diminutive Stature lived in caves in ancient times.[23] R.

Brown also states that according to popular tradition some of the Naga tribes came out of a cave which was at a place called Murringphy in the hills at about four day's journey north-east of Manipur.[24] Some scholars hold that the Negrito tribes (Naga) constituted the original substratum of the population of the Assam valley. The Negrito or Negroid race appeared in the North East India in the Palaeolithic Age. The Negritos of Philippines, the Malaya Peninsula, the Andaman islands, New Guinea and Equatorial Africa had a culture similar to that of the Negrito of North East in both Palaeolithic and Neolithic Age. J. P. Mills suggests that both the traditional and physical characteristics of some of the hill tribes bear a clear evidence to the fact that the earliest inhabitants of Assam were of Negrito stock-wandering folk. To quote him, "They have left behind them an immense number of stone celts, probably the blades of digging sticks. These are found on or just below the surface and differ in a most interesting way in different areas of the province. There is strong tradition, however, that the remnants of the race were blocked into a cave near Haflong by a Kachari king".[25] Again, "An archaeological characteristic of Assam of world-wide fame is its wealth of Megaliths, such monuments "hardly found in the world. Some of the old ones are of great age and interest. 'Among the monuments are groups of huge sandstone cists of a type unknown elsewhere".[26] Both on the Megaliths or rocks in Assam, Mills and Hut on found interesting drawings, contemporary representation of weapons, carving of figures, geometrical patterns, animals and birds etc.

All the above mentioned tribes lived in the Palaeolithic Age or old stone Age and Mesolithic Age or Middle stone Age known as transitional stage (here roughly between 10,000 B.C. and 5000 B.C.), which are generally character set by nomadic life marked by hunting and pastoral life with the formation of groups and associations. During this period the tribes concerned lived in the natural surroundings. They used to live in caves and sometimes in groups for defensive purposes. They had unsettled life. They used to move in groups from place to place in search of food, and shelter. Their stone implements were chipped with edge axe and rude in form. Sometimes they used to make weapons of bones also. The art of cave paintings and sculpture are believed to have taken shape at the rudimentary stage. They did not know the use of copper and iron, nor did they understand the value of settled and agricultural life. Any way this period provided the first thread which they wove in their early civilization.

Far different from the civilization of palaeolithic Age is the civilization of Neolithic Age, which falls roughly between 5,000 B.C. and 2500 B.C. here. A.H. Dani has elabornately dealt with the Neolithic cultures of the Khasi-Jaintia Hiils, the Naga Hills, the Cachar Hills, the Garo Hills, Sadiya Frontier Zone and Brahmaputra valley.[27] He has classified all the neolithic remains such as megaltithic remains, cists, dolmens, menhirs, and stone implements of various types of all the above mentioned zones. The Neolithic implements were studied by various other scholars also, notably, E. H. Steel (1870), Lt. Barron (1872), Lubbok (1867), Medlicott (1875), H. C. Das Gupta (1913-1931) J. C. Brown (1914), J. H. Hutton and J. P. Mills (1928-29), According to him the Neolithic culture of Assam was dictated by geographical factors. All the Neolithic relics present a picture of secluded cultures with mutual relations. K. L. Barua also refers to the relics of Neolithic stage such as Celts, adges, grooved stones, shouldered axes, hoes, sepulchral monuments like cairns, dolmens, menhirs, cromlechs, upright stones, flat and horizontal stones, male stones, female stones and some stones depicting carvings and designs on them.[28]

The Neolithic monuments of the Khasi-Jaintias have greatly attracted the attention of scholars. According to Iswari Prasad, the Neolithic weapons were made of stone but they were different from the primitive type.[29] They were sharper, better chipped and more polished than the weapons of their predecessors. The Neolithic people knew the use of bows and arrows. They used to make pottery with the wheels. Different metals were also used. Some carvings on rocks and caves constitute the monumental evidence to their acquaintance with the art of painting. Among these people mention may be made of the ancestors of the Santhals, Kols, Mundas, Khasis of Assam and the inhabitants of Nicobar islands. According to S. B. Sharma, all the monoliths and table stones which appear to be cenotaphs or memorials were hewn out of solid bits of rock and taper towards the top.[30] They did not bear any inscription. The ashes of the dead were deposited in cairns. S. K. Chatterjee also points out that the Austric Khasi had the custom of setting upright stones' and rock stone slabs, etc.[31] Their notion of life after death and idea of the plurality of the souls gave a new line of speculation to the Brahmanical thinkers and the Aryans who had no acquaintance with the doctrine before. According to him, the Khasis introduced developed primitive system of agriculture and terrace rice-cultivation on the hills and plains. Some tribes of present Arunachal Pradesh also developed Neolithic culture.

According to A.H. Dani, the discovery of Neolithic "facetted tools" in the Mishmi Hills indicate the cultural contacts of the Mishmi tribes as well as Sadiya region with Yunnan.[32] G. Bertrand, describes the Apatani enclave as a survival of late Neolithic culture.[33] In Subansiri frontier division, slow investigation of the human colonies living in time honoured peace unravels the truth that the Daflas and Apatanis were living in the stone Age. Recently two Neolithic implements - "Grooved Ground Axe" and "Oval chipped and Ground Axe" have been reported from the Subansiri District near a place which is inhabited by the Nishis.[34] R. D. Banerjee also mentions the occurence of stone tools in the Abor country. [35] It is not known whether proto-Austroloids, Mediterraneans, Armenoids, Mundas, Monkhmer Khasis and other Tibeto-Burman tribes brought the megalithic culture from south East Asia or developed it here. In the present state of knowledge nothing can be conclusively said.

One of the curious features to be noted is that these Neolithic stone monuments are associated with the cult of fertility, ancestral worship, theory of sacrifice, and worship of phallus—Linga and Yoni, later personifed as the Mother Goddess and Siva principles of Saktism. Bertrand has also pointed out that the "Khasi monoliths comprising memorial stones, menhirs, and dolmens like these of western Europe, northern Africa and western Asia are doubtless the emblms of that phallic cult of standing stones which were so widespread in ancient times. These monoliths in the shape of Linga-found in India are asscociated with the worship of Siva." [36]

Generally speaking, in the Neolithic Age the variety of polished stone tools of advanced workmanship, discovery of agriculture, the settled life, formation of villages, domestication of animals, weaving, pottery, farming, technological art, introduction of art of culturation, food crops, trade, crafts, other socio-economic achievements like development of exogamous clans, family, land-tenure system, principles of inheritance, the position of women, megalithic monuments, art, paintings, worship of phallic stones and other revolutionary innovations constitute the distinguishing features of the complex culture of the tribes in North-East India. B. Harrison has rightly said that the Neolithic Age heralded the beginning of "First Industrial Revolution in History"[37]

The Chalcolithic Age (roughly between 2500 B.C.—1000 B.C. here), is generally characterised by the development of metallugical art, use of copper, smelting of iron ore, urbanisation of society, contacts among cultures, development of power of thinking, speaking, invention of Alphabets and other technological development. During this age the Khasis knew how to smelt the iron ore. The use of copper was first made by the Chutiya tribes of Sadiya Region at a later stage which is not antecedent to llth or 12th-century A.D., which is evident from the details of the ruins of copper Temple appearing in the Archaeological Reports and other relevant sources.[38]

The real flower of the Neolithic and Chalcolithic civilizations blossomed in the gardens of the tribes belonging to so called Austro-Asiatic groups and Bodo groups in particular. The stone celts and megaliths associated with burial urns erected in memory of their deceased representing the phallic worship, the use of iron implements, the developed hunting, fishing, animal husbandry, the growth of clans and the marriage system, the erection of thatched buildings, the formation of groups under the leadership of headman, the art of cultivation, the primitive system of jhum cu'tivation, the introduction of matriarchal principles in the matter of administration and inheritance, the belief in the immortality of the soul or the spirit and practice of worshipping the mother cult led to the foundation of the Khasi-Synteng, culture and civilisation in the Neolithic Pariod. S.K.. Chatterji observed that "they were in the Neolithic stage of culture and perhaps in India they learned the use of copper and iron and later on they developed a primitive system of agriculture employing their primitive weapons"[39] This has been corroborated by R.C. Majumdar.[40]

Thus the tribes belonging to Austro - Asiatic or "Finno - Ugrian Austro-Asiatic" group or Pre-Mediterraneans, speaking Mon-Khmer and allied languages once covered a large part of the globe and gradually occupied various parts of India. The Khasi-Syntengs affiliated to this group have made several distinctive cultural contribution in the field of Neolithic shouldered hoe, megalithic burials, art of cultivation, iron-smelting, totemic religion and matriarchy- all indicative of advanced culture and civilization, The stone celts and megalithic monuments found in the Garo Hills, the North-Cachar Hills, the Mikir Hills, the Naga Hills, Manipur and Upper Assam establish their recial and ethnological links with South-East Asia, western Asia, Pacific and Mediterranean world and Europe during pre-historic period.

As a sequal to the arrival of successive hordes of tribes known as Tibeto-Burmese, the intermingling of races, languages and cultures in North-East India followed. According to K. L. Barua, the Bodo tribes came into contact with the Mediterranean Pundras of Northern and Central Bengal who had the same Chalcolithic civilization as that of the dwellers of the Indus valley.[41] They first came under the civilizing influence of the Mediterraneans, then of the Alpines and lastly of the vedic Aryan colonists in North Eastern India about 1000 B.C., if not earlier. He mentions that "The earliest pre-historic culture in Assam, so far known, was not a Paleolithic but a Neolithic culture spread throughout the length and breadth of the province as indicated by the wide distribution of Neolithic celts.

We do not know who the original authors of this culure were. Perhaps long after came a people much more advanced in culture who introduced the shouldered Neolithic hoe, terraced rice cultivation, megalithic burials, ophiolatry and matriarchy. These people began with a Neolithic culture but later they acquired the knowledge of iron-smelting. We do not know whether they developed this art themselves or borrowed it from others. They were speakers of a language which belonged to a family very widely distributed all over the world. In course of time, however, they were displaced and submerged, in most places by hordes of new comers from Tibet, Burma and Yunan. These new comers may have been actually inferior to the Monkhmer speakers in culture when they debouched from the hills on the North and settled on the plains of Northern Bengal and the Assam valley but gradually they came under the cultural influence first of the Mediterranean Pundras of Bengal, then of the Alpines and lastly of the Aryans by which time the historic period began.[42]

The trend of evolution of tribal polity through centuries of their segregated life also merits attention. Political evolution has always been preceded by social evolution as the law of nature and our history constitute the standing testimony to the fact. In the first stage of human life, the tribal people were organised into group of clans and during later stages different families got united and formed villages and thereby laid the foundation of organised civil administration which was the product of mutual agreement be'ween the groups. It is exactly like that of the political evolution of the Aryans during the early Vedic Age which can be traced in the following ascending series of formation of groups, *viz.* the family (Griha or Kula), the village (Grama), the clan (*vis*), the people (Jana) and the country. The fundamental principles of primitive democracy with minimum of authority or control, tribal organisation, multiple society, local government of the villages, judicial procedures, customary laws, crimes and punishments, oaths and ordeals were determined in both pre-historic and proto-historic periods.

L. Pareti states that the tribal organisation continued to be the basis of life among the peripheral people especially in the mountainous district.[43] The federation beween the set of tribes was achieved. Later they were converted into regional divisions for administrative convenience. The traces of the primitive ideas and institutions remained among the people of succeeding generations. Robert H. Lowie also holds the view that the primitive democracy, the kinship, the customary laws, body of civil laws, judicial system, and family association clubs etc. were shaped in archaric condition.[44] The age-old self-governing institutions of the tribal people of North East India developed along the lines of vedic bicameral bodies—the Sabha and the Samiti, the "parishads" of the Brahmanic and Upanishadic period, the Greek democratic system of the Homeric Age and Pericles Age (458 B.C to 451 B.C.), the Hindu Republican system of the Post-Vedic Age as revealed by Megasthenes, nonkingly form of Government of Epic Age, self government as revealed in Smritis, Sangha or Gana of Panini period (5th to 4th century B.C.) supported by Patanjali, Gan-Rajya Rules in

Buddhist India, the Republics of Northern India (650-325 B.C), the Sanghas occurring in Kautilya's *Arthaśāstra* (325-300 B.C.) and other tribal republican institutions, parliaments and federal assemblies of Northern India. Between 500-800 A.D. the tribal political and social institutions made remarkable progress. From 800 AD down to the coming of the Ahoms in the 13th century the territories in Assam were ruled by different tribal chiefs.

Equally .remarkable is the evolution of the religious and philosophical system of the tribal people of North East India. Hinduism and Buddhism flourished among the tribal people during the period concerned. According to some reliable sources[45] Saivism and Saktism were the prevailing religions among the Kirata people, especially the Khasis, the Jaintias, the Garos, the Kacharis, the Tipperahs, the Chutiyas, the Mikirs, the Akas and the Idu Mishmis in Pre and Post Naraka period. Actually all these tribes known as the Kirātas in the Epic Ages, were worshippers of Mother-Goddess, Kāmākhyā, the Chief Sanctuary of Saktism. No wonder the Kāmākhyā was an embodiment of the fusion of the Āryan and Non-Āryan beliefs and practices in the early times. These tribes lived in ancient Prāgjyotishapur where the holy shrine of Kāmākhyā is located.

The tribal rites were celebrated in a cave which sank lower and lower as the result of subsidence over which the temple of Kāmākhyā was built and rebuilt. This was a transition from primitive Paganism of the tribal people to elaborate Hinduism. The former symbolised the great monoliths of unhewn stones and latter symbolised the Hindu temples with the images and carvings. After being subjugated by Naraka in the war in Prāgjyotisha in pre-Bhārata war period (3100 B.C.), the Kirāta people were pushed back towards the mountains and jungles as far as the Dikkaravasini (the present Sadiya region). At the time of dispersing in different groups from Kāmarūpa into the hills the above mentioned Kirāta people carried away with them the cult of mother Goddess as replica of early life. They left some unmistakable imprints on the Brahmaputra valley. The hill culture and religion first flourished in the valley and then in the hills.

After Saivism and Saktism mixed with varied forms of Tantric rituals attained great popularity, Tantrikism developed among some tribal people of North East India. It was a system of magical or sacramental ritual associated with magic, sorcery, witchcraft, and exorcism etc. Subsequently, perhaps during the 8th—12th century A.D. Tantrikism got intermixed with Vajrayana cult of Buddhism. P. Bhhttacharyya observes that it was during the Pala rule that Kamakhya became the centre of Tantric Buddhism.[46] According to Nandlal Dey, the Tantrikism as an offshoot of Buddhism of Mahayana school developed about the 9th century under the Pala rulers of Magadha and from Buddhist university of Vikramśilā the Tantric doctrines spread to Kāmarūpa and Tibet.[47] But this view can be contradicted on the basis of the statements of both E. Gait[48] and Charles Eliot[49] who held that this doctrine originated in North-East India.

In the North Eastern Frontier region also the influence of Hinduism can be traced out. The Akas' progenitor Bana was an ardent devotee of Lord Śiva. Various archaeological discoveries of Siva ling (Phallic stone), Sculptured images of Hindu pantheon, such as Dasbhuja Durga, Ganesha, Kartikeya, Saraswati and magnificient Bull-Nandi (the vehicle of Siva) etc., bear an irrefutable proof of the prevalence of both Saivism and Saktism among the primitive tribes of present Arunachal Pradesh. T. Bloch also shows that in Sadiya region the images of Surya and Kali dancing on Śiva and Saraswati were worshipped by the tribes.[50] Here we find Synthesis of culture embcdymg the elements of Indo-Mongoloid culture and Aryan culture which was completed by the end of 11th century A.D.

B.K. Kakati states that Naraka drove away the Aboriginal Kiratas from his Kingdom up to the point in North-East Frontier tract which is at present inhabited by the Abors, Miris and the Mishmis tribes.[51] In ancient time there was an Aryanised colony in the north East Frontier which has been referred to in pauranic literature as Dikkaravasini and in Tantric literature as Saumere Pitha.

K.L. Barua[52] points out that "The Bodos as well as the Austria people when they came under the cultural influence of the mediterraneans (Dravidians), the authors of Pre-Aryan Indian cultures, perhaps copied the custom (Saivism and Tantrikism) from the latter..." It may be noted that "the cults of mother Goddess or Saktism and Saivism popularised by the Austrics and the Bodos before the Dravidians of the Mohenjodaro of the Chalcolithic Age and the Aryans of the vedic Age or Satayuga left any imprint on the Indian culture. R.M. Nath States that Kamakhya or Ka-cy-Khati was a sacred shrine in the western part of Sind.[53] She was worshipped as Ma Ma Ka-cy-Khati or copper goddess'ia the same sense as the goddess of Cyprus (copper Goddess) of the ancient Cretans and Cannanites was worshipped by a race of people as Satiyas or Chutiyas, distortion of Chattusas. In one of the Mohenjadaro seals he refers to Kshasaku tribe along with other tribes. Once the Chutiya tribes in Sadiya region also popularised the cult of Saktism and Tantrikism.

The cultural and philosophical patterns of the tribal people of North East India appear as a queer mixture of both the Āryan and non-Āryan elements. The assimilation of tribal polytheistical beliefs, animism, propitiation of both benevolent and malevolent spirits, the natural phenomena having the anthropomorphic attributes based on magico-religious system, eschatological belief, doctrine of Atman and Karma,'ritualism, priesthood, sacrifices and other indigenous faiths, into the Aryan religious system, popularly known as proto-Hinduism appear to be a cardinal feature of Indian civilization. Saivism, Saktism, and Tantrikism which emerged as popular religious cults during the' period concerned, co-existed with the aboriginal forms of worship and further flourished after coming within the pale of Aryanisation. We have every reason to believe that the concepts stemming from Pre-Aryan civilisation have found their way into Hindu doctrines, thoughts and scriptures just as the concepts of orthodox Hinduism have been assimilated by many of the primitive tribes of our country. Several Upanishadic. Vedic and Pauranic doctrines and even the Vedantic philosophy have got pre-Aryan features. S. K. Chatterjee has also drawn the plausible conclusion that "The ideas of Karma and transmigration, the practice of Yoga, the religious and philosophical idea centering round the conception of the Divinity as Siva and Devi and as Vishnu, the Hindu ritual of Homa - all these and much more in Hindu religion and thought would appear to be non-Aryan in origin."[54] Tylor[55] and Atkinson[56] have expressed similar views.

Some tribal people of North-East India could not keep themselves away from the forces of Buddhism which was greatly influenced by vedic thoughts, Brahmanical doctrines and Tantkrism. Those hill-tribes who professed Buddhism during the period concerned are the Monpas, the Sherdukpens, the Khamtis, the Singphos, the Tangsas, the Khampas and the Akas (all frontier tribes of present Arunachal Pradesh), the Chakmas of Hill-Tipperah and Mizoram, Mughs of Hill Tipperah and some Naga tribes of Manipur. According to Hannay, in the Sadiya region many temples of Buddhist origin were found.[57] The religion deteriorated in succeeding centuries and reached the condition which was observed by Hiuen-Tsang in the 7th Century. Buddhism spread through the country about the 9th century and gradually assumed a debased style due to the Tantric and Sakta forms of Hinduism. The frontier tribes were followers of both Mahaynna and Hinayana schools of Buddhism. The Khamtis and Singphos followed the

Hinayana school of Buddhism prevalent in Burma.[58] It is true that Buddhism during Pagan period was also tinged with Mahayanism and Tantrikism. According to Butler, the Sherdukpens and the Monpas were the followers of Mahayana school which was preached by Padma Sambhava (a great Acharya of Nalanda University) in the 8th century A. D.[59] Later in the 11th century Atisha Dipankara of Vikramsila University of Bihar preached it in Tibet. According to Pandit P. B. Vidyavinod, some of the mountain tribes of the North East of Brahmaputra valley known as the Bhutiyas and the Khamtis accepted Buddhism as a result of their connection with Tibet and Burma.[60] Kennedy in his Ethnological Reports of 1910 on the Akas , Khowas, Mijis and Monpas of Towang contended that their animism seemed to be mixed with appreciable amount of Tibetan Buddhism.[61] C.R. Macgregor has also referred to the acceptance of Buddhist tenets by the Aka tribes.[62]

The Chakmas were the followers of the Hinayana school of Buddhism. W.W. Hunter states that the Buddhist Chakmas worshipped Lord Siva and Kali vis-a-vis traditional deities.[63] Their religion on the whole appears to be a mixture of Buddhist, Hindu and old tribal customs. J. C. Ghosh has also given an indication that Hill-Tipperah became the great centre of Buddhism because of its contact with Bengal and Magadha in Bihar.[64] The Tibetan work "PAGSAMZON-JAN of SUMPA KHANPO" and "KAHBAB DUN-DAN" of Lama Taranath unravel the mystery that after the destruction of Nalanda, Odantpuri and Magadha - the chief centres of Buddhism, by Bakhtiar Khilji in 1197-98 A.D. and the attacks of the Turks in Central and Northern India, many Buddhists migrated towards the east and found a safe shelter in the land of the Kukis (Hill-tribes).[65] A small state comprising the Hill-tracts of Assam, Cachar and Tipperah was named "Naingata" which was inhabited by the Buddhists. This can be further confirmed by one verse in Sanskrit mentioned in one Bengali source.[66] The present Chakmas of North East India also came from Magadha after the attack of Bakthiar Khilji in the early Medieval period. They are also not Indo-Mongoloid as erroneously supposed by many scholars. Hiuen-Tsang brought to light a very interesting point that the tree and serpent worship of the old Nagas including the Manipur Nagas was based on Buddhist beliefs.[67] This Chinese source can be further supported by Greek source. The Periplus also states that the Tibetans of remote pre-historic time were worshippers of trees and serpents.[68] Their descendants have got connections with Bengal, Ceylon, Burma, Tibet, Siam and China as bulwarks of Buddhism.

The fabric of tribal civilisation has been woven by both internal and external threads. Besides the religious, cultural and other factors their contacts with the outer world largely affected the course and currents of their civilisation. During the Naraka period in the Epic Age, the migration of Aryans from Mithila to Assam greatly influenced the Austric and Bodo culture. Placing our reliance upon Native Chronicles[69] as well as other evidence[70], we can state that during the early period right from the time of Yudhisthira (about 5 thousand Years ago) the Jaintias were under the influence of Brahmanical rulers, as a result of which they accepted aryanised faiths and practices. Their religious customs, ceremonies and priesthood system are strikingly similar to-that of Hindus. From the Epic Age to the 12th Century A.D. the relations of the Khasis and the Jaintias with the rulers of Kamarupa, Bengal and other neighbouring rulers moulded their way of life. Both the Brahmin and Buddhist priests from Bengal, as a result of their frequent visits to these places and cultural fellowship, might have influenced the various grades of their culture. The Garos' relations with the rulers of Kāmarūpa between 7th and 13th Centuries gradually shaped their socio-cultural pattern.

The early rulers of the North-Cachar Hills maintained their relations with the Epic Heroes and the rulers of Hill-Tipperah by borrowing various cultural traits. On the basis of the literary evidence[71], Native Chronicle[72] and other historical evidence[73] it can be stated that Hill Cacharis had close contacts with Epic Heroes and Aryan rulers. As a result of this contact the process of their Hinduisation soon followed which can be proved on the basis of numerous evidences.[74] In the Mikir Hills innumerable archaeological finds of Hindu temples and images prove that they were under the control of the Varman, the Mlechha and the Pala dynasties. The Political and cultural relations of the Tipperah Kings with the rulers of Kamarupa, Bengal and with several Brahmins from Mithila greatly determined the shape of their early culture and civilisation. On the basis of some valuable evidence[75] it can be affirmed that as a result of the relations of Tipperah tribes with Aryan rulers as well as the neighbouring kingdoms, the process of Sanskritization soon began which gradually put its indelible imprint on the tribal beliefs and practices.

The vertical stone monobliths set up by the Nagas in the Neolithic Age reminds us of the cultural traits of the people of Indonesia, Phillipines. Sumatra, Malanesia and Polynesia. Thair contacts with the rulers of civilized countries in the plains in connection with trade influenced their culture, industries, arts and crafts, language and art of warfare. The imperial records furnish the evidence of the Nagas' trade relations with the plains of Assam, Burma, Manipur and other places which went a long way in changing their ways of life.[76] The Nagas are also traditionally believed to have established contacts with the Epic Hero Bhima and the Kachari Kings. It is very difficult to specify the particular period. A. G. Macall states that the Lushais were also deeply influenced by varied contact; with predominantly stronger civilisation through the earlier ages.[77] The archaeological records show the prevalence of Hinduism and its impact on Non-Aryan ways of living, which is confirmed by tradition and epigraphy.[78] According to Pandit Vidyavinod tradition records that a colony of Brahmins was set up in Sadiya region near the city of Kundin by Parasurama.[79] Kaundinya, well known as a founder of the Kingdom of Kamboja belonged to this Brahmin colony. The existence of Aryan colony in North-Eastern frontier region and the impact of Aryans on Mongoloid elements can not be denied. The Gauhati Copper - Plate inscription of Indra Pala=Varma-Dev (Circa-1038 A.D.) deciphered by Hoernle also corroborates this statement.[80]

It is worthwhile to note that when the process of aryanisation set in the North-Eastern Region tentatively between 2nd millennium B.C. and 7th century A.D., the hill religion, culture, language, manners and customs, beliefs and practices, arts and crafts were greatly modified. Their early contacts with both the Alpine and Vedic Aryans which profoundly contributed to the synthesis of culture can not be denied. It is generally believed that the Alpine Aryans coming from Iran to Eastern India before Bharata War of 3100 B.C. across the Himalayas diffused advanced culture known as "Vratya culture" before the advant of Vedic Aryans. After the coming of Vedic culture the synthesis of both the cultures took place. During the early centuries of Christian era and 5th century A.D., they introduced the Aryan language of Pisachi family and popularised the propitiation of both the natural objects and malevolent spirits. The Assamese term Deo or Deva signifying an evil spirit or a malevolent god was probably applied by the immigrants to the Gods of aboriginal Tibeto-Burmans who had to be appeased by crude worship and sacrifices. Hence the priestly class of Bodo tribes like the Chutiyas and the Tipperah later came to be known as Deoris or Deorais. The Alpine traits are discernible among the Nagas, the Bodos, the Lushasis, the Manipuris and others who are Tibeto-Chinese speaking Monoloids.[81]

B. Sahni writing on the "The Himalayan Uplife since the advent of Man" states that there is evidence of contact between early human cultures on the two sides of the main Himalayas.[82] Migration across these mountains was possible in Palaeolithic times. Himalayas were not a barrier for migration of Palaeolithic or even the Neolithic man. Direct contact was established not only with China but also with Iran across the Himalayas since the dawn of human existence. "The migration of Alpine Aryans to India is believed to have taken place before the advent of the Vedic Aryans and towards the close of Chalcolithic civilisation in Sind or nearly 5000 years ago", H. C. Chakladar also refers to the contacts of Vedic Aryans with the people of Bengal and Assam.[83] The Vedic Aryans settled in Assam about the beginning of Christian era. The Greek source also supports this view.[84] R. M. Nath also holds the view that Maithili culture "influenced the Austric and Bodo cultures-sometimes by annihilation and sometimes by assimilation.[85] Some of the Bodos and the Austrics held their own ground in the hill areas sometimes as vessals and sometimes as independent rulers. The Austric Ka-Meikha and the Bodo U-Mei-Ludai were gradually assimilated to the Hindu pantheon and became goddess Kamakhya and Siva Umananda". According to Pauranic evidence, Kuru, Panchala, Eastern Country, Kamarupa, Pundra, Kalinga, Magadha and Dakhisna had established mutual contacts in the early period.[86] The eastward movement of the Aryans through Bihar and North Bengal towards this region paved the way for the fusion of the Aryan and Mongolian culture. According to Native chronicle, "Debaka, one of the principal habitates of the Mikirs upto this day is believed to be a fragment of the Devaka Kingdoms, forming part of the empire of the. Imperial Guptas as we learn from the Allahabad Pillar inscription of Samudra Gupta; and the remains of old buildings and sculptures in the adjoining areas point to the existence of a flourishing Hindu state during time of Samudra Gupta and his successors."[87]

Syed Sayeed-ud-Din Ahmed is of the view that in the Epic Age Hidimbapur (present Dimapur) was the.capital of Ghatotkach, the son of Bhima and the Jantia Hills was occupied by the Aryans. Two other kingdoms, Naga Rajya (modern Naga Hills) and Manipur were situated side by side and occupied by civilized people.[88] The Hindu influence was all pervasive. This is what tempted. Arjuna to marry Ulupi the daugher of one Naga King and Chitrangada the daughter of Chitrabahana, the King of Manipur. C. J. Lyall writes, "I have already taken a lively interest in the singular oasis of comparative civilisation and organised society set in the midst of congeries of barbarous people over whom its rulers exercise an authority."[89]

The contact of North Eastern India with the rulers of Bengal, Orissa, Mithila and Magadha is a unque feauture of Eastern Himalayan civilisation. Right from the time of Ashokan period to the Sātavāhan Age the cultural contacts among various racial groups which were established in the regions stretching from Assam to China probably continued till the 13th century.

The various tribes belonging to the Austric group, Negroid group, Bodo groug, Tibeto-Burman group and semi-aryanised group evolved a mixed civilisation and developed various theological and 'philosophical doctrines which contributed to the growth of Hindu religion and culture known as Proto-Hinduism. The assimilation of non-Aryan religious beliefs and practices within the fold of Aryan culture and vice-versa later became the twin pillars of composite Indian culture and civilisation. This period also witnessed the progress of aboriginal art in North East India. Their monolithic marvels dating back to later Neolithic Age, Prehistoric finds, ancient monuments and relics of pre-Christian and Christian era scattered all over the region, architectural remains, sculptural and iconographic arts, decoration and paintings undoubtedly testify to their attainment of a high degree of artistic perfection. The observance of traditional ceremonies and festivals accompanied by music, songs and dances also formed the integral part of their civilisation. As a result of the political and cultural intercourse amongst the various racial groups a common pattern in repect of the society, economy, polity, art and architecture and religious beliefs can be noticed.

Notes and References

1. *Der Unterganj des Abendlandes*. Vol. I, p. 153, Ref. to A.J. Toynbee, *A study of History* (Abridgement of volumes - I-IV by D.C. Somervell, London 1946) p.p. 210-11.
2. *Decline of the West.* 2 Vols (London-1926-28), Ref. to R.G. Collingwood. *The idea of History* (London 1946, Reptd., 1973), p. 181; For further details also see *Decline of the West* Vol. I, p. 18-21.
3. Will Durant. *The Story of civilization*, our Oriental heritage (New york, 1954), pt 1, pp. 2.-3.
4. *The Use of History* (London 1946), p. 99.
5. *History as the story of Liberty* (Eng. Tran. by S. Sprigge, London, 1941), p. 19.
6. *What is history,* (Cambridge, 1961), p. 26, 32, 55
7. *Judgement on History and Historians* (1959), p. 179. Ref. to E.H. Carr. *op. cit.,* p. 24.
8. *Op. cit.,* p. 228, 282.
9. *Op. cit.,* p. 185 quoted by E. H. Carr. *op. cit.,* p. 55.
10. *The origin of the family, private property and the State* (Moscow, 1884, Reptd. 1891), pp. 35-41.
11. *Op. cit.,* p. 5, p. 90.
12. Quoted by R.G. Collingwood, *op. cit.,* pp. 87-88.
13. *Primitive culture* (London, 1871, 1903), Vol. I, pp. 35-38.
14. *Inda Aryan and Hindi* (Calcutta, 1969), pp. 32-33, 50.
15. On the basis of. Schoff, W.H.Tr. *The peripuls of the Erythraean Sea*. (Here-in-after abbrev as *The Penplus*) (London 1912) pp. 252, 278f; McCrindle, *Ancient India as described by Megasthenes and Arrian* (Edited by R.C. Jain, Delhi. 1972), pp. 80f. App.-4, pp. 230-33; McCrindle, *Ancient India as described by Ptolemy,* (Calcutta 1927), pp. 191-94; Gerini, *Researches on Ptolemy's Geog*. (London 1909) pp. 28ff; the Kiratas can be identified with the Khasi Jaintias, the Garos; the Kacharis the Chutiyas, the Hill Tipperahs, the Mikirs, the Nagas, the Akas, the Mishmis and probably the other tribes having the admixture of both Āryan and Non-Āryan-bloods.

16. *History of mankind, cultural and scientific development, Pre-history-and the beginning of civilisation,* (UNESCO, 1963). Vol. I. pt. 1, p. 3.
17. *Op. cit.,* p. 51.
18. *Op. cit.,* Vol. I, Ch. I, p. 1.
19. Robert H. Lowie. *Primitive Society,* (London, 1st Pub. 1921, Reptd. 1949) p. 1; Kroebar, A. L. *Anthropology,* (Newyork 1923, Revd; Edn; Calcutta 11967) p. 252.
20. *Assam District Gazetteer,* Vol. X, p. 6, p. 9.
21. *Journal of the Asiatic Society of Bengal* (hereinafter J.A.S.B) 1902, Vol. LXXI, Pt. III, p. 37.
22. *The Journal of the Assam Research Society* (hereinafter J.A.R.S), April, 1939, Vol. VII, N.I., pp. 10ff.
23. *The Peripus* pp, 278-79 See also McCrindle, *Ancient India,* p. 180.
24. *Statistical Account of the Native States of Manipur and the Hill Territory under its rule.* (Calcutta 1874, Reptd. Delhi 1975). p. 37.
25. J.A.R.S. April 1933, Vol. N.I., pp. 4-5.
26. *Ibid.*
27. *Pre-Hitory and Proto-history of Eastern India,* (Calcutta 1960), pp. 41-73.
28. J.A.R.S. April, 1939 Vol, VII., N.I., pp. 10-18.
29. *A new History of India* (Allahabad, 1965), p. 15.
30. J.A.R.S. July 1938, Vol. VI. N. 2., p. 56.
31. *Op, cit.,* pp. 38-39.
32. *Op. cit.,* pp. 44.
33. *Secret Lands where women Reign* (London 1958), pp. 182-83.
34. *Arunachal News,* August 1979, Vol. 8, N. 5, pp. 13-14.
35. *Annual Report of the Archaeological Survey of India* 1922-23.
36. *Op. cit.,* pp. 134-35.
37. *South-East Asia–A short History* (London, 1954), pp. 6-7.
38. J.A.S.B. 1845 Vol. XIV pt. 2. pp. 477-78; J.A.S.B. 1848, Vol. XVIII, pt. 1, pp. 462-68; Dr. T. Bloch *Report of the Archaeological Tour in Assam* (Abbrev. as RATA) 1905.

39. *Op. cit.*, pp. 37-38.
40. *History of Ancent Bengal* (1st Edn. 1971), pp. 251f.
41. J.A.R.S. July 1939, Vol. VII No. 2, pp. 38-39.
42. *Ibid.*, pp. 40-41.
43. *History of Mankind cultural and seientific development 1200 B.C. to A.D. 500.* (Translated from italian by GEF Chilver and Sylvia Chilver, UNESCO 1965) Vol. II. pt. I. p. 157.
44. *Op. cit.*, pp. 376-77, 385-83.
45. Kakati B.K. *The mother Goddess Kamakhya* (Gauhati 1967) pp. 5-6, 10-16, 37. Nath R.M., *The Background of Assamese culture* (Shillong, 1948), p. 4, 17, p. 95, p. 97, p. 99, p. 105, G. Bertrad, *op. cit.*, pp. 171-73.
46. Cf. J.A.R.S. 1962 Vol. XVI, p. 56.
47. J.P.A.S.B. (New series) 1914. Vol. X, p. 346.
48. *History of Assam* (Calcutta, 1926), p. 15.
49. *Hinduism and Buddhism* (London 1921) Vol, II, pp. 278-79.
50. R.A.T.A. 1905, vide Home 'B' Progs Nos.—702-708.
51. *Op. cit.*, p. 56.
52. J.A.R.S. Apr. 1938, Vol. VI, N.I. pp. 8-10.
53. *A Clue to the Indus Valley script and civilization* (Shillong, 1959), pp. 20-21.
54. *Op. cit.*, pp. 32-34.
55. *Op. cit.*, Vol. II, p. 164.
56. *The Himalayan Gazetteer* (Delhi, 1973) Vol. I. Pt, I. Preface.
57. Quoted by L.W. Shakespeare, *History of Upper Assam, Upper Burma and North Eastern Frontier* (London 1914), pp. 71ff.
58. *Asiatic Researches*, 1828. Vol. XVI, pp. 337-348.
59. *Asketch of Assam*, pp. 80-81.
60. J.A.R.S. Jan. 1936, Vol. III, No. 4, p. 117.
61. Elwin, V., *India's North East Frontier in the 19th Century* (Bombay 1959), p. 442.

62. *Proceedings of the Asiatic Society of Bengal*, 1884, No. XI, pp. 198-99.
63. *The Statistical Account of Bengal* (London 1876) Vol, VI, p. 45.
64. J.A.R.S. July 1936, Vol. IV, N. 2, p. 47.
65. Quoted in Nath R.M. J.A.R.S.; July 1936, Vol, IV, No. 2, pp. 36f.
66. *Srihatter Iti-Vritta*, 2nd Book, 1st Part Ch. 4, p. 56. Ref. to J.A.R.S. 1936, Vol. IV, N. pp. 36f.
67. S. Beal, *The Life of Hiuen-Tsiang* (London 1884), Preface-Xf.
68. *Ibid,* p. 279.
69. *Deodhai Assam Buranji* (Gauhati, 1932), pp. XXII-XXVI, pp. 169-175; *Jaintia Buranji*, (Gauhati, 1937), pp. 1-10.
70. J.A.R.S., July 1935, Vol. III, No. 2, p. 69.
71. *Skanda Purāna* (Kalyan Series), pp. 178-80; The *Mahābhārata Adi Parva*, pp. 452-461 Verses—2-5.
72. *Deodhai Assam Buranji*, pp. 1622-68, XXI.
73. Hunter, W.W., *The Statistical Account of Assam* (London 1879. Repotd. Delhi, 1975) Vol. II, pp. 403-4.
74. Montgomery Martin, *Eastern India*, (Reptd. Delhi, 1976) Vol. V, pp. 665, 690.; Assam Sec. Privatew Sec. Ofiice, Arch. Branch "B" Progs June 1910 No. 7-9.; *Proceedings of LT, Governor of Eastern Bengal and Assam,* June 1910, No. 18; J.A.S.B., 1900 Vol. LXIX, p. 45.
75. Hunter. Vol. VI. pp. 357-8, p. 463 Wilson H.H. *Vishnu Purāna* (Calcutta, 1961), Ch. XVIII. p 354., *Vishnu Purāna* (Kalyan Series) p. 732; Pargiter, *Ancient Indian Historical Tradition.* (Reptd., Delhi, 1972), Ch. IX p. 109; Aitchison. *A collection of Treaties, Engagements and Sanads,* (Calcutta. 1930), Vol. II. p. 173; Barua, K.L. J.A.R.S. October 1935, Vol. III. No. 3, pp. 90-97; *Imperial Gazetteer of India* 1908. p. 606, Report of E.F. Sandys Cf. S. Playne & C. *Bengal and Assam, Bihar and Orissa*, (London, 1917), pp. 460 F.; *Mahābhārata, Ādi Parvan* verses-35, pp. 233, 261-62.
76. Letters received from Govt. Vol. 8. Al. 1832, p. 368; Letters issued to Govt. Vol. II, No. 78, or 6, p. 265; Vol. of letters

received from Misc. Officers Vol. 5 (a) 1840 *Proceedings of Chief Commissioner of Assam* (Foreign Deptt.) 1890, No. 513.

77. *Lushai Chrysalis*, (London, 1949), pp. 34-35.
78. Bloch D.T., R.A.T.A. Jan. Feb.1905; Hannay S.F., J.A.S.B. 1848. Vol. XVII, pp. 466-67, 471-72.
79. *Kāmarūpa Śāsanāvali*. p. 27 (Introd.) Cf. J.A.R.S. July 1939. Vol. VII, No. 2, pp. 60-61.
80. J.A.S.B. 1897, First Plate, Vol. LXVI, Pt. I, p. 129 Verse-13.
81. J.A.R.S. Jan. 1936, Vol. III, No. 4, p. 115, pp. 131-32. J.A.R.S. July 1938, Vol. VI, No. 2, pp. 48-52.
82. *Current Science*, Aug. 1936, Vol. V. No. 2. J.A.R.S. July 1938, Vol. VI, No. 2, p. 46.
83. *The Aryan Occupation of Eastern India* (Calcutta, 1962), pp. 78ff.
84. Schoff, W.H., p. 253.
85. *Op. cit.*, p. 27.
86. *Vishnu Purāṇa* (Kalyan Series), p. 671.
87. *Deodhai Assam Buranji,* pp. 209-14.
88. J.A.R.S. July 1935. Vol. III, N. *2,* pp. 67-69.
89. *Ibid.,* Lyall.

12

A Study of the Tribal Republics in North-East India

The most distinctive and remarkable feature of tribal style of living in North-East India is fundamentally the smooth functioning of their age-old legal and political but free and representative institutions maintaining their republican character and spirit which indicates their highest attainment and skill in the art of self-Government running throughout their whole history and stands in comparison and contrast with the ancient Hindu Republican forms of Governments (from Vedic Age or in the true sense of the term from first Millennium B.C. to 300 B.C.) and Greek Democratic system (from pre-historic Age to 451 B. C.) in various respects, *i.e.*, equality before law, liberty of thoughts, freedom of opinion and expression, working patterns of councils and councillors, elective system, local Governments in the villages, judicial procedure, crime and punishments, oaths and ordeals, etc.

A succinct summary or sketch, I hope, would possibly suffice to give a real and vivid picture of the administrative patterns of both the Āryans and Non-Āryans of Northern, North-Western, and South-western and Eastern India respectively. While drawing a line of parallelism, it is quite indispensable at the very outset to discuss the similarities in the trends of political evolution which is always preceded by social evolution as a law of nature. History bears an eloquent and glowing testimony to the fact that in the first stage of human life, the tribal people were organised into a group of clans and during the later stage different families got united and formed a village and laid the foundation of civil organisation which was product of mutual agreements between the groups. Likewise, the political evolution of Āryans during the early Vedic Age may be traced in the following ascending series of formation of groups—the family (Griha or Kula), the village (Grāma), the canton or clan (Vis), the people (Jana), the country. The Āryans mostly lived in grāmas or villages. Several villages made up a Vis or settlement and number of settlements formed a Jana or tribe out of which some Āryan tribes (peoples) like Bharatas or Purus, Yadus, Anus, Turvasas, etc., living somewhere between Sarasvati and Yamuna were republicans. The early Āryan settlement or Visah came under the control of chief appointed by them. Similar was the system followed by the ancient Greeks. According to the picture depicted by Homeric poems, before the rise of city states (Hellenic) the Greeks lived in village communities. Each village in primitive times belonged to a group of families or household which was cemented by a tie of blood. The village was ruled by a headman. Such a group—constituting a village community—was called "Yevos" (Gens) or Clan. Several Clans constituted a lager group (tribus) or tribe the head of which was the king. The phratry was the connecting link between the family or Clan and the State. Homer calls the king hereditary chieftain and "shephered of the people" rather than a constitutional king. Side by side the king there existed number of other chieftains, heads of Clans or of tribes who equally bore the title (Basileus).[1] We also find the nobility in existence. It was on this foundation, conforming more or less to the "Social contract theory" of Rousseau, that magnificent edifice of Republican forms of Government was erected.

This democratic tradition and spirit finds best expression through and reflection in indigenous tribal administrative organisations. The institution of chieftainship and other local heads of the administration bearing different designations and maintaining corporate character as a body politic, their existence and dependence on number of advisers, high dignitaries and other offiicials, the supreme voice of the people in the deliberations of open councils—machinery for co-ordination and consultation—and their participation in the election reflecting the public opinion in the first instance provide real framework which certainly help us draw a comparative account of the working system of Republican Government.

First, mention may be made of the elaborate republican system of the Khasis and Jaintias. Khasi Syiems and other local heads of the administration have always carried on the administrative works in accordance with the advice and consent of council of ministers and other advisors in a better way than the system that existed in Hindu republics for a thousand years.

According to Manu a king must have "colleagues" and ministers in their midst and along with them he has to consider ọrdinary and extra-ordinary matters of the State (*Manu* VII 54-57). Manu says: *"Sosahain mudhain Lubdhanākrita Budhinā Na Shakdyo Nyāyato Netu Sȧkten Bishayapuncha. Shuchinā Satyasandhen Yathāshās-trānuārin̩ a Dandah̩ Pranayitun Shaktah Suśahayen Dhimata. Api Yatsukaraṁ Karma Tadapmyakena Duskara Vishestoṣaha Yen Kiṁtu Rajayaṅ Mahodayam.*[2]

According to Kautilya, the king should as a rule consult with three or four ministers (*Mantnbhishacha turbhin sahaba Mantrayat*)[3]. But the amount of latitude and freedom granted to all the ministers and advisers by the Hindu kings is little known whereas, on other hand, the freedom and powers exercised by all others officials among Khasis and Jaintias are obviously known. The elaborate elective system in its genuine form in Khasi and Jaintia Hills is also far more superior to what existed elsewhere in India during ancient period. Khasi traditions clearly reveal the fact that in many states both male and female (Syiem-Sad) Syiems were elected. Various Khasi states had both electoral and executive councils. The clans, who laid the foundation of states, were jointly responsible in runnig the administration with the Syiem maintaining the right to elect their Syiems. They formed the state electoral college to which each clan sent a delegate. The electoral council was further enlarged by adding village heads to it.[4]

An ounce of evidence is weightier than tones of theories. A notable and glorious example set by peoples of Cherra in case of election of Ram Singh will always be considered as a memorable recordand the finest example of the people's sovereignty. In 1856, after the death of Suba Singh, Ram Singh obtained the chieftainship of country with the sanction of British Government without being formally elected by the Elders in Durbar. This created unprecedented troubles and virtually a state of Civil war existed. All the twelve principal Clans refused to recognise Ram Singh as theit chief. Subsequently, the differences were patched up and all twelve principal clans took part in the popular election and re-appointed him as their chief[5]. At the same time the notable role played by the entire population in passing legislation and conduct of the judicial and administrative business in Durbars—open door councils, a parliament of the people and a supreme court—remarkably testifies to the existence of long standing republican system.

Equally remarkable are the village republics. All the local officials are elected. Thus it appears that Khasi people always governed themselves through their elected rulers, who were responsible to their respective durbars or councils. The administration of Jaintia Hills was also vested in the local chiefs called the Dolis and Sirdars who belonged to specials Clans and were elected. They were at the same time assisted by Subordinate officers like Pators, Sangot, Dan and others.

In North Cachar Hills, during the days of Kachari Rajas, the management of the Hills was entrusted to Senapati or General and chief law officer with a number of assistants. Each village had a headman called Kunang duly elected.

Large villages had an assistant headman called Dilo. In central Cachar the popular council "Forty Sem-pungs" used to appoint Raja according to established custom[6].

In Lushai Hills although chieftainship was hereditary, but in the administration of village the chief was assisted by a council of village elders called Upas who were appointed by him. Besides the Upas, there were other village officials. A strong chief was sensible enough to govern his subjects in accordance with customary Law, but a weak chief who tried petty tyranny on his subject soon found himself a king without any followers[7]. After the annexation of Lushai Hills, British also recognised the principle and value of election and put forward a novel scheme of constituting a Durbar composed of elected chiefs, one each from administrative circles. A cardinal principle for administration was to secure some expression of responsible clan opinion[8].

The Kukis of North Cachar Hills—"Rangkhois"—had also have republican Government. Villages are administered by a group of village officials, the Kalim or headmen, the Kabur or assistant headmen and their subordinate Chapia—Kalim and Chapia—Kabur[9]. According to report of Surgeon Mccrea, Kukis' nation was ruled by their principal hereditary chiefs or rajahs, but divided into clans, each under its own chief, whose officer was not hereditary but elective. The Raja was assisted by a council called "Thuspois" or Mantris and used to sit with them to administer justice[10]. In Manipur also, the tribal polity varies from tribe to Iribe. The democratic village councils of the Maos and semi republican gerontocracy of Kabuis are worth quoting. In general, the Nagas political institutions are more liberal than Non-Nagas in Manipur. However, Kukis of Manipur have unquestionably a democratic institution which works as a check on the appointed village official like Khulakpa, the chief of the village[11]. In Tripura also, a Panchayat system is headed by choudhary, elected by the members of the council. The seniormost male members of each family is entitled to participate in the deliberations of the Panchayat. Maghs, another tribe of Tripura, also have a village council in every three or four villages grouped together. The head of this institution is known as Bomarang or choudhary, duly elected by a council, and assisted by assistants known as 'Karbari' and a messenger called (Peada). Choudhary presides over the meetings of the council and awards the final verdict[12]. The Chakma chief called Sirdar also plays an important role in managing the aflairs of the community. Garos have also an open assembly popularly known as "Jingma Changga" in which chief and headmen of families sit together with equal right to decide administrative and judicial matters.[13]

It may be pointed out that the Nāgas had a long established tradition of republican system of government as we find that during 150 A.D. — 284 A.D. the Nāga Emperors fostered the republics which covered the whole of Eastern and Western Malwa, and probably also Gujarat (Abhiras), the whole of Rajputana (Yaudheyas and Mālavas) and a portion of Eastern Punjab—all connected territory to the West of the Gangetic Valleys—as the republican coins of "Eran" bear withness to this fact. The family of Ganapati Nāga of Padmavati was of Ṭaka—Vamsa. The Mālavas and the Nāgas spoke some dialect. With the origin and migration of the republican Mālavas from Punjab, the "TAKKA Nāga" had also migrated[14]. Ganapati Nāgas were called the Overlord of Dhara or (Dharadhisa). To the South of Malwa, the Nāga territory was spread out; their coins bear affinity with the Naga coins[15]. Their capital was Karkota. The name of Naga King was Nāgadutta. All the republican communities—Mālavas, Yaudheyas, Abhiras, Prarjunas, Sahasanikas, Kharparikas—belonged to tribal groups in Eastern Malwa. The *Bhāgavata* says that the rulers of above republics were called "Janadhipah" which means republican rulers[16].

The old form of government continues to prevail among some sections of the Nagas in present North East India. Dalton informs us that Lower Naga groups west of Dayang River acknowledge no chiefs rather they appoint as sopkesman of the village, known as Elders, without giving them real power[17]. The Council of Elders as a supreme body deals with all administrative problems.

This system exactly conforms to non-kingly forms of republics existing in various Hindu republics of Sixth century B.C. Besides, the Zeme Nagas consisting of some seven thousand souls scattered over the three areas of North Cachar Hills, Nagaland and Manipur have republican system of government. Each village or community is virtually ruled over by the Kadepeo with the help of village council. Till recently there was no appeal against the decision of these village councils[18].

In Arunachal Pradesh also, all the tribal or village councils of various denominations having certain features in common and as expression and reflection of the will and power of the whole people are, no doubt, self-governing institutions. The people composing the councils are accepted leaders of a village, and decisions are not taken by formal vote but discussions and debates continue untill general unanimity is achieved. The idea of electing people is very familiar among Monpas of Kameng who have a well developed village self-governing institutions at least for the last one thousand years and the power is excercised by the councils. Their democratic nature resemble the Kebangs of the Adis[19]. The example of the election of sorgens for a period of three years through the ballot system and provision for their removal on grounds of inefficiency or specific incorrect action as also his subordinate position to the General Assembly indicates the real republican nature of government of Monpas. Another notable example is of Apa-Tani buliangs acting as the representatives of public opinion[20].

The above mentioned system bears a close resemblance to the system prevalent among the Hindus of ancient India right from the Vedic age down to 300 B.C. In its comparable aspects the tribal councils of North East India can fairly be compared in the first stage with Vedic Sabha and Samiti — the two popular assemblies described in *Atharvaveda* (VII. 12.1,) as the twin daughters of God Prajapati. They were the original and earliest institution of Indian Polity. The Sabha functioned as an open assembly or hall or meeting place or as parliament for disposal of public business through debate and discussion. Decision was taken by vote of majority. The Samiti was the larger General Assembly of the people expressing the voice of the Vis or people in choice of their king. Both these assemblies of the people put a check upon king's absolutism. We have age - old history of the Samiti from the latter part of the millennium of the *Rig Veda* down to about 700 B.C. During the Brahmanic or Upanisadic period, this body came to be known as the Parisat. But the North Eastern tribal councils stand in a far better position to the Vedic Assemblies which practically assumed the character of Aristocratic Democracy. Here little comparision with the Greek Democratic system will not be out of place. Homeric Poem gives us the first glimpse of the political institutions of the Greeks. In the Homeric Age, the council of the Elders known as "Yepovia" represented by all the heads of clans and the Assembly (ayopa) of the folk, in which all the free men had the right to be present in the conduct of public affiars, were the two representative Assemblies. In the later period, Pericles Age (451 B.C. to 451 B.C.), the assembly—the general body of citizens—and the Senate of the Five Hundred, chosen by lot from the general body of citizens, were considered to be an asset of Athenian Democracy. But we find that on the one hand Homeric idea was more theoretical than practical whereas on the other with reference to the participation of general people of total population, the existence of a slave and alien, element that vastly outnumbered the citizens, rendered the designation democracy in the modern sense quite inapplicable. But such kinds of discrimination between freemen and slave regarding equality before law is completely absent among North Eastern tribes.

The real Hindu Republics were in existence in post-Vedic period as Magasthenes records that "Sovereignty (kingship) was dissolved and democratic governments set -up at various places"[22]. The non-kingly forms of governments as the essence and beauty of Republican Governments can be traced out here. The *Mahābhārata* (*Śānti Parvan*) speaks of the republican forms of goverment—*Ganas*—the sovereignty of many and confederations of republics. The *Mahābhārata* mentions five republican people - the Andhakas-Vrishnis, Yadavas, Kukuras and Bhojas (*Śānti Parsva*, chaps. 107, 16, 17 and 18). The leaders of *"Ganas"* adopted measures ensuring, the welfare of the *Ganas*. Monier Williams and Dr. Fleet have wrongly translated the word *"gana"* as "tribe". *Manu Smriti* also speaks of self-government of people to a considerable degree. Paṇini (fifth century B.C.) talks about *Saṁgha* and *Gana*. The *Gana* was a political Assembly or republic comprising all castes and the *Samgha* as Republic comprised population of all castes and performed the business in accordance with votes of members. As Patãnjali says, *Saṁgha* is so called because it is one body, a unity (Samhanana) (*Sahnane Britah*)[23]. Prof. Rhys Davids in his *Buddhist India* observed that in the country of Buddha and its neighbours, there Were *Gana-Rajya* Rules-rule of numbers and rule by many. This *Gana-Rajya* consequently turned into a government by assembly or parliaments or Senates[24]. In Northern India, during, 650—325 B.C. innumerable repulics existed. The Sākyas of Kapilavastu had a parliament which met in mote-hall (*Santhagara*); Mallas Republic had a new parliament house called *"Ubhatuka"* and Videhas (Mithila) republic was governed by Assembly of Elders. The Licchavis with capital at Vaisali had been republican long before the time of Buddha. *Lalita Vistara* remarks that Licchavis recognised no distinction and everyone thought that he was the raja, *"Sekaika eva manyate aham raja ham rajati"*. Besides the Federal Assembly, there was a smaller body of eight (ashta-Kula) or nine members. Actually, the council of eight was in charge of justice and council of nine of foreign affairs[25]. The Greek writers also mention some Hindu Republics. MCcrindle informs us that Audheyas (whose dominion ixtended eastward upto the frontiers if Magadha Empire) had a parliament consisting of five thousand representatives. In near about 325 B. C. had Alexander observed that all the states he passed trough right upto Indian frontier in jaluchistan, were "republics". Most powerful in those days were Kshudrakas, Malavas and Ambashthas or Abastani. Their democratice constitution allowed the upper Houses Elders to fuction freely. The system of government in the Punjab and Sindh with the exception of two monarchies was republican[26].

All these republics were more or less similar to the tribal republics of North-East India so far as the nature of councils, assemblies or parliaments and the people's voice in its delibarations and debate and working systems are concerned. Kautilya in his *Artha Śāstra* (325-300 B.C.) also mentions two clases of *Saṁghas*—one class with chiefs or kings and other without kings. Amongst the former were the Licchavikas, the Vrijika, the Mallakas, Madrakas, Kukuras, and others. And Kambhojas in eastern Afghanistan, Surashtras, the Kshatriyas, the Serenis and others belonged to latter group which were also republics in true sense of the term.

More striking similarities can be observed in respect of village administration, elective system and general working procedure. The self-governing villages were the cornerstones of both the Āryans and non-Āryans, political system. In both the cases, villages as autonomous bodies were administred by local men. The village communities of the Vedic period were controlled by Gramini. They were in the days of

Kautilya (as throughout the Hindu Period) the self sufficient molecules which formed the body politic. Politically they were self-governing. Village communities maintained their existence inspite of the powerful tide of Imperialism as Russian Mir survived inspite of the growth of most powerful autocracy in Russia. Under this system villages continued to exist as self-sufficient little Republics which remained the basis of higher political existence. The villages were regarded as a cooperative social unit and its heads were elected. Village people always followed the orders of the man who was working for common good. a *"Prakshayamanishadah, Sasawjana, Naprakhasate Prachhanna Shravane Kchhana, Cha, Sarvahite cha Karmi-ni, Nigrihen, Dwigunamansa Dadhata Sarvahita makasya burbatah kuryurajanam"*[27].

It is important to note that McCrindle, an authority on classical writings on India, refers frequently to "Indian village system" as "Free" autonomous or independent Republics. The Greeks took each of the rural units to be independent Republic but they never mistook a village Panchayat for Republic. The Greek writer described Kathaians to the east of Hydraotes or Ravi with area covered by District of Lahore and Amritsara at capital Sankala as republican units[28]. E. H. Walsh reveals that some of the minor republics occupied valleys of Himalayas and the Chumbi valley. He speaks of "Old form of elective" Government. According to him the villages assembled at a fixed meeting place and presented to the two Kongdus— heads of local administration - the list of elected headmen of the villages. Kongdus maitained that they did not derive power from the Tibetan Government but from the local deity[29]. V. A. Smith is of the opinion that tribal constitution may have been of tibetan origin. He says that "the customs of hill men gave the best clue to working of all ganas" and were of Mongolian origin like the tibetans. His appreciation of the tribal republics of Mongolian origin unquestionably stands to reason and logic. But his ethnological accounts of the republics is open to criticism. According to him, Licchavi and Videha have got affinities with Tibetans[30] which is not true. The elective system and working procedures of both the Āryans and non-Āryans were almost the same. We find that in both the republican forms of Governments, the governing power was delegated to a small number of citizens elected by the rest; they assembled and administered it by their representative agents; principles of representation were based upon a reasonably wide suffrage; idea of common good (republican) and public law (jus publicum) prevailed and all powers were exercised for the common good. All the issues were put to vote and decided by the majority verdict, substantiating the truth that the voice of true majority is always the proper motive force in any Government. The essence of republican forms of Government is that decision are taken on basis of discussion in public meetings or in open Councils and assemblies. In Hindu Republics, vote was called "Chhanda" which means "freedom" and voting was free. Voting was by tickets consisting of slips of wood distributed among the members. During Budha's time, election was based on ballot-voting where tickets were collected. The system exactly conforms to the election system of Monpas of NEFA (Arunachal Pradesh). Like all tribal chiefs and village elders with some exceptions, in ancient India also kings were elected, re-elected and deposed. Right from later vedic age to 600 B. C. numerous references in literatures are available regarding elective system.

Equally great is the similarily discernible in the realm of law and justice. The tribal customary laws can without any ray of doubt fairy be compared to *Dharmasūtras* (600-300 B.C.) which was the record of local customs and usages on which civil and criminal laws were based. As tribal justice is guided by customary laws, in ancient India in Pre—Kautilyan Age Hindu system of justice was also guided by *Dhrama—Sūtras*. In ancient India, upto 300 B.C. we have no history of evolution of law and our knowledge does not go beyond the *Dharma Sūtras* which contain for the most part customary laws but seem to be deficient in most branches whereas on the other hand tribal of eustomary laws seem to be very sound. The judicial procedure and nature of crimes and punishments are also similar to each other. The Vedic Sabha used to function also as a court of justice. The Elders or heads of families forming the Sabha used to administer justice. The *Taittriya Saṁhitā* mentions the village judge (Grama—Vadin) and Maitrahis Sabha or court (II. 21.) According to Kautilya, disputes were settled in four ways-*Dharma* or truthful acknowledgement of the disputed claims by the other party, *Vyavahāra*-or through the agency of witness, *caritra*-by following the time honoured customs (customary laws) and *Rājasāsana* - or by royal adjudication. To quote Kautilya: *"Dharmasacha Vyavahārasach Caritran Rājashāsanaṁ vivadarthasa-chanusapadh Panschimah Purvahdhadhakah Atra Satyaistheto Dharma Vyavarāhastu Sakchhisu caritran Sangrahe Pusan raganyāmaganya tu Shāsanam"*[32]. He further observed that republican chiefs in states had the beneficial propensity of justice. No doubt, early legal system was marked by sense and spirit of nationalism. Local customs received recognitions in all matters.

The tribal village councils or Durbars in North Eastern region also functions as an open court where disputes are heard and decided according to established customs and usages which form the part of their customary laws. In these open courts, all the male members and in some areas even women are also allowed to take part in the trial of a case. The judgement passed on an offender is regarded as the judgement of whole village and not merely of the chief and his advisers. This system of administration is suited to genius of the people as a whole.

Another similarity is regarding the practice of forming larger *Saṁgha* and reference to them of disputes for settlement. In ancient India, sometimes *Samgha* of a particular locality not being able to decide certain disputes by itself used to approach a larger *Samgha* of neighbouring locality with a request for the settlement of issues involved[33]. In *Atharva Veda,* occasional references have been made to assembled Samities of the whole land or those who assembled (*Samgramah*). The village as a collective unit was well known[34]. This practice exactly conforms to the Judicial procedures of Apa-Tani of Arunachal. In 1945, when in one theft case an accused person became a threat to the peace between Apa-Tanis and Daflas, the Joint Councils of the Villages including various clans and representative of people met and went from village to village to find out the public views and then decided the issue[35]. In respect of punishment of crimes like assault, murder homicide, theft, adultery, rape, stealing, there is a striking similarity in both the cases. Besides, cases relating to marriage, marital status, divorce etc., are also decided in same fashion. In ancient India, murder and other offences were regarded more or less as torts and could be expiated by fines which had the same nature as the "Weregilds" in the early Saxon or Teuton laws. Fines were levied on persons accused of thefts which varied from tribe to tribe according to their respective customary laws. Adultery and unchastity were similarly punished. In ancient India also king was no more than a clan - head or tribal chief. In northern India, during 650-325 B.C. the judicial practice of Licchavis was practiced. The council of Eight or Ashta-Kula formed a supreme court before whom criminals were sent up for trial after preliminary investigation by experts. *Vyavahārikas* were lawyers and *Sūtradhāras* kept up threads of law and customs. The accused found guily were punished by Senapati and from him up to Raja who used to punish according to the prevailing penal code called *"Paven - Potthaka"*[36].

The practice of oaths and ordeals are also to be found in both the cases. During the Vedic Age, the practice of ordeals was prevalent as the blaze to the fire which was kept in the court house for purpose of ordeals bears witness to the fact. Kautilya also refers to the practice of oaths and ordeals. In case of theft or in certain criminal offences, Judicial torture was applied to make the suspect confess.[37] Besides, theft of girls, adultery with women either unmarried or living with their husbands, rape and other cases were all tried in the criminal courts. But in ancient India there is no doubt about taking of oaths but regarding ordeals we have but the least evidence. Whereas on the other hand the North-Eastern tribal conception and practice of oaths and ordeals is very clear. We find the common forms of oaths and ordeals of differnt kinds among Garos, the Mikirs and Nagas. Besides, Khasi and some other tribes of Arunachal strictly adhere to the practice af oaths and ordeals which constituted a major part of their trial, inflicting punishment and judicial procedure as a whole. Without a high sense of justice, a cardinal principle, no republic can last very long. Plato rightly says in his famous work, *The Law*, that in Judicial organisation all citizens should have a voice in administration of justice. More or less same judicial procedures were applied in Greece and Tibet. The popular courts known as " Dikasteries" was considered to be corner stone of Athenian Democracy. Five thousand citizen, drawn by a lot from the general body, were divided into ten panels among which an important judicial business was distributed but this system was extremly complicated. According to Tibetan procedure, the accused person is arrested, sent to lock-up, strictly watched, kindly treated, mildly interrogated, and whipped at intervals. After confession, repeated whipping and cruel tortures of various kinds are practiced. The culprit is taken to the Kalons or Ministers court which suggests to "Gyal-Tshab" (Regent) which is the highest court of justice that one of three punishments mentioned in the decision may be approved[38]. But this practice is neither fair nor based on general body's decision. Moreover, the arbitrary methods are also being applied which go against the established customs and fair judicial procedure of various tribes of North-Eastern Region.

It is worthwhile to note that North-Eastern tribal republican institutions as free and representative institutions reflecting the supreme voice of the people and translating the Lincoln's maxim—Government of the people, for the people and by the people—into the realm of reality can unquestionably be considered far more superior not only to the Vedic bicameral bodies - Sabha and Samiti—which had aristocratic democracy but also to Hellenic institutions purely tyrannical, "Yepovia" or "Senatus", a council in conflict with king, and Folk Assembly (ayopa) unrepresented by all during Homeric Age, "Gerusia" of Sparta or its other oligarchical (partly royal and partly democratic) institutions-senate and assembly—Athenian democratic institutions of Pericles Age, not fully representative, Roman Senate, represented by only "Patrician", Comitia centuria - an assembly of one rich people—and "Comitia Tributa" represented by only Plebeians, political institutions of Venice-an Oligarchy of hereditary nobles—and Poland which was mixture of aristrocracy and Monarchy, public councils of Burma known as "Hiuttaw" and "Byedaik" a Privy council in both of which members were creatures of Kings, minor republics of Chumbi Valley of Tibet - a mixture of theocracy and democracy—Germanic Folk assembly, Folk assembly of Western Europe-unknown to debate—and various other senates, assemblies and Tribunals of ancient, medieval and mordern times.

Looking at the over-all picture of North-Eastern tribal polity and its distingushing marks and characteristics, it is quite heartening to note that their time honoured Self-governing institutions have remained more or less unaffected by manifold social changes and political turmoils in the course of many centuries or millenniums. The dymamic process of transition from monarchy to aristocracy and on to democracy-a thesis, antithesis and synthesis-rejecting the platonic ideal of Government—aristrocracy of intellect—and Aristotelian contradictory concepts of popular sovereignty and the political philosophy of Machiavelli expounded in his famous work *The Prince* as well as

Kautilya's propounded Treatise *Arthaśāstra* which champions the cause of the germ of republic in monarchy may be viewed in the context of ancient Indian political system. Tribals' republican institution has withstood the test of time without any major change by virtue of which they are being placed in more advantageous position and valuable possession of the finest Commonwealth ever heard of in any quarter of the globe. The majority of tribes have been consistently following the democratic system of government since time immemorial.

Notes and References

1. Wood House, *Tutorial History of Greece,* pp. 37-39, London, 1938.
2. *Manu-Smṛti,* Trans by Pandit Har Govind Sastri, chapter VII (Verses 30, 31, 55) p. 312, Dharma-Sastra Section-3, Varanasi—(1970).
3. N.C. Bandyo Padhyaya, *Kautilya,* p. 124, Calcutta, 1927.
4. Hamlet Bareh, the *History and Culture of the Khasi* people, pp. 252, 268. Calcutta, 1967.
5. Letter; dated 6th. Jan. 1859, From Hudson Esquire, Vol. 23 (a) 1859. Letter Received from the Miscellaneous Officers.
6. S. Barkataki, *Tribes of Assam,* p. 69, N. B. T. Delhi. 1969.
7. H.K. Barpujari, *Assam in the Days of Company,* "Appendix" "C", p. 99, Gauhati, 1964.
8. S. Barkataki *op. cit.* pp. 96-97.
9. M.A. Gilchrist McCall, *Lushai Chrysalis* pp. 246-254 London, 1949.
10. S. Barkataki, *op. cit.,* p. 73.
11. Dalton, *Descriptive Ethnology of Bengali,* pp. 44-45, Calcutta, 1872.
12. Roy, *History of Manipur*, pp. 192-193, Calcutta, 1973.
13. B.K. Roy Burman, *Demographic & Socio Economic Profiles of the Hill Areas of North-East India,* pp. 104-106, Delhi, 1970.

14. Hamilton, *An Account of Assam,* pp. 91-92 Edited by S.K. Bhuyan. D.H.A.S. Gauhati, 1940.
15. K.P. Jyaswal, *History of India* (150 A.D. to 350 A.C.) pp. 38-53-54, Pub. 1933
16. E. J. Rapson, *Indian Coins* Section 51. pp. 12-13, Varanasi 1969, V.A. Smith, *Catalogue of coins in Indian Museum* (Calcutta), 162, Oxford, 1906.
17. K. P. Jayaswal, *Hindu Polity,* pp. 160-161, Fourth Edition, Bangalore, 1967.
18. Dalton, *op. cit.,* p. 42.
19. S. Barkatati *op. cit.,* p. 75.
20. V. Elwin. *Democracy in NEFA,* pp. 18-56. Shillong, 1965.
21. Haimendorf, *Apa-Tanis & Their Neighbours,* p. 100, London 1st Pub., 1962.
22. J.W. McCridle. *Ancient India as described by Magasthenese and Arrian* [Trans. of fragments of Indika of Megasthenese and first part of Indika of Arrian Reprinted with and trans. form Indian Antiquary 1876-77, pp. 38-40, Rvd. Edn. Calcutta, 1960.
23. K.P. Jayaswal, *op cit.,* p. 24.
24. Rhys Davids, *Buddhist India.* Cf. *Hindu Polity,* p. 23.
25. R.K. Mukherjee, *Hindu Civilisation* pt. II pp. 231-40 Bhartiya Vidya Bhawan Bombay, 1957.
26. J.W. Mecrindle, *The Invasion of India by Alexander the Great,* pp. 121-292. M.D.C.C-CXC III.
27. N.C. Bandyopadhyaya, *op. cit.,* p. 259.
28. McCrindle, *op. cit.,* pp. 115-16.
29. E.H. Welsh, *Indian Antiquary* p. 290, 1906.
30. *Indian Antiquary* p. 233-35, 1903, Letter No. 25th Nov. 1917, Ref. to *Hindu Polity,* p. 170.
31. R.K. Mukherjee, *op. cit.,* P&I, p. 127.
32. *Kautilya Arthasastra* Trans, by Dr. Shamasastry, p. 150, [First Published in 1909, Mysore, Govt. Oriental Library Series, Bib. Sanskrita No. 37], Bangalore, 1915.

33. R.K. Mukherjee *op. cit.,* pt. II, p. 249.
34. Macdonel & Keith, *Vedic Index,* p. 245, London, 1912.
35. Haimendorf *op. cit.,* p. 104.
36. R.K. Mukherjee *op. cit.,* pt. II, pp. 240-42.
37. Shamasastry *op. cit.,* pp. 218-20.
38. S. C. Das, *Proceedings of Asiatic Society of Bengal* 1894, p. 5.

13

The Tribal Administration of Justice : A Historical Survey from the Vedic Age down to the end of the British Rule with Comparative Analysis

I. Preliminary Remarks

In the present paper, an humble attempt has been made to portray the vivid picture of the tribal administration of justice in the Khasi-Jaintia and Garo Hills (the present Meghalaya) from the Vedic Age down to the end of the British rule establishing suitable comparison with the judicial system prevalent in India from first millennium B.C. to 300 B.C. and Greece from Homeric Age to 451 B.C. in various respects. For our clear and convenient study the subject under review has been broadly divided in different parts. Here it has been clearly shown that the indigenous pattern of the judicial administration was of very simple nature in primitive times ; the dawn of Medieval Age marked the beginning of some new phases which remained almost intact till the end of the East India Company's rule in 1858 and in the post-Mutiny period it underwent certain modifications and changes, but basic feature was retained. The historical treatment of the subject is basedon ancient literary texts, Greek sources, Persian annals, documentary evidence and other published and unpublished sources.

II. Sources of Law

Sources of law determine the basic framework of judiciary. The whole idea of justice is based on law. Law is the cornerstone of judiciary. In judiciary the supremacy of law is a universally recognised factor. The tribal customs, conventions, usages, ancient practices, ethical codes, precepts, fables, antecedents, taboos, royal edicts, etc. constitute the main source of law. Brigadier Shower's Report[1] that "the savage tribes in whole North-East India had no law" is complete distortion of the truth. The social customs, social institutions, the social structure the clan system, economic condition, mutual agreements and contracts, family environments, kinship, religion, etc. have had distinctly played their parts in the evolution of jurisprudence or the science of law. The law of marriage and women's property, law of divorce, law of inheritance and succession, law of household property, law relating to buildings and houses, law concerning the non-performance of agreements, law of debts, law of deposits, law of crimes and violence, defamation and assault, law relating to border disputes etc. form the main part of the customary laws of the tribal people of North East India. An interesting line of parallelism can be drawn between the customary laws of the tribals and laws systematised and codified by Manu[2], the first law giver. The above mentioned laws mainly fall under the sacred law, secular law, civil law, criminal law und practical law. In aletter dated Shillong, 24.9.1902 to the Editor of the "Bengalee" Calcutta Mr. Hormu Rai Diengdoh[3] had rightly pointed out that "Though the Khasis had no written language yet they could prescribe their rites and ceremonies. And they framed their laws which are still practised by the Siems and chiefs in their Durbars...which are well known and respected by the British Govt..." Mr. C. Lyngdoh, while dealing with the rudiments of the Khasi law of inheritance observed that "Antiquity, certainty, reasonableness and continuity are essential to the validity of custom".[4] G. Bertrand, a distinguished ethnologist had made the customary laws of the tribals his principal object of investigation. He had proved that customs, usages, beliefs and social structure are all binding forces for a judge. The' customary law precedes the judges and their functions and courts of law. His worthy remarks about the tribal people of North East India in general and the Garos in particular are worth quoting here. To quote, "At first these laws are difficult to grasp. It might be thought that in practice they would work out as an accumulation of fragmentary vestiges traceable to a few racial fancies or idiosyncracies, but in fact the primitive laws are so coherent and logical that as soon as we begin to set them out and classify them even roughly, one can make out the principles which have governed both their inception and development. It then becomes clear that these principles are essentially rational, however ignorant the man who devised them. The tribes are living under some laws. The law of exogamy governs the group at all points and at all times. It is based on the values—the women—which are the values par-excellence both from the biological and social point of view without which life is not possible On the map of the world this little corner of the Garo Hills may' well be lost, but what a wealth of virtue and simple faith its primitive society has to offer. In some insignificant tribe, we see our own image and phenomena, the lessons of which we would do well to learn. We should find them recovering all their ancient novelty. By what break of memory was a society which could not write and able to transmit to generation after generation a code of honour which makes our cleverest lawyers blush and an elaborate yet harmonious code of laws, regulating daily life almost too well? To these laws the Garo society is and will long remain fanatically attached. The Garo laws can be classified in three words and these are a self-contained code of observances as well as a mirror of Garo mentality. They are asimalja, dakmalja and Nima. None of the words can be defined or translated literally. Asimalja for instance represents a moral rather than a legal force—a force which is an inseparable part of Garo history. The word is so potent that a Garo about to commit a crime thinks better of it and anyone who has yielded to temptation is stricken to the heart. Anything which disrupts the harmony of law and order affects not only the sinners but the whole community."[5] J.D. Baveja[6] has also thrown little light on the social laws of the Garos. Thus, the matrilineal society and exogamous clans of the Garos called "Chatchis" sub-divided into sub-clans known as Machongs and their kinship group called Mahari and the "Kurs" of the Khasis based on moral code, certain norms and definite ideas of right and wrong, greatly determine the course of mutual relationship and become the guiding factors in the adjudication of disputes.

In ancient India, the judicial administration was guided by the Vedas, *Dharmasūtras*, and Purāṇasmṛtis. The kings had to dispense the justice according to the regional laws, sacred canons, precedents, family, clans, moral laws, equity, good conscience, rules of justice, civil laws, etc. as evidenced by many sources authentic.[7] The tribal customary laws can, without any ray of doubt be fairly compared to *Dharmasūtras* (600-300 B.C.) which was the record of social customs and usages on which civil and criminal laws were based. As tribal administration of justice was guided by customary laws, in ancient India in pre-Kautilyan Age Hindu system of justice was also guided by *Dharmasūtras*. In Ancient India also up to 300 B.C. we have no history of evolution of law and our knowledge does not go beyond the "Dharmasutras, which contain for the most part customary laws but seem to be definite in most branches, whereas on the other hand tribal customary laws seem to be very sound. J.D. Mayne[8] has correctly stated that though it is not possible to affirm as to how far the hill tribes were influenced by the laws of smrtis, but the tribal customary laws had definitely some impact on Indian judiciary and law in the broader perspective.

III. Evolution of Judiciary

Equally great is the contrast obviously discernible in respect of the evolution of judiciary and in the realm of judicial practices and procedures. Here it is sine-qua-non to discuss first of all one of the vital questions as to what was the nature and form of the tribal judicial system during the ancient period and particularly when the courts of law were not properly constituted and graded, the institution of chieftainship had not fully developed, the powers and functions of the Chief and their councillors were not clearly defined, the concept of state as it was ruled by the various chiefs at comparatively later stage was conspicuous by its absence, the boundaries of the villages and territories were not clearly demarcated, etc., The modern sciences of sociology, ethnology, anthropology and the history of law have, no doubt, cast some light upon the dim past, nevertheless no clear picture emerges therefrom and nothing can be established with any authenticity. In spite of the uncertainty and the absence of positive historical proof concerning primitive political institutions, we can safely dwelt upon this aspect of the subject with the help of the slender thread of evidence at our disposal. Our dependence on" inferences and generalizations to a certain extent can't be avoided. There is consensus among all the scholars concerned that the social organisation had its origin in kinship which knit together clans and tribes. Kinship created society which in turn created state. The headman of the tribes of the different groups or clans formed a council of elders for the fulfilment of the two-fold objectives *i.e.* to discover the truth and adjudicate the disputes. The chief of the family or the patriarch later became the tribal chieftain with judicial authority. In course of time the heads of the families became the council of the community. "The family was the locus of the altar as well as of the workshop of the school as well as of the tribunal." History furnishes a clear evidence to the fact that in the first stage the tribal people were organised into group of clans and during the later stage different families got united and formed a village and laid the foundation of civil organisation.

The kind of justice which prevailed in early times was based on tribal conception of justice. In the older days all the disputes in the Khasi-Jaintia Hills and the Garo Hills were settled in the open Assembly of all the members of the clans. The people enjoyed a large measure of liberty. They were self-governing under the control of the panchayat. It has been conclusively established through the modern researches that in both pre and post Vedic Age or before and after the Aryan conquest of India 'Grama' or village was the smallest and 'Jana' or tribe was the highest social and political organisation. This seems to be a prominent feature of both the Aryan and non-Aryan polity of India. In ancient times administration of justice was not an integral part of the Govt. All the disputes were adjudicated or settled by compromise or by family or by individual vengeance. In primitive society justice was personal and private affair to a considerable context. It did not matter much whether the punishment was inflicted in proportion to the offence committed or not. The ends of justice were supposed to have been met simply by inflicting the punishment upon members of the offending clan or tribe. The judiciary went one distinct step forward when the idea of retribution came to prevail. The aggrieved individual or tribe used to take action whatever it was possible to take. But in many cases presumably there was no way of enforcing or imposing a decision. In primitive society sometimes the justice was not without force and the form of punishment was retributive and at later stage it became deterrent, preventive, reformative and so on. A little later the idea of compensation for physical injury also developed. The earlier system, no doubt, underwent metamorphosis. The judicial authority exercised by the family or the clan in the olden days came to be exercised by State but not exclusively in the tribal society. One of the unique features of tribal administration of justice is that the importance of clans in judicial matters has been throughout maintained, whereas on the other hand in the Aryan judicial system the clan particularly in post Mauryan Age lost its sanctity, identity and value. Thus it is evident that judiciary as an independent or full fledged body developed comparatively at much later stage with the consolidation of the machineries of the State.

However, the popular assemblies or the Panchayat which functioned as the court of judicature in open space sometimes consisting of stone circles in pre-historic and proto-historic times in the Khasi-Jaintia Hills and the Garo Hills can fairly be compared with the Vedic Sabha—a court of justice in which the heads of the families or the elders used to administer justice—and Samiti—the larger general Assembly—the Parisat of the Brahmanic or the Upanishadic period, the Ganas confederation of republics of the Epic Age, the *Saṁghas* and the *Ganas* as described by Pāṇini (fifth century B.C.) and supported by Patañjali, the Gana Rājya of Buddhist India, the classes of Saṁghas occurring in Kautilya's *Arthaśāstra* (325-300 B.C.), the Federal Assemblies of the Classical Age, the council of Elders known as *"Ye Povia"* represented by all the heads of clans and the folk Assembly known as *"Ayopa"* of the Homeric Age and the general body of citizens and the Senate of Five Hundred—the assets of Athenian Democracy of Pericles Age (458 B.C.—451 B.C.)—and the council of elders of the primitive races of Australia, Formosa, South America and Malaya Archipelago.[9]

As late as 1927, Subhas Chandra Bose[10] had observed that the tribal democratic republican institution known as *"Ganas"* in the time of *Mahābhārata* and based on homogeneous tribe or caste was "flourishing among the Khasi tribe in Assam in North-East India."

In the Khasi-Jaintia Hills, before the evolution of Syiemship all the cases of disputes were settled in Durbar or council by the Basan and the Lyngdoh with the help of all the male population who participated in the deliberations and decisions. Both the Basan and Lyngdoh were assisted by village headmen popularly known as Rangbah Shnong, Metabors, Majis, etc. in day-to-day administration.[11]

The Khasi-Jaintia Hills were later divided into a number of petty principalities which unitedly contributed to the formation of the confederated States—a congregation of little oligarchical republics subject to no common superior.[12] The Basans, Lyngdohs and other chieftains formed Syiemships. The powers and functions of the syiems and the duties of their councillors were clearly defined. The Durbar or the council which functioned as a court of justice was properly constituted. With the dawn of early Medieval Age the institution of chieftainship began to take shape which gradually took its deep root by the time of Mughal Emperor Jehangir (1605-1627 A.D.).' Thus the system which developed at later stage continued unabated till the end of the East India Company's rule in 1858. The judicial system underwent little change in post mutiny period.

About the early judicial system of the Garos, Playfair[13] has correctly stated that "in former times the villages met in conference to decide any matter in dispute between its members. Future method wats adopted as continuation of the ancient usages of the people. While in these meetings evidence could not be adduced, recourse was and is yet had to trial by ordeal."

According to Hamilton[14], the Garo chief known as Rajas around the Garo Hills in ancient Kamarupa, under the Ahom and the Moghul rule were the petty chief of the country. R.M. Nath[15] clearly states that each village had a chief and several villages acknowledged allegiance to a Raja or Bunniah or Nokma. There were four such Rajas in the whole Hills. Even in the 14th century Laskar was appointed. It appears that these four chiefs were playing important role in deciding all the disputes with the help of Panchayat in the Mughal period. During Modern period the judicial systems of the Garos unlike that of the Khasi Pnars were greatly modified.

All the tribal chiefs had the propensity of justice. No doubt the early legal system, marked by sense and spirit of nationalism, retained its value. Local customs received recognition in the adjudication of all the disputes.

IV. Organisation of the Judiciary

The democratic tradition and spirit find the best expression though and reflection in indigenous tribal administrative organisations. The institution of chieftainship and other local heads of the administration bearing different designations and maintaining corporate character as a body politic, their existence and dependence on number of advisers and other officials, the supreme voice of the male population in the deliberations of the open Durbar or councils or Assemblies, machinery for co-ordination and consultation, etc. certainly help us in forming a clear idea about the well-organised and an elaborate judicial system. In the Khasi Hills the chiefs styled as Syiems, Wahdadars, Lyngdohs and Sirdars used to hear and decide all the cases in Durbar with the help of councillors whose numbers vary in proportion to the size of population and importance of the State. Besides state Durbar the village Durbar consisting of Basan or Rangbah, Shnong or Sirdar as the head assisted by the councillors (Matabar) and the elderly men of the village used to decide all civil and criminal cases. The disputes relating to religion or inter-relationship were dealt with in clan councils. In the Jaintia Hills the Syiems with the help of the local representatives known as twelve Dolois used to adjudicate all the cases. The Doloi had an executive council consisting of local officials known as Lyngdohs, Basans, Pators, Sangots and Majis, who assisted the former as Sub-Magistrates also in the adjudication of all the cases.[16]

In the Garo Hills, the each clan was headed by the traditional chief Nokma. One of the noticeable feature of the Garo society is that in case of inter-clan disputes the protection of interest of the clan was the matter of common concern for all the members of the clans or Mahari council. The settlement of the disputes was primarily considered to be a matter of concern between the lineages of disputants.

The tribal village councils or Durbars functioned as an open court of justice where disputes were heard and decided according to the established coustoms and usages which form the part of their customary laws. In these open courts all the male members used to take part freely in the trial of a case. The judgement passed on an offender was regarded as the judgement of whole village and not merely of the chief and his advisers. This system of judicial administration was suited to the genius of the people as a whole. More noteworthy features can be observed in respect of village administration. The self-governing villages administered by local headmen constituted the self-sufficient molecules and formed the body politic of both the Aryan and Non-Aryan political system. Under this system villages continued to maintain their existence as self-sufficient little republics in spite of the powerful tide of imperialism as Russian Mir survived in spite of the growth of the most powerful autocracy in Russian society. Village people always followed the consent and respected the will of the man who was working for common good.

V. The Function of Judiciary upto 1857

In a developed administrative system the judiciary has got a recognised place. It occupies a crucial position among all the organs of the Government. The function of the judiciary depends on the nature of the Govt. The excellence and efficiency of the Government can fairly be tested by the excellence of the judiciary. It administers justice, interprets laws, punishes crimes, protects life and liberty and works as a vanguard of the constitution. Sir Henry Maine[17] was absolutely correct in stating that it will be wrong to say that "there was no law of crime or torts in ancient India". The functioning of the judiciary exactly conforms to the ideals set forth by both Manu and Kautilya. Both have greatly emphasised the fact that the King or the Judge should examine and cross-examine all the witnesses, enquire into the character and nature of the offences, apply the law in both the civil and criminal cases, protect the life and property of the innocent and dispense the justice according to the established customs. According to Kautilya, the disputes should be settled in four ways. Dharma or truthful acknowledgement of the disputed claims by the other party, Vyavahara or through the agency of witness to the transaction, Caritra or by following the time honoured customs and Rajasasana or by royal adjudication.[18] Manu[19] has also expressed more or less the similar views. On the basis of some authentic evidence[20] we come to know that in the Khasi Hills the judicial Durbar which acted like a Jury or as a Supreme Court of Justice was concerned and presided over by a Siem in the capacity of Judge to hear the appeal, try the cases and pronounce the judgement. The Siem and his ministers or councillors used to sit together in State Durbar to decide all the civil and criminal cases after instituting the proper enquiry and conducting the careful investigation into the matter; where the local headmen failed to decide any case then they had to refer the same to the Siem's Durbar which also functioned as Appellate court. First of all complaint was lodged before the Siem or Chief against a certain party or parties. All the facts were discussed in detail and if no compromise or reconciliation was effected, a courier or crier (U Nong Pyrta Shong in the Jaintia Hills e Sangot) was sent out to proclaim at the top of his voice regarding the sitting of the Durbar. All the grown up males of the village had to assemble at the Durbar. The proceedings were started by the headmen by a long speech. The complainants and the defendants each of them used to throw down on the ground a turban or bag containing betel and pan etc. in front of the Durbar which were regarded as the pledges of both the respective parties. The pleaders known as "Riewsaid" on both the sides addressed the durbar, the Siem acted like judge and the Durbar as a Jury. Witnesses and all evidence were thoroughly examined. The finding of the Durbar was recorded after the Siem summed up and sentence was pronounced. Fining was the general punishment. The condemned one in a criminal case lost his freedom and property and served the Siems as slaves or menial servants.

Very few of the Siems possessed jails for the receptions of the criminals. The punishment of adultery was the imprisonment for life or a fine of Rs. 1,100. The punishment for rape and arsons was imprisonment for life or heavy fine. The punishment for robbery and theft was the "Stocks", the imposition of fetters or a culprit was compelled to sit on a bamboo platform under which chillies were burnt. It is worthy of remarks that crimes detected were usually punished with fine. Sometimes murder, rape and adultery were punished with death. Sometimes the criminal was handed over to the friends of slain for them to wreak their vengeance. The civil cases or disputes concerning law or money were also settled in a remarkable manner.

The village Durbar presided over by the local headmen used to pronounce the judgment over the accused or offenders or criminals and inflict penalties on wrong doers. The village Durbar decided both the civil and criminal cases. Here it must be pointed out that the will of the people was the supreme.

In the Jaintia Hills, first of all cases were tried by a group of Basans who acted like Deputy or Sub-Dolois, but in case of failure the matter was reported to the Doloi who convened the Durbar consisting of entire male population to adjudicate the case. The Doloi had the power of deciding both the civil and criminal cases but certain cases were referred to the Siem and his council. At the village level all the cases were decided by the headman in village Durbar which functioned as Panchayati court.[21]

In the Garo Hills, the chief popularly known as the Nokma and the headmen of families assembled in a council called "Jingma changga" and endeavoured to reconcile the clans who had disputes. The punishment was not inflicted unless a man was detected in uttering a falsehood before them. In such case he was put to instant death. Dishonesty or stealing was rarely practised and the only source of dispute was the murder which was in those days an ordinary crime. "But the relations of the person killed, are, by custom, held bound to demand blood for blood and ought to put to death either the murderer or one of his kindred or at least one of his slaves. The other family then is bound to pursue a similar mode of retaliation. Although every head of a family has an equal right to sit in their assemblies, the influence of the chiefs or of one or two wisemen usually decides everything". Adultery, robbery and murder are said to be punished with death. Fines expiated all minor offences. In the Garo polity almost every form of wrong could have been atoned for by the payment of pecuniary compensation. Many troublesome cases arose out of old blood feuds and existing customs which could be only decided by a panchayat of hill-men. The most remarkable of these customs was that of "dai" or compensation; under this custom the village headmen demanded large sums for wearing the tar-an-iron ring on the arm which was regarded as the badge of respectibility. This system was prevalent in the olden days. Later the villagers refused to pay the dues.[22]

T. Mohammad Cazim[23] in his description of Assam also deals with the crimes and mode of punishments. He has also referred to the attempts made by various tribal chieftains for reconciling the disputing parties and imposition of customary fines.

VI. Importance of the oaths and ordeals in the decision of the disputes

In former times, the oaths and ordeals were the two popular methods employed in the adjudication of cases with great honesty and fairness. Practically when all efforts proved to be of no use in the trial of the case then these two methods were applied. The .most ancient form of oath and ordeal in the Khasi-Jaintia Hills was known as "U Klong." The individual wishing to take the oath before the Durbar or open court produced a jar of rice with an arrow stuck in it. He produced another bowl of fermented rice with an arrow or stake thrust in. Both were handed over to .the judge who addressed a goddess in the following terms "come down a Goddess among us we may see who is telling the truth. If the man's accusation is false he shall lose his life, family, clan etc. If he takes a false oath tear out his tongue, destroy his lips...." The pointed stake is then addressed, "Thou oh arrow if the man who is about to take the oath is a perjured or guilty, pierce him, tear his flesh." Then the man places the gourd representing "U klong" on his head and repeats the same invocations. Anyone prepared to undergo this oath and ordeal used to win the case, Ordeal by water was very fashionable among the Khasis. "The two disputants in a case would fix the spear under water in some deep pool. They would then dive and catch hold of the spear. The man who remained longest under water without returning to the surface was adjudged by the Siem and durbar to have won the case". This water ordeal was the common mode of the decision. It was lawful to use the services of[8] practised attorneys" in this mode of trial. The other simple form of ordeal was that two jars were filled with water into which two coins, one silver and one gold wrapped into little piece of cloth were dropped. Both tried to get this object out and the first man to succeed won the case. If they got it out together the durbar used to arrange a friendly settlement and if the ownership of the land was the bone of contention, these objects were fairly divided.[24] The Greek writer Ktesias the Knidian (398 B.C.), while showing the importance of this ordeal in his treatise,[25] has said that the king used this as a means to bring the accused to a confession.

The earliest trustworthy account based on eye-witness left behind by John Eliot[26] in 1788-89 clearly indicates that in the Garo country the punishment consisted mostly of fines. The Booneahs decided all the complaints except adultery, murder and robbery which were tried by general assembly of the neighbouring chiefs and were punished with instant death. Their mode of swearing at "Ghose gong" was very solemn. The oath was taken upon stone which they first saluted and then they folded the hands and uplifted fixed the eyes steadfastly to the hills and called on "Mahadeva" in the most solemn manners telling him to witness what they speak true or false. They again touched the stone with all the appearance of utmost fear and bowed their heads to it calling again upon Mahadeva. In some of the hills they put a tinger's bone between their teeth before they relate the subject to be disposed : others take the earth in their hand and on some occasions swear with their weapons in their hands.

According to Playfair,[27] when the evidence could not produce any result the last recourse was ordeal. Among the Garos two kinds of ordeals were prevalent, one was ordeal of hot iron and other was the ordeal of boiling water. In the first ordeal the Kamal or priest takes the red-hot iron in his hand and administers an oath to the person to be examined and informs him that no harm will come to him if he has sworn truly, but warns him of the dire consequence of telling a lie. The man undergoing this ordeal closed his hand and the hot iron was then drawn through it. In the second ordeal, an egg was placed in a deep pot of boiling water and the person whose veracity was to be tested was asked to plunge in his hand and pick it out. It is believed that the person revealing the truth did not suffer any harm even after submitting himself to either of the ordeal but if he was proved to be a liar, his hand was badly burnt or scalded. G. Bertrand[28] has pointed out that duels with knives are the survival of the trial by ordeal among the Garos. But he has not given any clear description of it.

The striking similarity can be noticed between these oaths and ordeals and that suggested by Manu and Kautilya. Manu[29] has also referred to the ordeal by fire or hot iron and ordeal by water. Kautilya[30] also says that the bearer of the evidence had to take oath in ancient India. The judicial torture was applied in both the cases to make the suspect confess his guilt.

VII. Pattern of Judicial Administration in Post-Mutiny Period

The indigenous pattern of judicial administration underwent some change in the post Mutiny period. From one of the unpublished sources[31] it is quite evident that till the end of the East India Company rule the British did not interfere with the indigenous judicial system. From indigenous source[32], imperial records[33] and other valuable sources[34] it is clear that immediately after the introduction of British rule there was no change in the traditional system. The Siems or Rajas were allowed to exercise their judicial authority according to the established customs. But after 1858 in judicial matters a good deal of jurisdiction was transferred to the British courts. Only petty criminal and civil cases in which the natives of the Districts were concerned were decided by the village authorities in the Native tribunals of the British Communes according to the indigenous system of village panchayats. But all criminal cases of grievous or heinous character were tried exclusively by the British courts. All serious offences and civil suits in which foreigners were concerned were tried by the D.C. and his assistants. The native tribunals had jurisdiction over civil disputes arising between common subjects or a Federacy or State but all civil disputes between subjects of different states were tried by the British courts. The Khasi-Jaintia Hills was administered by political officer under special rules framed under Act XXII of 1869. The jurisdiction of the High Court at Calcutta was not extended to the hills except over European British subjects. Section VI of 1835 vested the High Court with Appellate authority. In K & J Hills D.C. exercised his power under High Court Act XV of 1862. All the disputes between Chiefs of the states were tried by the D.C. in K & J Hills. The siems were not allowed to adjudicate those criminal offences which were punishable under the Indian penal code with death, transportation or imprisonment for five years and upwards, particularly when subjects within the limit of his state alone were concerned.

Thus we find that in criminal cases tried by the British courts the penal laws for British India were invariably applied but they were not in force in Native federacies or State. All civil and criminal cases arising within the limits of a state of Siem in which the subjects of other Khasi states or Europeans or natives of the plains may be concerned were adjudicated by the D.C. or any other officer appointed by him for the purpose concerned.

In the Jaintia Hills, the Dolois (12 in number) and the sirdars were placed under the authority of British Officer. They were responsible to the regular British police who started interfering in all the matters. The decisions of the Dolois in Civil and criminal cases became the subject of approval of the British Officer.[35]

Thus when all the leading Khasi-pnars felt that the indigenous judicial system based on democratic tradition is becoming very much corrupted under the rule of the British Executive Officer, they decided to place the demand before British Govt. for reform of the system of administration of justice by the British courts of the Districts of K & J. Hills. They wanted these courts to be placed under the control of Calcutta High Court who exercised jurisdiction over the courts into the whole of the plains of Assam. But this proposal was turned down by the Assam Govt. They submitted innumerable memorandums to the President and members of the Indian Statutory Commission or Simon Commission for the reform in the judicial system and the restoration of their lost traditional political rights.[36] Ultimately the jurisdiction of the Calcutta High Court was extended to the British Courts in K & J Hills in 1930. This system continued upto 1947 with little modifications here and there.

In the Garo Hills also minor changes took place in the judicial administration in post mutiny period. After the annexation of the Garo Hills by the British Government a body of men called Lashkars was formed who acted as a kind of rural police and also as honorary magistrates. They were authorised to settle some minor matters and unimportant disputes. "Their powers did not exceed those of inflicting fines and awarding compensation to injured parties." Petty criminal cases were tried by the Lashkars who could impose fine up to amount of Rs. 50. In civil cases they could have imposed any amount as a fine provided that the parties were the resident in their jurisdiction. All serious offences were tried by the D.C.[37]

VIII. Some Unique Characteristics

The most distinctive and remarkable feature of the tribal judicial administration is the smooth functioning of the time-honoured self governing institutions which indicates the highest attainment and skill of the tribal people concerned in the art of self-Government in respect of the equality before law, liberty of thoughts, freedom of opinion and expression, judicial procedure, etc. Their village Durbars as an open court of justice can unquestionably be considered far more superior not only to the Vedic bicameral bodies—Sabha and Samiti—which had the germs of the aristocratic democracy but also to the Hellenic institutions— "Yepovia" or "Senatus"'—a council in conflict with King, and Folk Assembly (Ayopa) unrepresentative during Homeric Age, "Genusia" of sparta or its other oligarchical (partly royal and partly democratic) institutions—Senate and Assembly—Athenian democratic institutions of Pericles Age not fully representatives, Roman Senate, represented by only patrician, political institutions of Venice—an oligarchy of hereditary nobles—and Poland which was mixture of aristrocracy and monarchy, public councils of Burma known as "Hiuttaw" and "Byedaik", a privy council, in both of which members were the creatures of Kings, minor institutions in the Chumbi valley of Tibet—a mixture of theocracy and democracy—Germanic Folk assembly, Folk assembly of western Europe unknown to debate, Tutonic councils, Anglo-Saxon institutions and various other Senates assemblies

Tribunals and Federal courts of ancient Medieval and modern times. The tribal people concerned are in possession of institutions which appear to be the finest commonwealth ever heard of in any quarter of the globe.[38] My remarks may appear to be an exaggeration but this is not so. Some more valuable and notable remarks given below will leave no room for doubt about its unique novelty.

The late viceroy and Governor General of India, Earl of Wellingdon in his address to the Khasi people at Shillong in 1933 said,... "It is a proof of the stamina and virility and competence of your people that when greater empires in the East and the West have throughout the ages come and gone you still maintain in your pleasant hills the freedom of your small Republics based on the ancient ways and tenets of your race."[39] His Excellency Sir L.L. Hammond in his speech at Jowai on the 9th Nov. 1928 also praised the "time-honoured distinguished social and political democratic institutions, customs, customary Laws and popular tribunals" of the Khasi-pnars.[40] Some leading Khasis in 1928 also said about themselves : "their institutions are standing out as a models for the rest of India in a great many respect. They would readily come first to any goal of self govt. in the common race with others of the Empire."[41] Captain White, an assistant to Mr. David Scott, being highly impressed by the judicial functions of the petty states or little oligarchical republics of the Khasis in matters of settling the disputes concerning succession or other problems, the trend of discussion therein and the participation of all the members and councillors, observed that such institutions have not been excelled or surpassed by any European society.[42]

Notes and References

1. Letters received from Govt. 1864, Vol. 47.
2. *Manusmrti* (Original Text with Parallel Trans. Trans. by Pt. H. Sastri and edited by Pt. Gopal Sastri Nene, Varanasi, Dharma Sastra section No. 3, 1970) Ch. VIII, Vs. 4-7, pp. 358-59.

3. *U Khasi Mynta* Risaw (Octo.) 1902, cf. Kynpham Singh, *Ka Jingsdang Ki Skul Ha Ri Ktiasi*, Pt. III, p. 20.
4. *Ka Syngkhong Jungtip (The Quarterly Journal of the Khasi Cultural Society)* (ed. Theodore Cajee) April-1938, Vol. 2, N, 5, p. 9.
5. *Secret Lands where Women Reign* (London, 1958), pp. 59-60, 88-89.
6. *Across the Golden Heights of Assam & NEFA* (Based on his Travels. Shillong, 1960-61), pp. 25-26.
7. The *Arthaśāstra* of Kautilya and the *Cāṇakya Sūtra* (edited & trans. by Sri Vachaspati Gairola, Varanasi, 1962), BK. III. Ch. I. vs. 55-57 (original), vs. 1, 2-6 (Trantlated) pp. 318-19; *Manusmrti*, Ch. VIII, vs 8 p. 360; or R.C. Majumdar, *Corporate Life in Ancient India* (Calcutta 1922) p. 6; R.K. Mookerji, *Local Govt. in Ancient India* (Varauasi' 1948) p. 16; Beni Prasad, *The State in Ancient India* (Allahabad, 1928), pp. 165-66; N.C. Sen Gupta, *Sources of Law and Society in Ancient India* (Calcutta, 1914) p. 11; J. Jolly, *Hindu Law and Customs* (Calcutta, 1928) p. 1; S. Vardachanar. *The Hindu Judicial System,* (Lucknow, 1946) p. 37.
8. *A Treatise on Hindu Law and Usage* (Madras, 1812), pp. 50.90.
9. *Atharva Veda* (original text with parallel trans. by Shree Ram Sharma Acarya, Bareilly, 1975), Vol. 1. Ch. 7, p. 357; Wood House : *Tutorial History of Greece* (London, 1838), pp. 37-39; K.P. Jayaswal : *Hindu Polity* (Bangalore 1967), pp. 22-24; N.C. Bandyo Padhyaya; *Kautilya* (Calcutta, 1927), p. 259; B.C. Law: *Ancient Indian Tribes* (Lahore, 1926) pp. 323f; D.R. Bhandarkar : *Some Aspects of Ancient Hindu Polity* (Benaras, 1929) pp. 142-46; V.S. Agarwal; *India as known to Pānini* (Lucknow, 1953) p. 399; Wovels; *Native Tribes of South Australia*, 1879, pp.34ff.
10. *Netaji's Life and Writings* (*The Indian Struggle*) 1920-1934 (Calcutta 1948) pt. 11, p. 17.
11. H. Bareh, *Khasi Democracy*, (Shillong, 1964), pp. 37-39.
12. Robinson: *Descriptive Account of Assam* (D.A.A.) (Delhi. 1977). Sec. XI, p. 407.

13. *The Garos* (London, 1909), p. 74.
14. *An Account of Assam* (1807-1814), (Gauhati. 1940), pp. 30-35.
15. *The Background of Assamese Culture* (Shillong, 1948), p. 111.
16. *Proceedings of the Govt. of Assam* Pol. Dept. June 1924. *The proceedings of the Foreign Dept.* 1874; *Proceedings of Chief Commissioner of Assam*, 1876; File 10 of 1874, No. 13. *Political Proceedings of March* 1867. No. 14; H. Bareh *op. cit.*, pp. 54-55.
17. *Ancient Law* (London, 1931) Ch. 10, p. 307.
18. N.C. Bandyo Padhaya, *op. cit.*, pp. 218-225. Sr. Gairola, *op. cit.*, pp. 318-19 ; *Kautilya Arthasastra* (Trans. by Dr. Shamasastry, Mysore, 1909, Bangalore, 1915) No. 37, p. 150.
19. *Manusmrti*, Ch. VIII, pp. 358-61.
20. P.R.T. Gurdon : *The Khasi* (1st Pub. 1907, Delhi, 1975) pp. 91-93; Dalton, *Descriptive Ethnology of Bengal* (D.E.B.) (Calcutta, 1872), p. 57; H. Bareh, *op. cit.* pp. 69-73; Lt. H. Yule; "Notes on the Kasia Hills, and People", J.A.S.B. 1844, Vol. XIII, pp. 627f; G. Bertrand, *op.cit.*, p. 144; See. also H. Lyngdoh, *Ki Syiem Khasi Bad Synteng* (Shillong 1964) pp. IV-V1I1 : G. Costa : *Ka Riti Jong Ka Riti Laiphew Syiem* (Shillong, 8.12.1937) p. 3f. U. Rabon Singh; *Ka Kitab Niam, Khein Ki Khasi* (Shillong, 1972) Ch. XXVI (*Ka Ainka Rikhasi Hyndai*) pp. 51-52; R.M. Roy, *U Khasi Hyndai*, pp. III-VII.
21. *Calcutta Review,* 1863, Vol. XXXVIII, pp. 280-81; H. Barch: *op. cit.* pp. 71-72; E. Gait, B.C. Allen & C *Gazetteer of Bengal and North East India* (Abbrev. as G.B.N.E.I.) (Delhi, 1979) p. 489.
22. Hamilton, *op. cit.*, p. 91; Playfair : *op. cit.*, p. 76; G. Bertrand, *op. cit.*, pp. 64, 111. G.B.N.E. I., pp. 509-10, A. Mackenzie, *History of Relations of the Govt. with the Hill Tribes of the N.E. Frontier* (H.N.E.F. Delhi, 1979, pp. 267f. D.A.A. Sec. XII, p. 418.
23. *A Lamgirnamah* (Trans. from Persian by Henry Vansittart) *As. Researches,* 1799, Vol. 2, p. 187.

24. J.A.S.B. 1844, Vol. XIII, p. 627; G. Bertrand, *op. cit.*, pp. 157-60. Gurdon, *op. cit.*, pp. 93-96.
25. J.W. McCrindle, *Ancient India as Described by Ktesias the Knidian* (London 1882), p. 80.
26. *Asiatic Researches,* 1794, (Repted, Delhi, 1979) Vol. III, pp. 30-32.
27. *op. cit.,* pp. 74-75.
28. *op. cit.,* p. 111.
29. *Manusmrti,* Ch. VIII, vs. 115, p. 386.
30. Sri V. Gairola, *op. cit.,* BK. HI, Ch. I, vs. 3-4, p. 319. Shamasastry, *op. cit.,* pp. 218-20.
31. A letter from more than 18 chiefs and their Myntries dated Mawkhar, Shillong the 15th October 1917 to His Excellency the Viceroy and Governor-General of India in Council—Simla.
32. *U Nongpynim* (The monthly journal in Khasi edited by Babu Sib Charan Roy) 1928, Maiwieng N. 9 and Jan. 1929, pp. 15-18.
33. Letter issued to Govt., 1967. vol. 34, Nos. 165, 171, 172, 224, 244; Vol. 35, No. 305; letters issued to Govt. 1834-35, Vol. 1.
34. Treaty executed on 10th of March 1824 between David Scott and Raja Ram Singh of J. Hills. Articles-2, No. IV; Treaty of 30th Nov. 1826 between David Scott and Teerut Singh, Art. 6, No. VIII and Sanad of 1877, N. LIX cf. Aitchison, *A collection of Treaties...* (Calcutta 1931) Vol. XII, pp. 118, 122-23, 180-81, See also K. Cantlie *Ka Ain U Khasi* (Shillong 1969) pp. 67, 70, 73-76; Hunter : *A Statistical Account of Assam* (London 1879) vol. 11, pp. 244f; G.B.N.E.I., P. 492; G.I. (Oxford 908) Vol. XV P. 264.
35. H.N.E.F., p. 243.
36. A letter from Nollen Roy, dated, Shillong, the 6th Jan. 1929 to the President of the Indian Statutory Commission; A reply from the Assistant Secy. Indian Statutory Commission (I.S.C.) to this letter, Calcutta, 11th Jan. 1929 (N.E. Assam, N. 939). A letter from Nawoon Lyngdoh and others, dated Shillong 15th Jan. 1929 to the President,

I.S.C. Resolutions of a public meeting of the Khasi Community assembled at the Seng Khasi Hall, Mawkhar, dated 12th Jan. 1929 and 22nd Dec. 1928 signed by Nollen Roy and others which were forwarded to the President, I.S.C. A Memorandum signed by the Sirdars of Nongpol and many others of British; cmmunes in Khasi Hills, dtd. Shillong 31st Dec. 1928 to the Chief Sejy. to His Excellency the Governor of Assam; Letter by U Seint Singh and others dated 2nd Jan. 1929 to the Chief Secy, to His Excelln cy the Governor of Assam. A Memorandum signed by Sardar and the Durbar of Nongpoh elaka and many others dt. 5th Jan. 1929 to the President and the members of the I.S.C.; A letter of K Suki Mohan Roy and 4 others dt. Shillong the 25th Dec. 1928 to the Secretary. Royal Statutory Commission Comp. India. Letter from U Sib Charan Roy and others dt. Shillong 15th Dec. 1928 to the Chief Secretary to the Govt. of Assam (Pol. Branch); Letter No POL 3350-8665, Appl, & Pol. Dept., Pol. Branch from H. Weightman, Secy, to the Govt. of Assam to U Sib Charan Roy, dt. Shillong 28th Dec. 1928; Letter from Asst. Secy, Indian S.C. Camp, Dt. 7th Jan. 1929 to U Nollen Roy about the visit of Sir John Simon and the. Members of the I.S.C, to Shillong.

37. *Assam Dist. Gazetteer* (1906) Vol. X, p. 59; G.B.N.E.I, pp. 509-10; G. Bertrand, *op. cit.,* p. 111. Playfair, *op. cit.,* p. 74; *Assam Report on the Garo Hills*, 1881-82; see also Agreement executed by the Garo Sardars in 1817 Ref to Aitchison, *op. cit.,* Vol. XII, N. 11, pp. 115-16.

38. G.P. Singh, *"A Study of the Tribal Republics in North-East India", North Eastern affairs (A Quarterly Study of Trends and Events)* 1976, Vol. 5, Nos. 1 & 2. pp. 79-101.

39. *U Nongpynim* No. 50, 1933, p. 6.

40. *U Nongpynim* Kyllalsngkot, 1937, No. 64, pp. 6-9.

41. *U Nongpynim,* Naiwieng, 1928, No. 9, pp. 15-16.

42. *Secret Proceedings*, 1829, May 8, No. 11.

14

The Tribal Sculpture and Iconography in North-East India

Prefatory Remarks

Sculpture, usually cultivated in India as an accessory to architecture, is an allied art conscipuous both for its conventional iconography and astonishing life quality. It is not until the second century B.C. when we are provided with clear conception of the history and development of sculpture as a tradition. Actually, after 300 A.D. Indian sculptured figures deserve to be reckoned as an art. The Tribal sculptural style and features in the hill regions of North East India is akin to the East Indian tradition. The primitive style of utilitarian-cum-religio-magical value in the form of wood works and stone works, the early medieval sculptural style in the form of human figures and other non-iconic figures and the Eastern School of art of Bihar, Bengal and Orissa in the form of wood carving, image work of varying degree, etc. can be noticed in the tribal art. The pivot of tribal sculptural art is their traditional beliefs and religious practices. For our convenient study we can divide tribal sculpture in various parts, *viz.,* sculpture of human forms including Gods and Goddesses and sculpture of animal forms, sculpture of geometric, floral and symbolic designs and other sculptures found chiselled on stone slabs, rocks and terracotta plaques. The figures were executed in conformity with the canons laid down in the *silpaśāstras.* Icons mostly chiselled on rocks and stones belong to four major cults, i.e., Vaishnava, Saiva, Sakta and Surya. Besides, some other different deities and numerous images of Hindu and Buddhist Pantheon have also been discovered in the North East Hill region having a marked affinity with the regional and other prominent school of art, notably the Pala-Sena school of Bengal (Post Gupta period—9th Century to 11th Century). The late medieval trends, the late Pala style and indigenous style of 16th century can also be observed in the tribal art of this region.

Here it is indispensable to point out that the early literatures, epigraphy, palaeography, meagre chronological datas, the perishable character of the then used materials, the colossal havoc caused to the monuments of the past by the periodic natural calamities help us very little in tracing the general progress of aboriginal art in North-East India. However, we can safely depend on the various objects of artistic importance exhumed as a result of series of archaeological exploration and excavations, discovery of some other ruins, recorded statements in both published and unpublished sources, etc. Regional variations in facial expression, appearance and treatment are noticeable to a greater exten. ' The extensive remains scattered all over the regions bespeak eloquently of the prolific sculptural and iconographic activities of the hill tribes which point to their attainment of the high degree of perfection and considerable progress in this branch of art in respect of artistic charm, beauty, designs, grace and excellence as well as testify to the synthesis of both Aryan and non-Aryan elements in their art and their aesthetic philosophy, glorious past and cultural heritage. Every possible attempts have been made to determine the antiquity from stylistic and epigraphical point of view.

Sculpture

In North-East Frontier region, in Bhismaknagar area the discovery of carved block of sand stone and the sculptured face of the stone placed upon the brick terrace close to the Eastern wall containing the figure of Krishna was really the fine specimen of the early sculptural art.[1] In 1905, Dr. T Bloch[2] trekking along the outer wall of it made an archaeological exploration of the area and collected some tiles bearing carving of animals, birds, human figures, floral and geometric designs. Major S. F. Hannay[3] refers to the elaborately carved stone gateway and the door of the copper temple (Tamreswari, lying 25 miles in dense forest to the North-East of Sadiya) of which the lintel carved on the edge in the chain of lotus flowers as well as some ornamented pillars containing the figure of an elephant carved out of a block of prophyritic granite of a hardness in the old tradition. He also refers to the brick tiles having stamped upon them in high relief figures of some of the "Hindoo Avatara". The principal figures were the caparisoned horss, some with warriors in high conical cap, Hanooman, the fabulous horse, the peacock fighting and one bird preying on the other, Nagasur in different forms etc. According to Dr. T. Bloch[4] the walls and buildings of this temple contained various sculptured designs including human figures, animals, birds, flowers and geometrical pattern evidently without any symbolical meaning attached to them. The style was of semi-harbarian kind as in the carving at Dimapur and other places in Assam. Various carved figures have close affinity with Mediaeval Indian Art. The carvings on tiles, 16 of them listed by Bloch represent figures of lion, peacock, bearded man in dancing posture, pair of dancers with musical instruments and various other designs in the shape of lotus flowers etc. The ornamental patterns of the tiles bear close resemblance to that of 'V columns pillars of Dimapur. F. J. Needham[5] also mentions that about two stones of the size 8×2×1′ were found standing at the entrance of the temple having human figures cut in them. These relics of the Sadiya region, which show the mixture of the Aryan and non-Aryan elements, can be placed llth and 15th centuries. Another piece of attractive stone carvings have been traced out in Malinithan Temple on the basis of recent archaeological exploration conducted in early seventies. The life-size lion figure in standing position on two elephants in crouching pose at each of the four corners of the Temple remind us of the similar motif found in old temple in Orissa. Several other stone carvings representing the pair of lion, female figures and dancing girls have also been discovered. In this region various tribes used to carve out beautiful images and pictures of their belief and imagination on wood, rock and stone wells. The wood carvings of Khamptis, the Wanchos, the Noctes, The Monpas, the Sherdukpens, the Konyaks and the Phom tribes connected with head hunting, decoration of Morung and funerary images erected for warriors, are well known for their exquisite beauty and artistic value. The carved features in low relief are fairly realistic. The main pillar of the roof and great horizontal beam running across the front of the Morung buildings were carved with fantastic variety of designs. The carvings of Mithum heads, hornbill tails, elephants, warriors with guns, tigers, monkeys, dancing couples, frogs eating the moon and human being on the pillars are fine examples of indigenous sculptural art. Some of the tablets of stone shrines of Sherdukpen tribes contain the figure of Buddha carved on them. In Kameng district stone sculpture of 9th-10th Century have also been noticed. The Khamptis wood carving of temple, musicians with instruments — guitar and drums in beating posture and ivory carving have got special place in the hierarchy of North-East Frontier tribal art, Dalton[6] specifically mentions about the Khamtis sculptural art. To quote him "The priest in their hours of relaxation amuse themselves by carving in wood, bone or ivory at which they are very expert.........with a creditable unity and gracefulness of design."

In North Cachar Hills the most astonishing remains of sculptural art inside the old fort of Diampur were the huge stone Monoliths, broken 'V' shaped chessman pillars — all elaborately, elegantly and profusely carved with representation of birds, animals spearhead etc.[7] The ornamentation on the columns was generally very simple. The pillars were decorated with carvings of degenerated workmanship after the Brahma-Tezpur School. The style of carving on the pillars was probably more or less indigenous with some light touches of Indian Art existing till the Ahom invasion of Kachar in the 16th century. Regarding the carvings of pillars and stones we find the similar features in Mathura-Gandhara School of Art (1st to 3rd Century A. D.), Hoysala style of Art (12th to 13th Century) Pallava Art (7th Century) and other arts in Asiatic tradition in general. On the basis of archaeological records[8] we find evidences of other sculptural works near Maibong. Twenty carved stones representing variety of subjects like elephants, horses, flowers and women in bass relief on them were discovered. The latter forms differ from the usual attempts of the Lushais. the Kukis and the Mikirs. Many carved statues of Goddesses, several carved bricks with animal figures and some curious crude stone carving of men have also been found there. Another specimen of Non-Aryan workmanship with Hindu influence are carved emblem of Kasomari Monoliths. Dr. T. Bloch[9] noticed a chessman pillar similar to those of Dimapur with a hemispheral capital containing the carvings of swords and daggers. The base had a horizontal band of ornamentation and the panel below it had some animal figures, elephants or lions carved upon it. Another attractive specimen is a Kachari Conch Shell bearing the carving of ten Avataras or incarnation of Krishna. It contains an inscription which proves that it was carved in Bir Darpa's (Hidimba Prince) reign in 1671 A. D.

In the Khasi-Jaintia Hills also we find beautiful specimens of sculptural art. Major H. H. Godwin Austen's information that.[10] "The only instance of carving I know on Monoliths of Khasi Hills is the simple circle with petaliform pattern" is not an adequate observation. The archaeological sources[11] testifies to the presence of statue of elephant carved out of solid rock. Their other carvings representing the sun and the moon, images of warrior, animals and other animate and inanimate objects some in Pauranic tradition stand as an ample testimony to the artistic perfection of the Khasi-Jaintia tribes in this branch of art. The most valuable information supplied by R. M. Nath[12] shows that stone boundary pillar with the image of Kali engraved on it with an inscription in Bengali script installed at Jamuagaon, now in Nowgong Museum is the manifestation of the victory of Jaintia Kings over the Mikirs as well as of their artistic grace. According to Dalton[13] the most conspicuous example of the triumph of art amongst the Garos are fantastically carved grotesque figures, ornamentations representing wooden images, animals, various kinds of fruits and vegetables on the post and beams of their larger Nokpantes and Houses.

In Naga Hills, Dr. T. Bloch[14] found several points of similarities between 'V' shaped pillars and memorials used by the Naga tribes to commemorate sacrifices. In the Sema Naga village he found large wooden shields cut out in the shape of the letter 'U' standing 7 or 8 feet high and covered with rough carvings, symbolising the sun, and, the moon lightning. The Rengma Nagas also used rows of stones carved of gradually decreasing size. Another carved stone near Lozema by the Naga tribe was also found[15]. A. Dabis[16] (Asst. Commissioner of Kohima) found one curious stone in 1887 A.D. roughly carved with Peacock. According to Report of R. B. McCabe[17] (D. C. Naga Hills), the front view of rich Angami Naga's houses were carved in slight relief representing various conventional designs, execution of life size human figures and etc. Clay dolls well suspended over the door and some wooden dolls with considerable elaboration dressed up in miniature reproduction of Angami costume were also made. The original manufacture of these dolls seems to have been a case of 'art for art's sake'. The village gates of the Angami Nagas were also carved with human figures. The pillars of the Morungs of Naga tribes notably the Angamis, the Aos, the Semas, the Bothas and the Konyaks were elaborately carved with human heads, hornbills, tigers, elephants, some other natural objects and so on. They were also skilful wood carvers. Various carvings recall the carving on the round Kachari Megaliths at Dimapur. The Paramount glory of the sculptural art of the Naga tribes lies in the techniques, symbolism and variation upon adopted themes.

Regarding the art of Naga tribes of Manipur no reliable information is available except for the rude stone-sculpture but distinctly belonging to Kabul Nagas discovered by Hodson[18] in the midst of jungle near the settlement of the tribes in the dim past.

In Hill-Tipperah carved rocks at Un-Kuti,Koilashaher was found[19] "Then excelled in the art of wood carving and stone sculpture."[20] The door ways of old Udaipur building contained the simple carvings.[21]

Here this fact must be exposed that all sculptural pieces of arts in North Cachar Hills, Naga Hills, Sadiya region and all rock sculptures in Khasi Jaintia Hills were brought under Ancient Monuments Preservation Act VII of 1904, passed by Lord Curzon.[22]

Iconography

The art of image making is as old as Hindu religion. Not only the Sutras but Patanjali describes these images of Murtis but the Brahmanas of Vedas also refer to. Though the cults of different deities of the Hindu pantheon in the early centuries of Christian era can be seen from the ruins of temples and other isolated icons in the hill region of North Eastern India, yet we can't deny this fact that the artistic revival of the Gupta period ushered in a new era in this field of art. Leons mostly chiselled on rocks and stones belong to four major cults, i.e., Vaishnava, Saiva, Sakta and Surya. Besides some images of Vedic Gods and Goddesses are also found. Numerous images of Buddhist pantheon have also been discovered in the North East Frontier region. The study of extant images show the influence of anthropomorphism here.

The art of iconography in the hill regions of North-East India developed along the lines framed by Ancient Indian Texts. In North Cachar Hills the Golden image of the Goddess Durga, installed in a temple in the earstwhile newly established capital, named Sonapur, the stone image of Vishnu, the Lord of Lakshmi - the Goddess of wealth, an image of Durga and a stone image of Ganesha — the elepeant tusked God on Dimapur can fairly be ascribed to 15th century. The images of Ranchandi Durga and Vasudeva in the rock-cut temples of Maibong belong to 16th Century[23]. Both architecture and sculpture were of the old Brahma Tezpur School as testified by the specimens lying at Maibong and other places. L. W. Shakespear[24] while corroborating this statement observes that most of the statues and ornamented stones looking like Goddess were excavated at Maibong in North Cachar Hills. G. H. Darnant [25] also refers to the brass image of Ranchandi in Cachar. Frank EDE[26] found Hindu Temples and two older images one representing Ganesha and other Hanuman on a hill bordering Cachar on the east known as Bhoban Parbat, 3000 feet high. The other two much larger crude one represented Parvati. The injury to the images was caused by the Nagas. Along the northern skirts of the Mikar Hills sculptures are ascribed to the Gods.

In the Khasi-Jaintia Hills, the art of image making was not very much popular. We find few specimens of images. The Hindu shrines of Nartiang temple were adorned with the images of Krishna, Durga, Kali, Mahadeo, Jaya, Bijaya and etc. The practice of Hindu religion has profoundly influenced their art. Archaeological record[27] also confirms this traditional evidence, as it also refers to the image of Goddess Kali in shrine in Jaintia Hills, In Garo Hills some terracotta pieces contain' ing the figures of Siva, seated on bull, Ganesa, Manasa, Kartikeya and other human figures have been collected by G. N. Bhuyan[28] near a locality called Bhaitbari. The ruins of the city and temples ascribing to llth to 12th century is attested by local traditions. These "Terracotta fragmentation bear close affinity with the late Pala and Sena artistic idiom in stylistic tradition."

Dr. T. Bloch[29] among his findings in Tamreswari Temple specifically refers to the lintel and jambes of its door bearing the two carved images of Siva and three statues, two of which represented the images of Surya and Kali dancing on Siva, while the other represented that of Saraswati with indistinct object in her right hand, perhaps musical instruments. This archaeological evidence has been further corroborated by R. M. Nath[30], who also mentions about the images of Surya and seven rampart horses below and stylistically datable to perhaps 7th-8th century, carved in Pala Sena idiom, Kali and Ganesa—all ruins of Tamreswari Temple in Sadiya region. Malinithan (situated in the lower region of the Siang Distt. of NEFA) has proved to be a store house of large number of historical ruins. The archaeological excavations and explorations conducted by L. N. Chakravarty (Research Deptt. Arunachal Pradesh) during 1970-71 have revealed over one hundred carved images of Gods and Goddesses of Hindu pantheon demi-Gods, Yaksas in dancing postures, figurines, Gaja, Ratha, animal motifs of bull, lion and elephants, sculptured panels, good number of geometric and floral designs on stone used extensively for decorative purposes, carved panels, lintels, columns, pillars etc. Among the impresstive remains are the life size lion on elephant motif, also found in Dimapur and various parts of Orissa, the images of Kartikeya seated on Peacock, like that of Pala-Sena School of art of 12th Century and Orissa School of art of 11th century (bothin Indian Museum, Calcutta) Indra seated on his carrier elephant (Airavata), Nandi-Bull in sitting posture, sun God—Surya standing on a chariot with Aruna as charioter Ganesa with its carrier Mouse, Goddess Dasabhuja, a statue resembling Saraswati with Bina and number of other erotic relief figures or sculptures signifying "Tantricism of the fertility cult of the primitive tribal society upholding the mother principle as the procreative power of nature." The style is simple, representation fairly lively and the ornamentation resembling the Hoysala style. All these remains do not belong to the same age, for the relics differ from "crudity to excellence in artistic conception and accomplishments." These remains may tentatively be placed in between 6th century A.D. to 14th century A.D. The art of making the image of Buddha was very popular among the Buddhist tribes of NEFA. The wooden image of Lord Buddha carved by Khamti, "the large size images of Buddha cut out of solid pieces of amber and other glass images based on documentary evidence[31], the clay image of Buddha made by Memba Monk, wooden images of Buddha by Monpa artists, and some other bronze statues and another Buddha icon of sand stone discovered from various places, some of them on display at the Central Museum, Shillong are well known for their elegance, grace, artistic beauty and great sculptural merit. These remains ascribed to 16th to 17th century speak eloquently of their attainment of perfection in this field of art. Some figures of Buddha with iconographic marks and attributes like that of Graeco-Roman pantheon are of identical character.

R. Reid[32] has brought this fact to the fore that in temple of Jadonang, a Kabui Naga of Manipur, the clay image of Mithun and various other figures of Naga men and women dressed in festival clothes were carved out.

In Hill-Tipperah the life-size figure of some of the tutelary Gods and Goddesses like Siva, Durga, Vishnu, Lakshmi, Saraswati, Kartik, Ganesha, Brahma and other ascribed to early centuries of Christian era all kept in the temple of old Agartala were the objects of veneration by the Hill-Tribes till recently.[33] According to W. W. Hunter[34] other white stone-images representing the deity Mahadeo or Siva was kept in the temple of Udaipur. AtUnakuti colossal figures representing Siva, Kal Bhairab, Hanuman, Ram Lakshman and Ganapati carved into rocks, date back to the early Buddhist and Hindu periods.

Conclusion

The foregoing brief description of the sculptural and iconographic art, utilitarian and functional in nature, of the hill tribes of North-East India constitute monumental evidence to their artistic attainments and distinctions which have contributed a lot to the enrichment of Indian art and architecture as a whole composite in nature. A marked similarities between the tribal art of this region and that of the contemporary Eastern School of Bihar Orissa and Pala-Sena art of Bengal can be observed. Both indigenous and external elements—the influence of Hindu art—contributed alike to the development of tribal art-non-Āryan in form. Several exhumed relics as a result of archaeological discovery testify to the great synthesis of cultures—Āryan and non-Aryan—which prevailed in this remote corner of India from time immemorial, their cultural intercourse and fellowship which provided the threads in the fabric of their artistic civilisation and the prevalence of Hinduism which played considerable role in shaping the body of aboriginal culture.

Notes and References

1. S. F. Hannay, JASB, 1848, Vol. XVII, pp. 471-72.
2. *Report of the Archaeological Tours in Assam* (hearafter abbrev. as R.A.T.A), : Jan-Feb. 1905.
3. S. E. Hannay, *op. cit,* PL-XXX. pp. 466-467.
4. *Op. cit.,*
5. Home, 'B' Progs, June, 1905, No. 638/675, pp. 40-41.
6. *Descriptive Ethnology of Bengal*, (Calcutta, 1872, Reptd, 1960), p. 11.
7. Dr. T. Bloch, RATA, 1905; *Annual Report of the Archaeological Survey of India* (Abbrev. as A.R.A.S.I) 1903; J.A.S.B., 1874, Vol. XLIII, Pt. I, pp. 3-6.
8. A.R.A.S.I., 1903; General Deptt. Rev. 'B' Progs July, 1902 No. 4441448; Arch. Br. 'B' Progs, June, 1910, Nos. 7-9. File No. 24-A.G.; Assam Sect., Gen. Deptt. Rev. 'B' Progs, Sept., 1902, Nos. 334, 335; Report from S.O. Haflong, No. 827.
9. R. A. T. A., 1905.
10. J. A. S. B., 1874, Vol. XLIII, p. 5.
11. Arch. Br. 'B' Progs, June 1910, Nos. 7-9.
12. R.M.Nath.The *Background of Assamese Culture* (Shillong, 1st Edn,1948) p. 104.
13. *Op. cit.,* pp. 61 ff.
14. R. A. T. A. 1905.

15. Arch,, Br. 'B' Progs, June 1910, No. 7-9.
16. Cf. L.W. Shakespear, *The History of Assam Rifles,* (London, 1929), p. 262.
17. Arch. 'B' Progs, May 1885, No. 175, 181.
18. *The Naga Tribes of Manipur* (1st pub. 1911. Reptd, Delhi 1974), p. 42.
19. Somerset Playne, *Bengal and Assam Bihar and Orissa,* London, 1917), p. 479.
20. S.K. Chatterjee, *KIRATA-JANA-KRTI*, (A.S.B. Calcutta 1974), pp. 138-39.
21. W.W. Hunter, *Statistical Account of Bengal,* Vol. VI, (London, 1876), p. 498.
22. *Proceedings of the Lt. Governor of Eastern Bengal & Assam,* June 1910, Nos. 15, 18, 35, 77, 2711 E.
23. R. M. Nath, *op. cit.*, pp. 71-73.
24. *Op. cit.,* p. 268.
25. *Indian Antiquary (The Journal of Oriental Research),* 1875, Vol. IV, p. 115.
26. J.A.S.B., 1902, Vol. LXXI, Pt. III, p. 36.
27. Arch. Br. 'B' Progs, June 1910, Nos. 7-9, File No. 24, A.G. 10.
28. *The Journal of the Assam Research Society* 1972, Vol. XX, pp. 8-13.
29. R. A. T. A., 1905.
30. *Glorious Assam,* pl. XXV.
31. Foreign Proceedings, 1894-Diary Recorded by J.E. Gray, 1892-93.
32. *History of the Frontier Tribes Bordering on Assam*, 1883-1941, (Shillong, 1942), p. 169.
33. Vide, Report of Somerset Playne, *op. cit.,* p. 463.
34. *Op. cit.,* p. 499.

15

Tribal Decorative Arts, Paintings, Terracotta, etc. in North-East India

The Buddhist and Brahmanical literatures of pre-Christianera contain abundant references to the art of decoration and painting in the secular and religious forms. This is the most important form of artistic expression by means of developed craftsmanship. As an intrinsic aspect of art, it is the product of the faculty of mind. It is said to have originated from the "Darsana activity of mind". This is an anthropocentric art portraying the varied life of everyday, hence it may be literary and illustrative in purpose. The early tradition and practice eventually led to the formulation of definite principles, theory, techniques, etc. The art of terracotta provided the most popular object for decoration. Quite different attitudes, of life and artistic visions are revealed by deluge of terracotta relief. Terracotta finds are supposedly archaic or of primitive type the study of which from the standpoint of historical and archaeological sequence is rendered difficult. In this paper, sincere attempt has been made to portray the pen-picture of various forms of tribal decorations, paintings and some terracotta finds which eloquently bespeak of their high degree of perfection, skill and efficiency in this form of art. The study is based on both published and unpublished sources.

The intense passion for beauty and artistic work inspired the different tribes to decorate and paint almost everything used in daily life. In the North-East Frontier Region, we find Monpa paintings on wooden cups, bowls and masks representing birds, animals, human beings, leaves of flowers, scenes and scenery which appear to be very attractive.

Painting and mural decorations are unique art treasures of the Monpa people. The Khamptis' paintings of bricks in red-blue, green and yellow colours, the Wanchos', the Konyaks' and the Phoms' decorations of Morungs or men's communal houses and funerary images are other examples of this form of art. The Phom drinking mug containing representation of stylized mithun-head and mask design, the pillars of Chang tomb decorated with tattoo designs, the Konyak's wood carvings whitened with clay and wooden figures coloured in dark, red and blue colours, the Wancho's carvings of dark wood with decorations in white line and wearing red and white beads, etc. are other attractive pieces of this form of art.[1] As a matter of fact, the head-hunting was the main inspiring source of decorative and ornamental works. Bamboo-drinking-mugs were carved with extraordinary skills but the central motif was always the human head. The Phoms and Konyak tribes excelled in making grave effigies. The figures were' realistically carved with the usual tattoo marks and ornamentations. The Nishis, the Khamptis and the Noctes used to carve and paint beautiful images. The Akas drawings on wood and houses are also praiseworthy. The official record[2] also reveals this fact that the Khamptis Lukkun Rajah used to make ablong box ornamented and studded with small coins, coloured beads, diamond shaped mirrors and profuse gilt. The, official document[3] bears evidence to the fact that the drawings of Membo Abors' houses were of high order. The front "Chang" too contained beautiful drawings. The drawings of small leaves of tree on the small houses have also been frequently referred to in the document. The paintings shown look like flowers and allied objects. Besides the representation of human figures and carvings on pillars of their morungs, we find mural paintings on them. Tribal morungs with mural paintings stand as "Ajanta" for them in the limited sense with some reservation. According to M'cosh[4], the Singphos used to decorate their ruder temples with ruder idols of all religions. But this fact has not been corroborated by any contemporary source.

However, decorations with geometric, floral and foliar designs and patterns, no doubt, left their indelible imprint on the hearts of the Europeans. The beautiful designed plinth of Malinithan temple was also artistically decorated. Here too, various geometric and floral designs have been noticed in course of recent archaeological explorations carried out by the Research Deptt. of the Govt. of Arunachal Pradesh.

The Buddhist paintings based on the ideals of Hindu paintings are also worth mentioning here. The episodes connected with the life of Lord Buddha painted on the walls of "Kakling", a village gate and monasteries in Kameng district as a whole, constitute the finest specimen of the Buddhist painting[5]. Among all the tribes of N.E.F.A. only the Monpas learnt the art of painting as an archaeological profession. The Daflas, the Akas, the Mijis and other tribes have been trying their best to attain the standard of the Monpa art. The village gates in Rupa and Shergaon villages were also elaborately and profusely painted with conventional designs and images of the Buddha. The four side-walls of "Kakling" or village gate contained the paintings of the images of previous Panchanlama, previous Dalailama, Lord Buddha's mother, etc. All the painted rectangles representing a Gompa with four gates bears an "Ashoka Chakra". All public buildings were elaborately painted with conventional Buddhistic designs and themes in different .colours which gradually became fashionable in the area. The paintings of various images on the potteries of the tribes of Kameng, Tirap and Lohit districts of MEFA exhibit a high degree of artistic inspiration and vision.

In the North Cachar hills, we find the entrance gateway of the ancient historic city of, Dimapur as a fine solid mass of masonry with a painted arch and representation of swords or daggers on the chessmen pillars—memorial columns closely resembling the old Naga knife.[6] A fine specimen of it was also found on some of the monoliths at Kasomari. G. H. Damant[7] points out that the iron swords of the Kacharis, worshipped as God's incarnation, was painted with red and white. Regarding the decorative art of the Mikir tribes R.M. Nath[8] informs us that "the feathers of the long tail of the Bhimraj bird, azure blue in colour, is prized as the most valuable decoration for the turban of young men on festive occasions".

In Hill-Tipperah, we have got the only instance of oil-painting, the most popular art in progress during Raja Bir-Chandra Deo-Burman Manikya[9].

The hillmen, especially the Naga tribes of Manipur, used to decorate their Morungs with trophies of war and games. It also contained the representation of animals. The houses of rich people were decorated with carvings, in some cases, of animals and with paintings of rough geometrical patterns such as circles, squares and oblong lozenges. R. Reid's[10] information in this regard is very valuable. According to him Jadonang's house-front made of wooden planks was painted with scroll patterns and pictures of men, mithuns, elephants, tortoises, etc., in blank. On each side of the door were white slabs of wood stuck in the ground bearing a representation of a sepoy with a rifle, in red paint.

In the Khasi-Jaintia hills, the main door of the palace of the Siems (Rajas) were duly decorated with flags and images and painted with blue-yellow colours which represented mainly the flower leaves. The famous limestone caves of Rupasor near Syndai village contained the mural decorations. Many rock caves in Sonphar in front of Bosara were full of decorations and paintings. The walls of stone cremation platforms contained floral and other decorations. The chariot of the Jaintias used in their Beh-Dien-Khlan festival contained the fine decorations which very much conforms to Tazia of the Muslims. The painted posts of Morungs and woodwork containing the life-size figure of man and animal belonging to the Garo tribes, are also considered to be of high order.

Art in the sense of decorative art and painting was very much popular among the different Naga tribes. Apart from the carvings on the front beams of average Angami house there was also a little ornamentation. Rich men used to adorn the fronts of their houses with painted representation of men, women, shields, mithun hornbill — features and geometrical designs in the form of concentric circles. The Eastern Angamis adorned the fronts of their houses with little clay models of men in ceremonial dress, mithuns, dogs and other animals executed with considerable ingenuity. J. H. Button[11] compares it with the adornment of the houses in Madagascar. The Eastern Angamis' memorials surmounted by life-size wooden grave effigies decorated with symbols, revealing their powers and achievements in love and war, were noticed by Mr. McCabe[12] during his tour in their country. This is a faithful record of what modern civilization would term, his virtues and vices. The Naga art of wood-carving was very much associated with the practice of headhunting and mortuary rites. The Thankul Nagas also used to decorate their houses with full artistic sense. Both Angami and Konyak Nagas' morungs were adorned with carvings associated with symbols in red, black and white. The Konyak morungs had a number of erotic motifs such as representation of men, animals, dancing couples, etc. The Sema Naga's decoration of Ganna Posts in the form of highly conventionalised representations and ornamentations of their weapons with very simple engraving and punch-marks, are the perfect testimony to their passion of art. On the basis of the report of Lt. R. G. Woodthorpe[13] we can affirm that the Eastern Nagas evinced their keen interests in .the decoration of their spears and shields with red hair. The cloth paintings of the Lotha, the Aos and Rengma Nagas are worthy of attention. The colourful designs and beautiful patterns are really of artistic value. The figure of elephants, tigers, mithuns, cocks, daos, spears and human heads painted with black on the white medium band and the Rangma Nagas' cloths containing the decorations representing the warrior's tail, tiger's eyes, a cow, an elephant, mithun, etc., are beautiful specimens of cloth painting. Mr. B. K. Bhattacharyya[14] has rightly pointed out that "the Naga art contains all the characteristics of a primitive-cum-peasant art which according to Herbert Read are there. Firstly, this art shows a tendency towards abstraction or geometrical forms. Secondly, it is more or less an applied art, specially in its origin, and thirdly, it is conservative. The art is akin to the art of primitive and unsophisticated peoples of the world. The basic beliefs behind the art is magical, being connected with cults that were and are practised to redeem the primitive emotion of fear. Nevertheless there is an unconscious tandency in the art to be utilitarian."

The Lushia tribes are also believed to have cultivated the art of decorating their tombs with Mithun's head. The tomb contained the representation of figures. The old Kuki clan also practised little drawings. The archaeological details as regards their artistic activities are conspicuous by their absence in all the reliable records.

The terracotta deer plaque discovered from Bhismaknagar during the excavations of 1969-70, now on display in Central Museum, Arunachal Pradesh, Shillong, is of decorative Indian style. Some tiles with inscriptions and incised designs are also on display in the museum, The terracotta referred to is an earthern deer-plate. Another terracotta plaque found near Tamreswari Temple in Saiya region contained the life-size divine and human figures as well as representation of birds, flowers, etc.[15] Other terracotta pieces collected by G. N. Bhuiya[16] from Bhaitbari, Garo Hills, containing both divine and human figures, are decorative in style.

The artistic value of coins as an aesthetic object is almost negligible. Yet its artistic standard, simplicity, refinement, elegance, structure designs, decoration, ornamentation and workmanship warrant us to assign a proper place to it in the school of art. This is really tribal in origin and primitive in conception. Its artistic designs, animal devices and human figures in the best Hellenistic tradition can be seen in the coins of the Jaintia Kings and Hill-Tipperah Kings as illustrated by V. A. Smith in his *Catalogue of Coins in Indian Museum.*[17]

Notes and References

1. V. Elwin, *The Art of N.E. Frontier of India,* pp. 68ff.
2. *Foreign Proceedings,* May, 1949.
3. Foreign Dept. 1885. "Extl" "A", "Pros" March 1185. No. 254.
4. *Topography of Assam* (Delhi, 1975), Sec,—VII, p. 152.
5. S. Johri, *Where India, China and Burma Meet,* (Calcutta, 1933), pp. 260-62.
6. J.A.S.B. 1874, Vol. XLIII, Pt. I, pp. 3ff.
7. *Indian Antiquary,* 1875. Col. IV, p. 115.
8. *The Background of Assamese Culture,* (Shillong, 1948), p. 109.
9. W.W. Hunter, *The Statistical Account of Bengal,* (London, 1879) Vol. VI, p. 471.
10. *History of the Frontier Areas bordering on Assam,* 1883-1941 (Shillong, 1942), p. 168.
11. J.A.R.I. (London) 1965, Vol. 95, Pt. I & II, pp. 26-27.
12. Foreign Dept, "Ext." 'A' "Pros" May-June, 1885, Nos-175-181. No. 697.
13. *Proceedings of the Chief Commissioner of Assam* (Foreign Dept.), Aug. 1876.
14. *Eastern Horizon* , p. 197.
15. R.M. Nath, *Glorious Assam,* pI. XXV.
16. *Journal of the Assam Research Society,* 1972, Vol. XX, pp. 8f.
17. Vol. I, (Oxford, 1906), PL—XXIX, p. 308.

16

New Light on Architectural Remains of Dimapur

Architecture can be described as an art of organising space not only functionally but beautifully too. Architecture like Sculpture, painting or poetry is the result of prevailing attitudes and fashions as evidenced from its history dating back to B.C. 250. Each age brings forth a style which clearly reflects the tastes of makers, their faiths, ideals and various stages of civilization whose stylistical examination and appreciation is necessary.

Of all the ruins of Assam that have excited the interest of archaeological savants, the old fort or ancient citadel of Dimapur (the capital of Kachari kings till the last quarter of 16th century) popularly known as the relic of forgotten civilization and representing Megalithic culture undoubtedly stands as the masterpiece of architectural monuments not only in North East India but in whole Asia. In this paper, all possible attempts have been made to make an indepth study of the subject for throwing new light on its workmanship, ornamentation, artistic and historical importance, antiquity, points of striking similarities with other contemporary architectural styles and patterns, etc. The historical researches carried out in the second and third quarter of the 19th century and early 20th century have no doubt thrown some considerable light on the subject under review, but there are some points of our enquiries which still stand as most obscure and beclouded. No systematic account and accurate picture of the subject on the basis of elaborate research has been presented so far. The study is based on archaeological evidence, documentary evidence—both published and unpublished—periodical reports, standard historical records and other contemporary sources and collateral evidences.

The first archaeological exploration was undertaken by Mr. Grange in 1839-40 and Lieut. Biggs in 1841. "The remains of Dimapur" observes Mr. Grange "consists in some pillars of various patterns, a gateway, the ruined town or palace wall and a small fort to the north besides a few tanks both within and without the walls. The fortification is surrounded on three sides by a dry ditch about thirty feet wide, a bund and a second ditch. The gateway which faces the river is in a tolerable stage of preservation but the inner passage or guard room has fallen in and lies a heap of ruins. The pillars are in three parallel rows, those of two rows arc of a circular form and in the third row the pillars are square."[1] While describing the ruined city in 1874, Mr. Johnstone remarks that it was surrounded by solid brick walls, twelve feet in height and six in thickness. The bricks were admirably made and burned. The walls enclosed a space seven hundred yards square entered by a Gothic archway. He found one or two sacrificial stones for offerings associated with flowers, water etc. Near the gateway some huge carved monoliths— one eighteen feet in height—were also discovered.[2] While supporting this statement, H. H. Godwin Austen (Dy. Supdt. of Topographical Survey of India) observes that the old town was bounded on the North by a brick wall 900 yards long on the South by the Dunsiri and the western wall was followed for 250 yards from the N. W. Angle. But it must be quite 1400 yards up to the river. The Eastern wall is 700 yards long with an obtuse salient angle. The finesolid brief gateway was situated on the side 150 yards from the N. E. Angle. The hill was in occupition of Kachari race. The entrance gateway was a fine solid mass of masonry with a pointed arch. It was flanked on both sides by octagonal turrets of solid brick work and intervening distance to the central archway was relieved by false windows of ornamental moulded brick work. All the moulded bricks were of very fine clay and well burnt. From the appearance of architecture it appeares that Muhammadan artisans had been employed on its construction.[3] The architectural beauty, designs and workmanship no doubt bear the stamp of Medieval Indian art. All the ornamentation was simple scroll. Not a single representation of any bird or beast was noticed, very much in conformity with Quoranic injunction or Purāṇic belief. The entrance gateway was beautfully executed and the palatial building of the capital was in a state of excellent preservation till recent time. The scattered blocks of stones and brick pieces with various designs were discovered by various explorers. While corroborating the Austen's statement about the structure and its architectural style, E. Gait asserts that "The curved battlement of the gateway, as well as the pointed arch over the entrance point distinctly to the Bengal, style of Muhammadan architecture."[4] It is further confirmed by archaeological evidence.[5]

The documentary evidence[6] also testifies to the existence of the old ruined city of Dimapur of great archaeological beauty. The other valuable descriptions about this old fort have been given by L. W. Shakespeare who saw it in 1897 and Major A. Vickers who made and archaeological survey of the area in 1919. This hill-fort discovered by Major Vickers[7] was probably a defensive post for the old Capital.

Mr. Fergusson's inclination to call this fort as a temple[8] appears to be a ridiculous affair. He probably misconstructed the whole thing. This has been further disputed by Godwin Austin[9] who remarked that this is perhaps questionable whether this was a temple at all ? No Hindu or Buddhist deity was found in sculpture nor was found any idol. So it was a town of an aboriginal race (old Kachari). But here we must provide the place for accomodating or incorporating Mr. Fergusson's[10] description of this monument. According to him, "it consists of a long corridor about 250 ft. In length and 21 ft. wide, the roof of which was supported by pillars richly carved spaced 15 ft. to 21 ft. apart." The architectural style in all limited sense reveals a striking similarities between this ancient kacbari fort and wooden architecture of Sweden and Norway.

Equally remarkable architectural remains discovered were the Chessmen "V" shaped carved pillars, monoliths etc. On the basis of archaeological evidence[11] and other varied sources[12] it is to be noted here that the most astonishing and distinguishing remains and other relics were the huge stones called as monolithic pillars, all elaborately, elegantly and profusely carved with representation of birds, animals, spear-head etc. which have withstood the weathering of many centuries. The chessmen pillars had for the most part merely garlands of flowers and jewellry, rosettes bells, crosses daggers or purely geometrical figures, while on the "V" columns a number of animals were inserted between .the floral arrangements. The figures were those of peacocks, elephants, deer, tigers etc. These megaliths like that of Naga megaliths were predominantly associated with elaborate rituals and fertility cult as evidenced from their phallic shapes. The phallic megaliths and monoliths as well as ornamental stones of Dimapur have a close affinity with the Naga Posts[13]. According to Mills[14] there was close affinity between the Kachari and N:iga culture based on identical beliefs in the cult of fertility and animism. Dr. T. Bloch[15] discovered amazing similarities between the architectural style and carving of Dimapur relics and monuments and Tamreswari Temple in North-East Frontier region. The pillars were decorated with carvings of degenerated workmanship after the Brahma Tezpur school. The style of carving on the pillars was probably more or less indigenous with some light touches of Indian art. Regarding the carvings on pillars and stones we find the similar features in Mathura Gasdhara School of Art (1st to 3rd century A.D.), Hosyala style of art (12th to 13th century), Pallava art (seventh century) and other arts in Asiatic tradition in general.

Its most remarkable features are two rows—one of sixteen, the other of seventeen monoliths standing in front of this. In the two rows each of monoliths with arounded top appropriately called "chessmen columns" and of bifurcated pillars shaped like Roman initial "V" and hence called "V" columns are the excellent specimens of architectural remains. These four rows run parallel to each other from North to South and a little to the west of them is a long ditch, perhaps the remains of an old tank. On the opposite border of this ditch stands an isolated chessmen column, which has now fallen down and further to the west is another isolated chessmen column, the largest of all, 16 × 6 in height with a girdle of 23 '7'. Lastly there was another double row of chessmen columns but without the corresponding "V" columns, running also from north to south. Its position is to the North west of the first and larger row. Dr. T. Bloch[16] classifies the monoliths of Dimapur into "sword blade" chessman "Y" shaped and "buffalo horned colomns." The ornamentation of the former type are floral and geometrical, and sometimes the ornamental bands hanging down the columns have the carving of swords and daggers..... On the latter type there are animal designs carved between the three rosettes whici have divided each half into separate fields of ornamentation." The ornamentation is completely different and with it rosettes resemble the pillars at Kasomari Pathars. The sword or dagger which is often found representing on these memorial columns closely resemble the Naga knife. R. M. Nith[17] observes that inside the compound the triumphal monument and lot of small stone triumphal pillars now known as Mushroom and chessmen pillars corresponding to the number of chiefs subdued were installed there which later on became bifurcated. Actually it was during Lord Curzon's viceroyalty whose interest for the preservation of ancient monuments is well known that these broken pillars were once again set up in their places, broken portions being fixed with iron bands and the surrounding gound was cleared and fenced in for their preservation. L. W. Shakespear[18] states that in the year 1902 Lord Curzin restored all the scattered broken pillars to its original place in Dimapur.

The two rows to the east are not unlike gigantic or huge "lingam" stones in shape, the western rows taking the form of "V" are believed by some savants to be evidence of ancient phallic worship. These monoliths have really bafflcd many savants. No trace of inscription or written character of any kind has ever been found on these monoliths or pillars. It still remains a puzzling and ticklish question to explain as to what purpose these curious rows of chessmen and "V" columns served. The diagram provided in archaeological report[19] shows the following arrangement of columns in each row. As the principal four rows run parallel to each other from north to south the distance between each row is equal.

The first or easternmost row of chessmen columns consists of 6 and the next of 17 columns. The same number prevails among the two corresponding rows of "V" columns but in the first row two columns have now entirely disappeared. A further peculiarity is that the position of the chessmen columns of the first line corresponds to the of the "V" columns of the first line and equally the position of the pillars in both the second lines. It must be however remarked that this arrangement has been somewhat destroyed by the columns having fallen down or otherwise became dislocated but it is still evident that the diagram shows their original order. Further it deserves to be noted that the central columns of each line are both higher and thicker than those towards the ends, thus the central chessmen columns showed an aveiage height of 13′ and a circumference at base of 14′ but at both the ends corresponding figure went down to 9′ or 10′ on the average. The top portion of the chessmen pillars was rounded, and it is evident that they did not support any other structure. The "V" columns on the other hand did so undoubtedly, as the upper portion of each beam bears a mortice hole for the reception of some other piece of stone or wood. What this may have been, it is difficult to say anything with any amount of certainty and conviction. If they supported an open verandah in front of some building, this building can't have been from stone or bricks as no other stone or brick are found there except broken pieces or portions of the pillars. If it was made of wood or mud it strikes one as rather peculiar that such a strong support was chosen for a comparitively light structure. The roof if one existed must have been sloping according to the Bengali fashion as shown by the arrengement with regard to the height of the columns. The building if any, cannot have had any great depth, as the old ditch is very close to the second or western most line of "V" columns.

The ornamentation on the columns was generally very simple. The chessrmen pillar have for the most part merely garlands of flowers and jewellry, rosetts, bells, crosses daggers or purely geometrical figures, while on the "V" columns a number of animals are inserted between the floral arrangements. It should be mentioned that no figure or animal particularly sacred to any Hindu deity and of any undoubted religious bearing is referred to in the original report, but it can't be denied that the scroll pattern shows an advanced style of Hindu art.

Inspire of the sincere attempts made by Lord Curzon in 1902 to restore the bifurcated broken pillars to its original place into better order the preservation of these curious pillars was found in bad state comparitively at later period. Many chessmen columns and "V" columns were found entirely broken which perhaps now lie around their base and partly buried under ground. The stendlng pillars were out of perpenticular.

Its artistic character shows that it belongs to the "Eastern variety prevalent in the Ninth century A.D." over the larger portion of Northern India[20]. The worthy remark by Mr. Fergusson is worth mentioning her. To quote him "......no similar monument exists anywhere for the pillars seem perfectly useless, though attached to two rows of stone that may have borne a roof; otherwise they look like these rows of rude stone monuments which are familiar within this country and in Britanny, but which, more artistic people may have adorned with rude carvings instead of leaving them quite plain, as our forefathers did. As for their carving, the only thing the least like them, so far I know, in India, are the pillars in the temple at Moodbidri and in other places in Canara but there the pillars are actual supports of roofs, these are round headed and evidently never were intended for any utilitarian purpose."[21] Further about its artistic and historical importance Mr. Fergusson remarks, "They are unique of their kind in Asia set up by a race long forgotten but still venerated by those who came afterwards owing perhaps to the mystery surrounding them."[22] Dr. T. Bloch opines that "They are to my mind the most interesting remains of the province and quite unique in India and moreover they enjoy the rare advantage of being easily accessible and so situated that a great number of travellers annually must pass them."[23] Godwin Austen says that ruins are extensively interesting and not having seen elsewhere buildings or sculpture bearing any resemblance to those of Dimapur.[24] Dr. T. Bloch's observation that "Dimapur is a relic of a stifled development of Tibeto-Burman civilization"[25] looks utterly fanciful idea and merely hypothetical view. As there is no reasonable ground and positive evidence to support this working hypothesis, this idea can be easily disapproved and hence dismissed. Here Dr. Maheswar Neog's remark, that the monoliths and rums of some forgotten places stand as testimony to the Non-Aryan impact on Hindu art,[26] appears to be very much palatable and hence it should always be welcome. Here ths impact of Indo-Aryan culture through the process of suaskritization on Non-Aryan culture can scarcely be denied. As a matter of fact, most of the specimens and relics of Non-Aryan workmanship with a touch of Hindu influence bear an ample testimony to the evolution of synthesis of Pan-Indian art and tribil cultural value during the early and later medieval periods. Here we can't fail to quote Hutton, "The carved monoliths at Dimapur seem to represent the final efflorescence in Assam of a forgotten civilization of which survivals appear sporadically from the Eastern Himalayas through South-East Asia and Indonesia down to the Paccific and which seems to have spread from Indonesia to Medagaskar and even to West Africa. It seems to have reached Assam partly at any rate from South-East and represented there by the Monolithic stone jars of the North-Cachar hills which are clearly related and that pretty closely to the stone jar necropolises of Vietnam, Celebes and Sumatra and also no doubt to the monoliths of Dimapur and the latter group at Jamugari. The North Cachar Monoliths contained the ashes of the dead and bears a resemblance to stone cises and monoliths of Khasi Hills ..."

About its destruction Mr. Grange has observed that after building of the city Chakradhvaj heard of the approach of the famous Hindustani warrior and invader Kalapahar when he fled away with his effect to Mybong in the hills, where he subsequently built a fort. Kalapahar not finding his foe pillaged and profaned the place, desecrated everything to the ground and withdrew and then Dimapur was deserted.[27] But this statement has not been corroborated by other sources. However possibility of this occurence can't be ruled out or precluded in view of the fact that after Kalapahar got converted to Islamic faith owing to the most dogmatic and orthodox approach of a group of fanatic Brahmins of Bengal took a vow to destroy the vestiges of Hindu culture and civilization. E. Gait also mentions that tradition supports its destruction to Kalapahar but simultaneously he admits that they were defeated by the Ahoms about the same time.[28] Austen's information that it was destroyed by the Nagas from the south[29] seems to be based on false assumption. L. W. Shakespear equally seems to hold the hypothetical view that the capital of Kachari kings was destroyed by Ahoms in 1570 A.D.[30] The only trustworthy information in this regard is that the early capital of the Kachari rajas was sacked by Ahoms in 1536 A.D. during the time of Detsung (A.D. 1531-36). On the basis of what we have adduced, Dr. P.C. Chowdhury's supposition that "most of the remains appear to be contemporaneous with the Kachari civilization established before the Ahom invasion in the 13tn century"[31] can fairly be disputed. The Ahom invasion took place in the 16th century, not in the 13th century as suggested by him.

About its antiquity, all the views put forth so far are absolutely incorrect and hence untenable. The Dimapur Monoliths was neither Prehistoric as erroneously supposed by J.H. Hutton[32] nor was the city built in 4th century or even earlier as unreasonably presumed by L.W. Shakespear[33]. Mr. Ferguson's statement that judging from the gateway and other remains of the town of Dimapur in which these pillars are found, they cannot be of any great or any remote antiquity[34] can be held as correct, but his observation that the gateway of Gaur type with a pointed arch is probably of the 16th or 17th century obviously appears to be fantastic and far from truth. Actually, it was a medieval architecture of the 15th century ascribed to the Kachari King Vikramaditya—Pha (1400-1460). This chronological date has been also attested by R.M. Nath[35].

This fact must be brought to light that all the archaeological remains from North Cachar hills including the monoliths, pillars, sculptured stone, and other relics of antiquarian interest of Dimapur were brought under Ancient Monument Preservation Act Vll of 1904[36] passed by Lord Curzon and declared protected.

Notes and References

1. Ref. to William Robinson, *A Descriptive Account of Assam* (1st Pub. 1841. Reptd. Delhi, 1975), p. 404.
2. *My experience in the Manipur & Naga Hills* (Delhi, 1971), pp. 8-9.
3. *Journal of the Asiatic society of Bengal* (hereafter Abbrev. as J.A.S.B.), 1874, Vol. XLIII. pt. 1, pp. 1-6.

4. *History of Assam* (Calcutta, 1926), p. 250.
5. Dr. T. Bloch (Archaeological Surveyor, Bengal Circle) *Annual Report of the Archaeological Survey of India, Bengal Circle.* (Hereafter Abbrev. as A.R.A.S.I., (B.C.) April, 1903, pp. 5-6.
6. Govt. of Eastern Bengal & Assam, Arch. "Br" 'B' Progs, Aug. 1907, Nos. 1-3.
7. Cf. L W. Shakespear, *History of the Assam Rifles* (London, 1929), pp. 259-60.
8. *History of Indian and Eastern Architecture* (H.I.E.A.) (London, 1876), p. 309.
9. J.A.S.B. 1874. Vol. XLIII, Pt. I, p. 5.
10. H.I.E.A., pp. 309f.
11. A.R.A.S.I. (B.C.) April, 1903, pp. 6-7; Dr. T. Bloch, A.R.A.S.I. Sept. 1905. No. 58, pp. 1-5, File page 13-17. File No. 'V' A—8, No. I Regr. No. 712 'R'.
12. H.H.Godwin Austen's Report Cf. JA.S.B. 1874, Vol. XL11I, Pt. I pp. 1-6; Annual Administrative Report, 1880—1 Vide *Imperial Gazetteer of India*, 1908 (Eastern Bengal & Assam) pp. 585-86; L.W. Shakespear, *op. cit.*, pp. 256-58.
13. Education Dept. File No. A/39, 'B' "Progs", July 1918, Nos. 13-16; General Dept. Rev. B" "Progs", July 1902, Nos. 444-448.
14. *Assam Review*, April 1928, pp. 26f., Cf. Dr. P .C. Chowdhary, The *History of civilization of the people of Assam* (Gauhati 1959), p. 74.
15. A.R.A.S.I., 1905.
16. A.R.A.S.I., 1906-7, pp. 19f; Godwin Austen, J.A.S.B. 1874, Vol. XLIII, pt. 1, pp. 5-6.
17. *The Background of Assamese Culture* (Shillong—1948), pp. 71-72.
18. *Op. cit.*, pp. 258-59.
19. Vide A.R.S.I., April, 1903.
20. *Epigraphia Indica*, 1925-26, A.R.A.S.I., 1925-26, Vol. XVIII? (Edited by Rai Bahadur H. Krishna Shastri) p. 329.
21. H.I.E.A., p. 310.
22. Ref. to L.W. Shakespear, *op. cit.*, pp. 256-57.

23. A.R.A.S.I., 1905.
24. J.A.S.B., 1874, Vol. XLIII, pt. I, p. 2.
25. Vide Home "B" "Progs", Sept. 1905, Nos. 702-708, A.R.A.S.I., 1905, Proc. No. 705.
26. *Assam Quarterly,* Jan.-March 1967, Vol. IV, No. I, pp. 14-15.
27. Vide, Robinson, *op. cit.,* p. 404.
28. *Op. cit.,* p. 251.
29. J.A.S.B., 1874. Vol. XLIII, p. I.
30. *Op. cit.,* pp. 16-17.
31. *Op. cit.,* p. 73.
32. *Man in India (A quarterly Anthropoliogical Journal,* Ranchi) Sept. 1922. Vol. II, No. 3, p. 150.
33. *Op. cit.,* p. 260.
34. H.I.E.A., p. 310.
35. *Op cit.,* p. 71.
36. P.E.B.A. (Dept. of Archaeology), 1910-11.

17

Tribal Socio-Religio-Cultural Renaissance and Reform Movements in North-East India in the Nineteenth and Twentieth Centuries

To begin with, Pandit Jawaharlal Nehru was absolutely correct in stating that the so-called European civilization had the disastrous and paralyzing effect on the tribal people. The March of modern civilization destroyed the traditional way of their lives and put an end to their arts, culture and simple way of living. He was totally opposed to the assimilation approach to the tribal people of India. He emphatically justified the attempts of the tribesmen to keep their pride in their own traditions. To quote him, "I am alarmed when I see not only in this country but in other great countries too-how anxious people are to shape others according to their own image or likeness, and to impose on them their particular way of living ... I am not at all sure which (the modern or the tribal) is a better way of living. In some respects I am quite certain theirs is better. There is no point in trying to make them a second rate - copy of ourselves".[1] R.S. Rattary, while exhorting the tribal chiefs and people said, "Guard the National soul of your race and never be tempted to despise your past. Therein I believe lies the sure hope that your sons and daughters will one day make their own original contribution to knowledge and progress".[2] In the light of the above remarks, the view of Marx, that "the tradition of all dead generations weighs like a mountain on the brain of the living",[3] can be disapproved here.

Dr. Hutton *(Census of India Report* 1931) pointed out that some changes were indeed taking place in the aboriginal societies of India for centuries before the advent of the British rule but its process was very slow which made the gradual and proper adaptation possible. He opposed isolationism and supported assimilation. He upheld the theory of culture contacts of the tribal people. He categorically stated that until and unless the aborigines come into contacts with peoples of advanced culture they cannot make any satisfactory progress. O' Malley *(Modern India and the West,* pp. 417, 438) has spoken about the effect of British rule on the primitive tribes. He wrote, "Far from being of immediate benefit to the primitive tribes, the establishment of British rule in India did most of them much more harm than good". J.P. Mill admitted the evil effects of Missionary activities in Assam. H.B. Rowney (*Wild Tribes of India*, pp. 7, 9, 14, 216) did not uphold the theory of assimilation. He rather supported isolation of the tribal people from the cultural standpoint. He wrote that some aborigines who were not protected more or less similar results had followed, i.e. the introduction of Hindu culture in close contact with them. D.N. Majumdar *(Journal and Proceedings of the Asiatic Society of Bengal,* New Series, Vol. XXV, 1929, pp. 150-55) had strongly pleaded for the protection of the indigenous culture of the "primitive tribes" and emphasized the need to enable them to stand against the onslaught of foreign ideas. Thakkar Bapa favoured a policy of assimilation for the tribes. "The aborigines", he said in 1941, "should form part of the civilized communities of our country, not for the purpose of swelling the figures of the followers of this religion or that, but to share with the advanced communities the privileges and duties on equal terms in the general, social and political life of the country. He said that "Separatism and isolationism seem to be dangerous theories and they strike at the root of national solidarity". *(The Problems of Aborigines in India,* pp. 7, 26.)

The early part of the 19th century marked the opening of a new chapter in the religious and cultural history of the tribal people of India. The rise and expansion of the British rule in general and the introduction and growth of western culture and civilization in particular had a disastrous and paralyzing effect on the indigenous socio-economic, political, religious and cultural systems of the tribal people of India. It was a period of struggle between the process of westernization and detribalization on one hand and the rediscovery of indigenous tribal culture on the other. In the 19th century, missionaries started converting the tribal people to Christianity in the name of spreading education. Towards the end of that century and in the early decades of the 20th century, the tribes found out that missionaries' basic purpose was to root out the native culture, bring the tribes under western influence, denationalize them and thus to place the British rule on a secure footing. This set off a chain reaction by way of rediscovery of their own socio-cultural roots as well as the religio-cultural tradition. The tribal reactions to the process of conversion as resorted to by the missionaries found popular expressions in the form of various socio-religious reform movements, as a result of which tribal religion, culture, language, literature, arts, crafts, education, etc. entered upon a new phase of orientation. The period under notice witnessed the reawakening of a large section of tribes in India including those in the north-east for the preservation and protection of their traditional religion and culture.

The history of tribal renaissance and reform movements in north-east India during the period under notice is the history of socio-religio-cultural awakening or revivalism as well as of social and religious reforms introduced by various associations, organizations and institutions. It is worthwhile to note here that the hill areas of north-east India saw the beginning of the revitalization movement in the 19th century much after the advent of the British rule in 1826 which in an intermittent manner continued upto the second quarter of the twentieth century. As a matter of fact, after the introduction of the British rule and further subjugation and annexations of different hill areas in north-east India, the psychological and cultural downfall and degradation of the tribal people began. The alien culture dominated the indigenous culture which being detrimental to their tender sentiments greatly jeopardized their interests reflected in the age-old traditional systems of high order. The conflict between two civilizations representing traditionalism and modernism ensued which appears to be an unique phenomena of the tribal history and civilization of north-east India. The British policy of alluring or inducing the tribal people by introducing all the apparatus of western civilization led to the crisis of faith, disillusionment with the traditional values, cultural neurosis and spiritual insolvency. This necessitated the beginning of a new movement—a movement to revive the archaic civilization and pristine glory of the past—by flashing beacon of light and kindling the spark of consciousness among the people for protecting, preserving, reviving, strengthening and developing all that was the best in their society, religion, culture, art, language, literature, etc. They illumined the gloom of ignorance and superstition and removed the haziness that enveloped their old glorious past and cultural heritage. It was a period of transition from westernization and detribalization to tribalism. Actually, they had two-fold objectives, one to protect their culture which was on the brink of extinction and the other to endeavour sincerely for the eradication of prevalent social and religious evils which were primarily based on superstitious beliefs and unscientific understanding. The contemporary socio-religious reform movements and other external influences set the wheel of progressive machineries in motion. The remarkable progress was achieved in different fields by different means. In the north-east too, the nineteenth century witnesses the dawn of a new era-an era of spectacular progress, gradual developments and miraculous changes in social, religious, educational and cultural fields. A successive wave of epoch-making events started taking place which still continue to exist in some tribal areas. As a whole, it was a period of social, religious and cultural renaissance. Though it is undeniable that its nature and course differs to certain extent from the 19th century tribal renaissance in other parts of India and Bengal Renaissance and the 16th century European Reformation Movement, nevertheless its paramount importance in a limited sense in the historical perspective as amply substantiated by available data can never be dismissed nor can we lose sight of those facts which have profoundly affected the course of their cultural history. In this paper, all possible attempts have been made to provide a brief, systematic and graphic account of the subject under discussion and to focus on both the forces and the personalities which directly or indirectly got involved in this tribal renaissance and reform movements on the basis of both published and unpublished sources.

First of all we will throw light on all the significant socio-religious changes that occurred in the Khasi-Jaintia Hills. The Khasi-Jaintia tribes (of the present Meghalaya state) played a conspicuous role in the history of renaissance and reform movements. After the partial annexations of both the Khasi and Jaintia Hill in 1833 and 1835 respectively, the British started interfering with their traditional social customs, religious practices and political system. At the very outset, it is an imperative to understand the political background of the movement. As a matter of fact, after the acquisition of Assam in 1826 the British started making serious attempts to capture the Khasi Hills, but Tirot Singh, who is still venerated as a freedom fighter, strained all nerves to resist and defy the British authority. He fought relentlessly and incessantly from 1829 to 1833 against the British and sacrificed his life at the altar of his motherland. He died in Dacca (Dhaka) jail sometime during 1840-41. His purpose of starting the anti-British movement was not only to throw off the iron yoke of colonial rule but to preserve the traditional Khasi culture, religion, customs, etc as well.[4] He wanted to maintain both political and cultural identity of his people. After the annexation of the Khasi and Jaintia Hills in 1833 and 1835 respectively, the British started encroaching upon their social customs, religious practices, political system and other traditional values. H. Onderson Mawrie[5] has also pointed out that after the fall of Tirot Singh the Missionary began to preach Christianity which led to the destruction of not only political system but traditional religion and culture of the Khasis. On the basis of some reliable sources[6] we can stated that the proselytizing activities of the Serampore Baptist Mission and the Welsh Presbyterian Mission in the Khasi-Jaintia Hills brought the indigenous religion and culture of the tribal people to almost a brink of extinction. Actually the first Christian Missionary to settle at Cherrapunji in the Khasi Hills was Alexander B. Lish of the Baptist Mission from Serampore. This Mission started its works in the Khasi-Jaintia Hills in 1832 and continued up to 1838. During this period they opened three Elementary Schools at Cheera, Mawluh and Mawsmai. The Gospel of St. Matthew was translated into Khasi with the help of Bengali script. But the real Missionary Zeal began from 1841 when the Welsh Presbyterian Missioin sent Rev. Thomas Jones at Cherrapunji to bring the tribal people within the fold of Christianity by conversion. This Mission translated Khasi Vernacular into Roman character replacing the Bengali script and opened the English Normal School at Cherra. By 1850 Evangelization brought the whole Khasi and Jaintia Hills within the pale of Western civilization. The other Mission under the denomination of Roman Catholic and Anglican Church continued their works in the following years. The tribal way of life, thoughts, manners, traditional institutions, religion and other indigenous practices were greatly transformed in tune with modern civilization. This stirred the conscience of both the tribal populace and potentates and created a strong sense of urgency for starting reform movement. They adopted hostile attitude towards the British and made all possible attempts to oppose the propagation of Christianity. Their vehement opposition to the spread of Christianity is evident from the religious persecution of the Neo-converts to Christianity. All the converted Christians were contemptuously looked down upon by the non-Christian population who were keen to maintain their traditional Khasi culture. They were also opposed to the new system of western education imparted through Missionary. The non-Christians aroused the feeling of consciousness in the hearts of the people in the Khasi-Jaintia Hills which had its impact far and wide. In 1862, U Kiang Nongbah, another reformer and liberator, started socio-politico-religious movement in the Jaintia Hills against the British' pernicious attempt of establishing the Christian Mission and their interference with the traditional values, social custom, religious practices and festivals.[7] The noble example set and the bloods shed by these two martyrs as well as reformers became the fountain head of inspiration for the posterity. When the unwanted interference of the British with their ceremonies, rituals, beliefs, usages, traditional system of inheritance, customary laws and mode of succession reached the climax in the eightees and ninetees of the 19th century, the non-Christian felt it warranted to start revitalization movement to resist the onslaught of Christianity and western civilization for maintaining their cultural tradition and heritage.

The life and activities of Raja Ram Mohon Roy, Swami Dayanand Sarasvati, Swami Vivekananda and others, who were foremost among the notable personalities of the 19th century Indian Renaissance, constituted the source of inspiration for the intellectuals among the Khasis. The Brahmo Samaj, Arya Samaj, Ramakrishna Mission and Hindu Mission greatly attracted the Khasi and Jaintia tribes to their folds. Various socio-cultural organizations appearing as a prototype of these also flourished and gave fillip to the socio-religious and cultural awakening.

The British Missionaries remained throughout active in propagating their religion, disseminating their culture and imparting their education based on British model by establishing educational institutions in the Khasi-Jaintia Hills. Faced with menace of being swallowed up by a new religion, a new culture and a new education, the soul of the Khasi and Jaintia people revolted. The first visible embodiment of this movement was Babu Jeeban (or Jeebon) Roy (1838-1903), the spiritual father of the modern Khasi. The emergence of this prominent figure on the socio-religious platform heralded the dawn of new age in the history of the cultural awakening of the Khasis. He was the prophet of the new age and an apostle of Khasi cultural renaissance. His appearance before the public was destined to have a great influence on the future course of the new awakening. He tried to infuse into the new generation a sense of pride in their glorious past and cultural heritage, of faith in future, and a spirit of self-confidence and self-respect. He acquired proficiency in Bengali, Khasi and Sanskrit languages. He was deeply influenced by the philosophical thoughts set fourth in all ancient literary texts in general and the Hindu scriptures in particular. He was greatly moved by the teachings of Hindu classical literature like *Rāmāyana, Mahābhārata, Gitā, Upanishads,* Vedanta and other instructive Sanskrit and Bengali religious literature. The study of the classical religious texts inspired him to defend the past, to check the denationalizing effects of missionary activities and to bring the Khasi within the fold of Sanskritization. He preached the gospel of the fundamental unity of all religions and urged for the cessation of inter-religious strifes. He advocated all round regeneration of the social and religious life and the acceptance of all that was useful for keeping the light of their traditional culture aglow. He played a notable role through his writings, mass-media and non-sectarian educational approach for arousing the social and religious consciousness in the hearts of his countrymen. As a result of his untiring efforts, the Khasi religion, education, culture and literature entered upon a new phase of reorientation.

According to some valuable sources,[8] it can be pointed out that he vehemently opposed the English education or Bible education spread by the Welsh Mission. There was only one M.E. School at Shillong. Regarding upgrading of that school, the Rev. Thomas Jones of the Welsh Mission said, "We have come here for religion ant not for education. As a befitting reply to this, he and his Bengali associates established the Shillong High School in 1878 for imparting the non-sectarian and secular education to the Khasi people. He started Ri Khasi Press in 1896 for publication of all those works which might help in arousing the cultural consciousness. In the Brahmo Samaj Hall at Mawkhar (Shillong) he founded Mawkhar Bengali Middle English School in 1899 for encouraging the Bengal education. He also encouraged the teaching of Sanskrit. Many Khasi people, while writing to the editor of *U nongialam khristan* pointed out that we do not want only Christian education; there should be a education for all—Hindus, Muslims, Khasis, Bengalis, Brahmos, Cathlics and Unitarians.

Babu Jeban Roy fulfilled the aspirations of his people. U Rai Sahib Sivanath Dutta has rightly observed that "His name should not be allowed to sink into oblivion. Jeeban Roy was the father of the modern Khasis. He was the pioneer of the modern Khasis. It was he who first had the vision of a glorious Khais race and he strove hard for their uplift in all spheres. He was a seer—and a farsighted seer—and it was in this that his greatness lay. With his keen insight he knew that the Khasis have their future linked with that of the Indian (U Dkhars) specially foreigners those of Sylhet, their nearest neighbours, because the Khasis have to live with them and rise or fall with them. He accordingly started a school for the Khasi pupils in which Bengali formed an important subject of instruction. We allowed him the use of the Mawkhar Brahmo Samaj building close by this hall for this school and it continued there for some years. He came to read the Sanskrit and *Hitopadesha* and he was so much charmed with it that he had to traslate into Khasi. He once told me that he knew of no other book like it for the moral training of our young hopefuls... he approaches the great Pandit Iswar Chandra Vidyasagar of revered memory. Though he had the opportunity of coming into contact with the westerners he was never dazzled by the glamour of their civilizations. He was ever national in his outlook, in his costumes and other things...."[9] According to H.R. Diengdoh, he believed in the fundamental equality of all religions. He extended equal respect to Hindus, Mussalmans, Christians and Brahmos.[10] S.C. Das has rightly pointed out that "spiritually Babu Jeeban Roy was an humble and unassuming man. His religion was pure and simple. It is true that he did not profess any creed, join any denomination or sign any articles of faith, but there is no doubt that he sincerely believed in God and the efficacy of prayer. Verify he has often been seen in his closest sitting in a state of deep communion with the deity. Babu Jeeban Roy was never partial to any particular religious body. A truly religious man be he a Hindu, a Mohammedan, a Christian or a Brahmo was always an object of his love and admiration"[11] J. Soloman called him the "leading Patriot of the day" "His spirit of patriotism was not less marked. There was not a wholesome movement in these hills which was not touched upon by his sacred hand. He did all that lay in his power for the amelioration of the distressed condition of his ignorant countrymen".[12]

Jeeban Roy was a great advocate of unsectarian liberal education. To improve the literature of the Khasi as well as to inculcate some moral values among the people, he composed several original works in Khasi and translated some English and Bengali books in his veranacular. By writing a book titled *KA NIAM JONG — KI KHASI* (The religion of the Khasi) in 1897, he advocated the re-introduction of old religious beliefs, rites and rituals, festivities and ceremonies, etc. His another book *KA KITAB SHAPHANG U WEI U BLEI* (A book on one God) published in 1900 incorporated the monotheistic beliefs of the Khasis.

This book is considered to be a Jewel of monotheistic theology. His other books like *KA KITAB NYNGKONG* (Bengali-small book for villagers published in 1897), *KA KOT PULE NYNGKONG* (book for villagers) published in 1899, *KA KITAB KHASI KABA AR* (Khasi Primer Pt. II) and *KA KITAB KHASI KABA LAI* (Khasi primer Pt. Ill) published 1899 served as the guide lines for common people to understand his objects and philosophy. Besides the books mentioned above, he translated a number of sacred classical texts and scriptures of the Hindus in tribal language (Khasi). By translating *HITOPADESHA* Pts—I, II, III and IV (1898-1899), *KA RAMAYANA* (1900), *KA KITAB CHAITANYA* (1900), *BUDDHA DEB CHARITA* (1901) and *KA HISTORY JONG KA RI INDIA* (History of India, 1900), in Khasi, he afforded an unique opportunity for the people to draw inspiration from them for the sake of preserving and protecting their traditional culture. He also translated some portion of the *KORAN* for the Muslims but unfortunately it is not available. From some of his original works it appears that he greatly encouraged the teaching of *Ramayana,* Lord Buddha, Gauranga Prabhu Chaitanya, *Hitopadesha* and *Koran* among the Khasi people for having the broader concept of religions and higher understanding of all the moral values. He also advocated the abolition of the caste system, which, according to him, proved to be detrimental to the unity of India.[13]

His all works paved the way for cultural re-orientation. He was, of course, the brightest star in the socio-religious firmament of north east India. Actually, it was he who first of all dispelled the dark cloud of misfortune hovering on the cultural horizon of north-east India. He spared no pain in vivifying the indigenous culture. He came in the forefront to refurbish the tarnished image of Khasi culture during the period concerned. His broad vision, catholicity of outlook, amplitude of mind, vivacity, tenacity, dedications, unostentatious disposition, unfailing courtesy and unflagging zeal earned him great love and admiration. He was enshrined in the hearts of his followers as a true champion of their cause. If he is to be studied properly, I do not have any doubt that he may be canonized as one of the foremost saints in the National Calendar of India.

He died in 1903 before attending the Delhi Durbar of Edward VII.[14] In the Memoirs of the late Babu Jeebon Roy, it is stated that "A marked commonsense and tenacity of purpose characterized the man in all his undertakings. Such a strong personality has passed away from amongst us at a time when the whole Hills are crying in one voice for his powerful guidance. It is not known if ever there will be one among the Khasis who can fill up the vacuum caused by the death of Babu Jeebon Roy."[15] He was "the most remarkable personality of nineteenth century Assam".

The establishment of the *SENG KHASI,* — a socio-cultural organization —on 23rd Nov. 1899 by Jeebon Roy, his son Chandranath Roy (founder Secretary) and other illustrious Khasis, in order to preserve the traditional religion, culture, beliefs, practices, songs, dance and customs, to maintain mutual unity, to heighten the image of the Khasis and to know about the religion and culture of others, constituted a distinct landmark in the revivalist movement of the Khasi-pnars. This organization urged a return to the original principles of the Khasi culture. It stood for the total rejection of all the socio-religious impurities that had crept into their culture. This popular institution provided an excellent opportunity to the tribals in the Khasi-Jaintia Hills to understand and protect their traditional values. It still continues to play a notable role in preserving and developing the traditional Khasi culture. It is more or less like the *Arya Samaj* of Swami Dayanand Sarasvati which exhorted the people in the past to go back to the Vedic culture. Babu Jeebon Roy, Sib Charan Roy, Rash Mohon Roy (First Chairman), U. Chandra Nath Roy—all true champion of tradition—were among the great patrons of this organization.[16] The aims and objects of this organization find reflection in its permanent constitution. The Journal *SENG KHASI* has been its mouthpiece and its flag, which is still being unfurled very high, reminds the new generation of their past glorious heritage and exhorts them to raise its honour. By holding periodical discussion on Khasi religion and culture and publishing several booklets, pamphlets and monographs highlighting all the noble features of its past history, religious beliefs, customs and traditions, this organization has been playing a commendable role in the socio-religio-cultural renaissance of the Khasi and Jaintia people since its inception.

One of the notable features of the organization is that it still organizes *Shad Suk Mynsiem* (Thanks giving Dance) in the month of April for three days every year as a symbol of the continuity of ancient Khai culture. "We must know that although the dance is organized and managed by Seng Khasi, it is actually the dance of the whole Khasi nation which we hope will further the preservation of our customs, usages and culture and which will be held annually". In 1912, the Seng Khasi clearly spelt out the purpose of this dance "to advance the culture of the Khasi race and to reveal our gratitude and joy to God, the Creator, that He has protected and taken care of us during the year and that He has provided in abundance to meet all our needs". Though this annual dance the Khasis foster among themselves a sense of unity and take pride in their religion and culture which was abhorred by the Christian missionaries. The Christian missionaries saw in this dance as in other religious, social and cultural activities of the Khasis, a major impediment in their proselytizing activities. To missionaries, Khasi music was "barbaric" and Khasi dance "baying of dogs". The missionaries defended their action by publicly declaring, "... it is one of our bounden duty to condemn not only this art of the Khasis but also their religion and the rites thereof." The comments by the editor of the Khasi Christian paper *Ka Pateng Christian* provide an eloquent proof of missionary attitude.

The Seng Khasi valiantly preserved their traditions (including the matrilineal family pattern) and arts despite opposition from the colonial government. Even today they continue their work through education, cultural celebrations and social service activities. The aims and objectives of the Seng Khasi are "to foster a sense of brotherhood among the Khasis who still retain their socio-cultural and religious heritage, to work for the advancement of education, to encourage traditional cultural dance and other social festivals, to undertake such welfare and development activities as maintenance of cremation grounds for those who dispose of the dead bodies according to traditions and religion". The Seng Khasi organisation right from its birth till today has been playing a very vital and praiseworthy role in preserving the indigenous culture by organizing different programmes and conducting various intellectual activities.

Sri Jairamdas Daulatram, while visiting the Seng-Khasi School on Octob. 18, 1955, said about the Seng Khasi people that "I am greatly pleased to learn that you have undertaken the work of collecting all your find indigenous songs reviving your own beautiful tunes and giving fresh vigour to your dances and other cultural activities. You have your share to contribute in developing the cultural wealth of India... and I have hope that your share will be worthy and substantial one".

Some unpublished letters[17] bear an eloquent testimony to the co-operation of the Khasi people and their genuine interests in the works and activities of the Seng Khasi. One of the very important unpublished lettes[18] shows that when Dacca (Dhaka) became the capital of Eastern Bengal and Assam in 1906 as aftermath of the partition plan of Bengal put forward by Lord Curzon in 1905, many of the Seng Khasi members in Govt. service were transferred there but here also all of them used to evince keen interest in the cultural revival of the Khasi people under the banner of the Seng Khasi. All of them residing at Dacca rallied round under the banner of Rash Mohan Roy who presided over the meeting held at Dacca on the Anniversary Day (23rd Nov. 1911) of the Seng Khasi. Twenty one people attended this meeting. Actually, Rash-Mohan Roy always played memorable role, as one of the patrons of the Seng Khasi, in bringing together all his brethrens on a common platform for reviving the ancient faiths, religion and culture.

Hajom Kissor Singh (1865-1923) started another religious movement known as "Unitarian" in the Khasi-Jaintia Hills for the spiritual and moral development of the people. The Orthodox Calvinist Mission had converted him to Christianity in tender age. But after coming in contact with *Brahmo Samaj* in his twenties and going through the liberal religious views of various scriptures he decided to break away from Christianity and to start a Unitarian movement based on the monotheistic principles of the Khasi religion. He raised his voice against the rigid and sectarian principles of the Calvinist Mission. He named his new movement "Ka Niam Mane Wei Blei", *i.e.* the religion that worships one God. He declared the Unitarian character of God as the antithesis of the Trinitarian character of God as propagated by the foreign missionaries of Calvinistic Methodist faith. The teachings of great men including Raja Ram Mohan Roy and selected passages from the *Bible* and other scriptures greatly moulded his thoughts. He maintained frequent contacts with the Unitarians of Bengal, Europe and America. He said, "There is only one God-Father and Mother of Humanity... All religions are equally good because God reveals His truth to Christianity in the same way as to Unitarianism, to Hinduism, to Islam, to Judaism, to Buddhism, to Zoroastrianism as well as to Confucianism... Jesus was not the only son of God. Krishna, Mohammed, Chaitanya, Confucius, Zoroaster, Ramakrishna Paramhansa, Raja Ram Mohan Roy, Vivekananda, Guru Nanak were all sons of God..." He drew inspiration from the universal aspects of Vedanta. Nilmani Roy, a Bengali Brahmo of Shillong, and other Bramo Sanyasis who preached the teachings of Raja Ram Mohan Roy in the seventies of the 19th century greatly influenced his religious thoughts. Between 1887 and 1900 he achieved remarkable success. A good number of the Khasi-Jaintia and Mikir tribes joined his Unitarian movement. In 1936, Miss Margaret Bar came from England, joined this movement and rendered very valuable services to the tribals in the Khasi and Jaintia Hills. It is worthy of note that various talented Khasi scholars of great excellence through their writings and movements of varied nature not only postulated the basic doctrines of religion or preached and popularized the old religious beliefs and customs but also proved to be a moving force in reviving the old glorious past and thus saved the Khasi race from cultural extinction.

Many contemporary non-Christian Khasi writers and intellectuals belonging to traditional school of thought representing serenity and syncretism played conspicuous role in the revitalization movement by writing books and bringing out magazines, journals, periodicals, pamphlets, etc.

The revitalization movement started by Jeeban Roy was carried forward by many other prominent reformers. The name of Sib Charan Roy (1862-1952) also figures prominently in the galaxy of all the reformers. Like his father Babu Jeeban Roy, he was also the defender of rich cultural heritage of the Khasi-pnars. He was an arch-enemy of Christianity. He was determined to resist the denationalizing and proselytizing activities of the Christians. He also acquired proficiency in the Sanskrit language. His monographs titled *Ka Niam-Ki khasi (Ka Niam Tip Blei Tip Briew* (1919) - a book on religious philosophy about one God and man—and *Ka Kot Toh Kit Tir-Tir* (1920) helped the people know about their religious doctrines, philosophical thoughts, supreme being, monotheistic beliefs, etc. These two books provided the correct interpretations of the original religion of the Khasis and focused on moral, spiritual, ethical and philosophical values. His other work like *"Ka Jingpyni Ka Kmie bad Ki Khun"* (Teachings of the forefathers, Pub.

in 1911) and a collection of lectures on Khasi religion and culture delivered in 1912 and 1913. (Published, in 1914) also proved to be valuable for the common people. The two noted monthly papers, *U Nongphira,* (watchman or caretaker) and *U Nongpynim* (a saviour) started by him in 1903 and 1928 respectively highlighted mainly those aspects of religion, rites and customs which were misinterpreted and misrepresented by the missionaries. Besides, these two also elaborately dealt with the traditional political, social and religious system of the people. In *Ka Jingiakyr-Sieu* (1903), he made a sincere attempt to trace the linguistic affinity between the Khasi, Sanskrit, Bengali and Hindi and ultimately proved that the Khasi rites, ceremonies and rituals are based on the Vedas and Sastras to a considerable degree. His *Ka Chanakya Niti Darpana* (trans. into Khasi in 1902) deals with the basic principles of the ancient polity as enunciated by Kautilya or Chanakya. His famous work *Ka Bhagavad Gita* (trans. into Khasi in 1903) - a *Magnum Opus* — proved to be a treasure — house of spiritual values, knowledge and wisdom. This work was his greatest contribution to the enrichment of the Khasi literature. He earnestly appealed to all the youths and elders in the first decade of the last century to learn the teachings of the *Gitā.* He was profoundly influenced by the ideals of Rāma, Krisna, Arjuna and Buddha and the teachings of the *Mahābhārata* and Vedas. The teachings of the *Gitā* exercised tremendous and persuasive influence on the minds, thoughts, views and actions of the people. Consequently, they started discarding the importance of Biblical doctrines. He was very much rational in his general outlook. He laid great stress on the truth and purity of the religion. He really made an earnest attempt to modify and simplify the religious practices of the Khasis by proving himself a harbinger of new age.[19]

From some valuable indigenous sources[20] it transpires that he was greatly influenced by the characters of Rama and Buddha. He was also deeply moved by the instructive stories narrated in the *Ādi Parva* of *Mahābhārata* and the

Yajurveda. The critical and comparative analysis of Hinduism, Christianity and Islam in *Satyārtha Prakāsh* written by Swami Dayananda Sarasvati greatly impressed him. He was also the vice-president of the Shillong branch of Brahmo Samaj for sometime.

On the occasion of the 39th anniversary celebration (23rd Nov. 1938) of the Seng Khasi held at Mawkhar (Shillong) he said "Khasis are free people. They need no religious despatches from foreign lands. Fundamental conceptions of their religion is to know God and know man... If there was no Seng Khasi the name Khasi would have been extinct or gone to dogs. It is because there is the Seng Khasi that all know that there are Khasis in the Khasi Hills and desire to study our culture and know our ideas and opinion regarding various social and political mattes... don't be swayed by the tide of foreign religions and beliefs..."[21]

The letter written by Rev. Robert Evan's to him in 1915 clearly illustrates his attitude towards Christianity, "You have for years shown great enmity towards Christianity and Christians but of late you have actually won the notoriety of being the archenemy of this country". His reply was, "as a friend I advise you to fear God, the creator and the Lord. Love him and follow the truth..."[22] It is very interesting to note that he filed a case against Christian Mission on 5th Octob. 1925 for disparaging remarks against the Khasi religion. A. Cosgrave (the then D.C.) in his letter dated, 9th Nov. 1925 wrote to him that now I decline to interfere with what people used to preach about their traditional religion and culture.[23] The speech delivered by Miss Margaret Bar on 20.4.1952 at the time of paying tribute to Sib Charan Roy is worth-quoting here: "a landmark in the history of the Khasi people has been removed with the passing of Sib Charan Roy of Shillong, whose work for the Khasis should be far more widely known than it is. Following the example of his illustrious father Jeebon Roy, who translated the *Hitopadesa* and published books on Buddha, Chaitanya and the *Rāmāyana* as well as several on Khasi religion, and whose little book *Shaphang U Wei U Blei* (concerning one God) is a jewel of monotheistic theology; Sib Charan Roy also wrote several similar books and as his master piece has left to his people a Khasi version of the *Bhagavad Gitā...* It is not likely that Sib Charan would have devoted time and labour to the translating of it unless his own religion had been in harmony with its message, and he had wanted his fellow Khasis to attain the same liberation from fear whether of Khasi demons or Christian hell... No Khasi home whatever its religious affiliation should be without it *(Gita);* and they should be proud to know that a great treasure-house of spiritual wisdom is accessible to them in their mother tongue... there are great spiritual riches enshrined in other books besides the *Bible.* When that time comes Jeebon Roy and Sib Charan Roy will be given their rightful place in the annals and the loving memory of the Khasi people."[24]

Rash Mohan Roy (1872-1962) as one of the mighty pillars of the Send Khasi organization played a vital role in the reform movement of the Khasis. His coming gave a fillip to this movement and the socio-cultural renaissance of the Khasis. As the education imparted by the Christian Missionaries was opposed to the fundamental ideas and primary objectives of the Seng Khasi organization, he started Seng Khasi Free Morning School on 20th Jymmang (May) 1921 to impart such non-sectarian education which might help the people in protecting the indigenous religious and cultural system. The British Govt. started making every possible attempts from 1924 to stop the grants-in-aid to this school in order to stem the tide of the progress of this movement. In 1925, Rash Mohan Roy issued an appeal for some donations for the smooth functioning of this school and furtherance of his objective. Lala Laj Pat Roy was the first man to respond to this appeal. Due to his initiative the British Govt. extended the grant of Rs. 50 to this school. Bharatiya Adimjati Sevak Sangh also agreed to give a monthly grant of Rs. 5 to this school as a token of solidarity.

This grant was given for several years before 1949.[25] In 1940, Rash Mohan Roy issued a circular in which he openly accused the Govt. for refusing to give grants-in-aid to the school and not allowing to include non-Christian religious books in the curriculum. A copy of this circular reached Mahatma Gandhi also. The extracts published in his *Harijan* issue of 9th March 1940 are exactly reproduced below. "The British Govt. gave education grants to the Christian Missionaries for spreading education among the people of the Khasi and Jaintia Hills District. The Missionaries printed Text-books for school according to their likings and choice, *viz.,* History of Jesus, Abraham, Isaac, Jacob and so on and so forth. They translated the *Bible* into Khasi language and made it a text book for schools... Fortunately for the Khasis, some pure Khasi gentlemen of hallowed memory took the initiative of providing national education for the Khasi children and started the Seng Khasi Free Morning School as early as 1921 with a view to preserving Khasi National culture. They wrote books containing the ideas of ancient Khasi culture and religion. Ever since its starting the school has been doing its humble service in the line of education. The books written by the late Babu Jeebon Roy, late Radhon Singh Berry and U Sib Charan Roy are being taught in the Seng Khasi school. It is matter of great regret that the Deputy Inspector of School compels this school to teach Missionary books and frustrates the very object with which it was established." Gandhiji commented, "I advertise the circular not for the sake of emphasizing my argument. I do so in order to ventilate the grievance of the Secretary of the school. Surely he has every right to object to teaching proselytizing literature prepared by the Missionaries..."[26] As a result of this attempt the Govt. sanctioned a monthly recurring grant of Rs. 20 to this school. His book *U Khasi Hyndai* (The Khasi in the past) extensively dealing with important aspects of the traditional religion, culture, polity, usages and customs of the Khasis contributed a great deal to the socio-cultural awakening of the Khasis.

While paying tribute to Babu Jeebon Roy of hallowed memory and the founder of the Seng Khasi, Rash Mohan Roy remarked, "The Seng Khasi is the congress of all the Khasis, who preserve the *Khein Kur Khein Kha* (blood relation from the maternal line) which is standing from the beginning of creation. The Khasis are free people, free from all sorts of prejudices and absurdities—caste system, untouchability, purdah and so on... There is no poverty of religion among the Khasis and they do not stand in need of embracing religions dispatched from foreign lands and become blind believers of those creeds and dogmas. It is the Seng Khasi and the Seng Khasi along".[27] He passed away in 1962.

Chandra Nath Roy (1873-1959), the second youngest son of Jeebon Roy, and the founder Secretary of the Seng Khasi, was also one of the pillars of this movement. His great contribution was towards the literary and educational development of the Khasi people. For some time he was in-charge of the Ri-Khasi press established in 1896 and encouraged the reading of the books on traditional culture. For acceptance of the Khasi as one of the second languages by the Calcutta University in 1908 the credit goes to him. Thus the Khasi language was brought to prominence. His only literary contributions are the two books, *Grammer ban hikai ktien phareng* and *Jingmlien ha ka kam.* In 1907, he along with Dohory Ropmay and others set up *Synjuk Khasi-Synteng (Khasi-Synteng united Guild)* a—precursor of the Khasi National Durbar which was founded in 1923.

Babu Radhon Singh Berry (1854-1904), a great poet, philosopher and original thinker, by writing a book *Ka Jingsneng Tymmen* on moral code, and composing songs for Brahmosamaj, Seng Khasi and Unitarians played a very important part in this renaissance. Though in search of truth he became Christian, but again reverted to the old faith or the Khasi religion. His book *Ka Niam Wei Blei* proved to be the original scripture of the Khasi Unitarians. He was a close associate of Nilmani Cakravarty of the Brahmo Samaj, and helped the latter in preaching the doctrine of the Brahmos in the Khasi Hills. He never associated himself with the Seng Khasi so actively but accepted the Khasi Unitarian as Khasi religion and strove hard to retain some of the old Khasi religious rites, rituals and customs.

Another social and religious reformer was U Rabon Singh (–1910), the first cousin of Radhon Singh Berry. He also played some considerable role in this movement. Inspite of being a Christian, he never blindly followed any dogmas, creeds or the Christian faiths. Nor did he accept the various restrictions or prohibitions on the cultural activities of the fellow Khasis by the foreign Missionaries. He always raised the voice in support of the preservation of rich cultural heritage of the Khasis. In his three valuable books, *Ka Niam Khein Ki Khasi, Ka Kitab Jingphawar* and *Ka Kitab Jingiathuh-Khana Puriskam* the threw a good deal of light on old religious beliefs, usages and practices which contributed a lot in arousing the consciousness among the Khasi-Pnar towards the preservation of their old culture. In all his works, he stressed the need of maintaining the traditional socio-religious system comprising ceremonies, customary laws, rituals, code of ethics, sacrifice, ordeals, divinations, etc.[28] His all works became valuable source of inspirations for the future generation.

Some other Khasi intellectuals (protagonists of this movement), notably, H.R. Diengdoh, Dr. H. Lyngdoh, Hari Charan Roy and many others carried on the task of reviving the traditional Khasi culture with considerable degree of dexterity and success.

H.R. Diengdoh played unforgettable role in this revitalization movement. He contributed innumerable articles which primarily aimed at preserving the originality of the Khasi language and proving the great similarity between it and Sanskrit.[29] Dr. Lyngdoh's classical works known as *Ka Pomblang bad Thang Siem* (1928) and *Ka Niam Khasi* laid emphasis on the preservation of the traditional religion, festivals and other ethical and moral values. Haricharan Roy's *Ka Savitri* also went a long way in creating the strong feeling of urgency in the minds of the people for maintaining their old religious faiths.

It may be specifically mentioned that Mass-Media played a vital role in providing a momentum to this movement in the Khasi-Jaintia Hills. When the Welsh Mission circulated the first paper *U Nong Kit Khubor* in 1894 for the purpose of spreading the Christianity, H.R. Diengdoh started a monthly paper popularly known as *U Khasi Mynta* (The Khasi Today) in 1895-96 to counter the propagandist activities of the Christian Missionaries. He was himself the editor of this paper. He always inspired the people through his writings to preserve the traditional Khasi culture by checking the proselytizing activities of the missionaries. The Ri-Khasi printing press set up in 1896 by Babu Jeebon Roy enabled all the protagonists of this movement to disseminate their views through the Mass-Media, This was the first printing press in the Khasi-Jaintia Hills. This press played a notable role in the revivalist movement of the period concerned. Many important works particularly againt the onslaught of western influences were published. Besides *U Khasi Mynta,* two other important papers *U Nongphira* and *U Nongpynim* edited by Babu Sib Charan Roy as stated earlier helped a lot in keeping the light of traditional culture aglow. All these three papers strongly championed the cause of the preservation and revitalization of the traditional Khasi culture.

With the establishment of the Khasi cultural society in 1936-37, this movement started gathering momentum. This society was founded primarily for arousing the consciousness among the people for reviving their traditional culture as well as for extending respect to the culture of others. In 1937 another journal named *Ka Syngkhong Jingtip* was started at the behest of this cultural society by a number of talented and creative geniuses for the preservation and consolidation of the traditional Khasi culture and heritage. When Swami Satyananda, President of the Hindu Mission, said about the envelopment of the Khasis by Christian culture and English

Education and the formatin of a little England in the lap of Shillong, T Cajee observed that "the existence of this society is the best proof that conversion to Chritistianity has nothing to do with our culture and nationality."[30] Mr. C. Lyngdoh, associated with this society, opined that "we must confess to our shame thzt inspite of the proud position which we hold as the most enlightened and most forward of all the Hill-tribes of India, we have not seriously attempted to present to the world the culture or the beauty of our political and social institutions which our forefathers have left to us as a glorious hertiage. We may have embraced other religions but true Khasi religion has more to do with the practical aspect of human relationship than with any thing else...Changes, political, social and otherwise are pouring in form all sides and before long we shall lose our individuality as a race unless we preserve our culture, It is, therefore, high time that members of a society like ours should put their heads together and rescue our country's name from oblivion and forgetfulness."[31]

It is worthy of remark that in the Khasi-Jaintia Hills various distinguished and talented scholars of perfect excellence through their writings not only postulated the basic doctrines of religion or preached and popularized the old religious beliefs and customs but also laid great stress fundamentally on continuance of their traditional dances, songs, colourful festivals, etc. without being swayed by alien influences and other external interventions. The Khasi literature was reckneod as valuable treasure house of the teachings of their ancestors and old ethical and spirtitual values. Their romantic secular literature constituted a cultural milieu in their history.

In 1887, U.H. Kissor Singh raised his voice against the "Calvinistic Methodist — faith" propagated by western Missionaries who proclaimed the Trinitarian character of the God. According to one reliable evidence,[32] Kissor Singh declared the Unitarian character of the God.

In 1926, one of the Khasi leaders observed the traditional system of cremating the ruler or prince at Cherrapunji simply to demonstrate before the people as an antithesis of the new western system of burial.

Thus, we find that all these attempts no doubt proved to be a moving force in reviving the old glorious culture and saving the race from cultural extinction. Actually all efforts aimed at keeping the cultural heritage of the Khasis intact and protecting it from the forces of proselytism during the imperialistic regime of the British.

It is worthwhile to mention here that U Lad Singh (1878-1955), and his sister Ka Tewmala (1876-1951), Ka Sikijer (1889-1973), Ka Thaen (1890-), U Maj Bud Singh (1893-1942), a Sirdar or village chief of Sohbar, U Willison Roy (1898-1962) and U Kerison Roy (1896-) - all these prominent figures in the East Khasi Hills - advocated the Secular education imparted in New India School founded in Sohbar in April, 1928 by T.K. Purkayastha and managed by Ramkrishna Mission Ashram. They strongly protested against the establishment of Christian school in their areas, opposed all the attempts of the British Govt. to close down this school and time to time organized the villagers to raise the voice against the British policy of encroachment on their traditional rights. They were the great patrons of this Ashram. They believed in the harmony of all religions. They were profoundly influenced by the philosophy of Swami Ramakrishna Paramhansa and Swami Vivekananda. They always aroused the consciousness among their countrymen for making them feel proud of their culture, heritage and national feelings. Miss Margaret Barr of the Unitarian church (1936-1973) also opposed the imperialistic and colonial policy of the British Govt. And supported the growth of secular education imparted in the said Ashram. This school is still popular among the tribal people of that area. Moreover, the tribal people of Shella, Nongwar, Umwai, Nongsken, Jowai, Nongtalang and other adjacent area helped by all means in the growth of the schools managed by the Ramkrishna Mission Ashram. The people of all these areas went against the British attempts to open their institutions and always fought for the secular education.[33]

It is because of the renaissance and reformation movement of the 19th and 20th Centuries that the traditional religion, culture, dance, songs, customs, beliefs, etc. are still very much alive among some sections of the Khasi-Jaintia people. The Seng Khasi organisation right from its birth (23rd Nov. 1899) up to the present time has been playing very praiseworthy role in preserving the indigenous religion, culture, customs etc. by organizing different programmes and conducting some other intellectual activities. Sri Jairam Das Daulatram and Sri Nagesh (both the then Governors of Assam) while visiting the Seng Khasi School on 18th Oct. 1955 and 21st May 1962 respectively highly praised the cultural activities of this organization. Prime Minister, Smt. Indira Gandhi, while visiting this institution on 18th Oct. 1956 said "It is good to love our ancient traditions and customs and we can grow better when we do not forget them. We have, of course, to study and learn the progress of other countries and adopt the good that is in them, but we should not forget our past heritage.[34]

The most balanced views as put forward by B.C. Allen, E.A. Gait and others are also worthy of our attention. To quote them "The people have shown themselves extremely receptive of Christianity, but have little taste for Hinduism. One of their chief characteristics is a dislike of all restraint including the restraint of tradition, which is of such binding force among most of the inhabitants of the East. There are few people less conservative than the Khasis and they are ever ready to take up a novelty. To this healthy spirit of enterprise is due the marked progress they have made in the development of material comfort and the extent to which they have outstripped the other tribes on the North-East frontier in their progress towards civilization."[35]

In the Jaintia Hills also, a remarkable progress was made in the field of preserving the traditional culture. In the whole of north-east India, amongst the tribal people the Jaintia consciousness in maintaining their Hindu-oriented traditional culture in all fields, despite the British attempt to encroach upon their religion, is a living example of their affection for their glorious past and heritage. It is a well authenticated fact. According to R.M. Nath, many educated Brahmins from Sylhet and other places were encouraged to settle in the Jaintia Hills and to propagate education and religious teachings. "Burra Gossain and his queen Kasamati were initiated into the Tantric cult by Harekrishna Upadhaya... They became mendicants in the Kali temple at Jaintia (Jaintiapur) under the theological guidance of the priest Lilapuri."[36] Ram Singh II (1790-1832), the ruler of Jaintia, preached the cult of Saivism in the Jaintia Hills which had tremendous impact on the tribal people. History records that the tenets of Hinduism due to influences of Brahmins and local conditions attracted thousands of people within its fold. Later on, the Brahmanical influence spread far and wide. Tradition also confirms the truth stated above.

From the middle of the 19th century the missionaries stated interfering too much with the old religious customs of the Jaintias. Their forcible conversion also began. They were not allowed to worship their gods and goddesses in their own traditional ways. When everything went beyond the limit, U Kiang Nongbah started a political-cum-religious movement against the Briths Raj in 1862 in order to maintain the political and cultural identity of the people. He was hanged at Jowai by the British. In the early part of the 19th century, Saivism, Skatism and Tantricism also thrived well in the Jaintia Hills because of the brahmanical influence on the Jaintia tribe. A socio-religious organization known as *SEINRAJ* was also founded in 1935 in Jaintia Hills with the prime objective of preserving, promoting and practising the old Jaintia religious rites, customs and festivals.

In 1891, a group of Khasis living in the areas bordering on the plains of Sylhet adopted a Vaishnava form of Hinduism after coming under the influence of a preacher of their own race.

The Bengal Renaissance of 19th century greatly inspired the Khasi, Jaintia, Garo and other tribes of north-east India and left its indelible imprint on them. Branches of the Brahmo Samaj, Arya Samaj, Hindu Mission and Ramakrishna Mission were also established in different parts of the Khasi-Jaintia Hills.

Brahmoism or the Brahmo movement based on natural or universal theism became very popular in the Khasi-Jaintia Hills. Both E. Gait and Shivanath Sastri have reveald this truth that a small Brahmo Mission known as Sadharan Brahmo Samaj set up in May 1878 was working among the Khasis and the Jaintias and later it drew within its fold many other hill people too. The first letter dated, Laban, Shillong, October 8, 1930 written by Mazumdar Sastri to Kshitindranath and the other letter written by Prasanna Kumar to Kshitindranath on August 22, 1931 (both mentioned in *Tattva-bodhini Patrika, Journal of the Adi Brahmo Samaj}* bear glowing testimony to the fact that a big group of the Khasi formed under the inspiring leadership of Babu Sib Charan Roy (Vice President of the Shillong local Committee of the Brahmo Samaj) made all possible attempts to stem the tide of the progress of Christianity and to preserve their own tribal religion and traditional system. They were not at all influenced by the Christianity, rather they were monotheistic and non-idolatrous. They did not like to follow casteism. Sib Charan Roy belonging to the Khasi community played a leading role in the revivalist movement of the Khasis and Jaintias. Sadharan Brahmo Samaj was mainly doing its work in southern Khasi Hills, particularly in Sheila and Cherrapunji areas, while the Adi-Brahmo Samaj was active in and around Shillong. Babu Jeebon Roy, Sib Charan Roy, Chandranath

Roy, H. Kissor Singh and many other illustrious Khasis became close associates of Babu Nilamani Chakravarty, the founder of the *Khasis Brahmo Mission,* and took a leading part in the revivalist movement of the Khasis and Jaintias. For the first time a big compilation of Brahmo hymns in Khasi dialect was published. A good number of Brahmo Temples, Schools and Ashrams were founded at Shillong, Cherrapunji, Mawlong, Laitkynsew, Nongiri, Nongwar and Shella. The simple code of the Brahmo Samaj highly impressed the Khasis and Jaintias concerned.

The "Brahmoism was a compromise between the ethical or social teachings of western Christianity and traditional values of Hinduism... The two socio-religious factors, *viz.* Monotheism and castelessness brought the Brahmos and the Khasis closer together and provided Brahmoism and easy way of infiltration among the latter." The spread of Brahmoism among the Khasis in particular has its own historical importance.

Babu Jeebon Roy, a pioneer of the Khasi literature and a noted Brahmo, came under the influence of Mr. Nilmani Chakravarty (born in 1859 near Diamong Harbour, South of Calcutta) who was sent to Shillong on a pious mission to preach Brahmo philosophy, thoughts and ideas. He for the first time published a "big compilation of Braho hymns in Khasi." Babu Jeebon Roy extended his full support to him for accomplishing his task. All these facts have become a forgotten and neglected chapter of history.

Assam Census Reports of 1881, 1891, 1901, 1911 and 1921 are authentic sources to prove that in Khasi-Kaintia Hills there were quite a good number of followers or adherents of the new faith. The available Census figures show the prominence of Brahmoism among the Khasis and Jaintias. In 1881, 15 out of 177, in 1891, 95 out of 239, in 1901, 83 out of 360, and in 1911, 252 out of 428 Brahmos in Assam were living in the said hills. Brahmoism, however, seems to have made very little progress in the adjoining

Garo Hills. Only 1891 Census Report records the presence of 5 Brahmos in the Garo Hills. In his Report of 1911, J. Mcswiney observed that the Brahmos were "strongest in the Khasi and Jaintia Hills. "In 1921, total 559 Brahmos were living in Assam. In his Report of 1921, G.T. Lloyd records that nearly half of the Brahmos in Assam were residing at Shillong.[37] In his Census Report of 1891, Edward Gait opines that "Brahmoism is a modified form of Hinduism... There is, however, a small mission at work amongst the Khasis which is said to be meeting with fair success. Some tribes on the frontier were under the influence of Hinduism". From the letter written by Prasanna Kumar to Kshitindranath, dated Bejura, Aug. 22, 1931, it appears that along with the Khasis and Jaintias many other tribes, namely, the Garo, the Naga, the Kuki and the Lushai were also proselytized and admitted to the *Adi Brahmo Samaj.* This bears glowing testimony to the fact that apart from the Khasis and Jaintias many other tribes were also brought within the fold of Brahmoism.

The Ārya Samāj founded by Swami Dayanand Sarasvati also made its appearance in the Khasi Hills. That Samaj was at work in the beginning of the last century. It popularized the ideals and teachings of Dayanand Sarasvati by conducting regular meetings and discourses. But it did not make much impact on the Khasi-Jaintias. At Barabazar in Shillong, the Arya Samaj Mandir still stands. In the twenties of the last century, Lala B.K. Dey and some other intellectuals of Shillong started the Hindu Sammelan. Babu Chandra Kant Roy, a noted nationalist and enlightened Khasi, was actively associated with this Samelan. Pt. L.N. Shastri, a Hindu Mahasabha leader, was also one of the patrons of this Sammelan. Dr. Shyama Prasad Mukherjee, while visiting Shillong at that time, highly praised this movement. Many Khasis were attached to this movement. Besides, the Hindu Mission of Calcutta also started its branch at Shillong which later on merged with the Hindu Sammelan. The Hindu Mission functioned as a popular organisation in Shillong. Swami Vivekananda and Subhas

Chandra Bose, while paying visits to Shillong in 1901 and 1938-39 respectively, greatly inspired the Khasis and Jaintias to pursue their movements for rediscovery of their roots.

Among all the Hindu Missions, the Ramakrishna Mission achieved far greater popularity among the Khasis and Jaintias. It is really very interesting to note that when Swami Prabhananda popularly known as Ketaki Maharaj was undergoing training at the Mission branch of Dhaka and planning to co-operate with Gandhiji in the Non-cooperation Movement against the British Raj in 1920-21, some leading Khasi gentlemen invited him to establish the Ramakrishna Mission in the tribal areas and to work among them by starting schools in the hills "to which they could send their children without any danger of being exposed to the propaganda of any sectarian religion as it happened in existing schools in their hills". The Khasis gave much preference to Ramakrishna Mission over the Christian Missions which were already entrenched there, for the obvious reason that as a result of the work of the Christian Mission many of their children were converted to Christianity and a large number of them though nominally loyal to their own religious traditions were getting influenced by Christian dogmas.

We learn from *Golden Jubilee Souvenir* (1924-74, Ramakrishna Mission Ashrama, Sheila, pub. By Ramakrishna Mission, Cherrapunji, 1974, pp. 2-12) that in order to fulfill the cherished aspirations of the Khasis and to save their race from Christian influence, Ketaki Maharaj reached Sheila (Southern Khasi Hills) in 1924 from Dhaka. His purpose was to spread the light of national and liberal education by upholding the cause for saving their culture from the foreign cultural conquest. The Wahdadars of Sheila, Gauri Charan Roy, Jogidhan, Joydhan and many leading Khasis like Satyendra Roy, Chaitanya Roy and others extended all support to him. Many Hinduised tribes, who had earlier come under the influence of Vaishnava preachers from Bengal, rallied round under his banner for starting Ramakrishna Mission Schools. "He let every body know that he had come there without any ulterior motive, without even the motive of trying to Hinduise them, though it was true that if anybody having already been under Hindu influence wanted to study Hinduism further, he was ready to help him. It pained him to see that conversions often took place because the people were poor and ignorant. It pained him more when he saw that those who embraced Christianity became thoroughly denationalized". Soon the word spread to other villages that a strange young man had arrived at Sheila who was running schools without any attempt to convert the pupils to any particular religious beliefs and he was anxious like the Khasis themselves that they should preserve their ancient religion, culture and traditions. Ketaki Maharaj recalling the prophetic message of Swami Vivekananda made them understand their real condition. He opened Schools and Ashramas at Shella between 1924 and 1925, in Nongwar in 1928 and in Cherrapunji and Shillong between 1933 and 1936. He wrote books like *Ka Rukom Durga Puja, U Siva Ka Durga, Ka Sarasvati* and *Ka Jingrawai India* and composed songs on Ramakrishna, Mata Sarada Devi and Vivekananda which profoundly influenced the Khasis. He popularised Durga and Kali puja. He also used to send Khasi boys and girls to Calcutta, Dhaka and Belur Math to receive education and Diksha. He passed away in 1938.

A good number of Khasi men and women in the East Khasi Hills also extended their support to T.K. Purkayastha in starting New India Schools and Ramakrishna Ashram at Sohbar near Cherra in 1928 for receiving secular and liberal education. The Schools and Ashrams managed by Ramakrishna Mission helped the Khasis maintain their traditional culture. The Khasis strongly protested against the establishment of Christian Missions in their areas, opposed all the attempts of the British government to close down the new school and from time to time organized the villagers to raise their voice against the British policy of encroachment on their traditional rights. They were great patrons of the Ashram. They believed in the harmony of all religions and were profoundly influenced by the philosophy of Ramakrishna Paramhansa and Vivekananda. Miss Margaret Barr of the Unitarian Church (1936-73) also supported the growth of secular education imparted in the Ramakrishna Mission schools and opposed the proselytizing activities of the Christian Missionaries in all these areas. Thus, with the help of the Ramakrishna Mission a section of the Khasis were able to save their religious faith from the onslaughts of foreign missionaries.

The revitalization movement has been described by A. Wallace as "deliberate organized conscious effort by members of a society to construct a more satisfying culture."[38] According to Mathur, this movement among the Khasi appears to be a 'Nativistic Movement in a narrow sense."[39]

Jadonang (1905-31), a young Kabui Naga leader popularly known as "Messiah" and a great social, political and religious reformer, started a movement in 1920's in the western Hills of Manipur. His movement aimed at introducing reforms in political, social and religious fields. He embarked upon a career of Mystic leader and introduced excellent reforms in the social life, and religious worship and the practices of the Zeliangrong people. He was an apostle of socio-religious and cultural awakening in his community. According to G. Kabui "In the beginning of 20th century the social condition and religious life of the Nagas was at its lowest ebb. The detestful treatment of the Hindu neighbours towards the backward Hill Men on the one hand and the advance of proselytizing Christianity on the other hand brought the darkest hour for the zeliangrong to defend and preserve their traditional and religious beliefs... their zeliangrong religion had been submerged in superstitious custom and useless taboos. Jadonang's political aim was to establish "Naga's Raj" by expelling the foreign rulers, social aim was the integration of the three tribes, the Zemeis,

Langmeis and Rongmeis by putting an end to inter village feuds and ill-feeling and religious aim was to abolish many unnecessary taboos of birth and death"[40] Because of his painstaking efforts, foresight, wisdom and prudence all the said three tribes got combined under the banner of zeliangrong. In religious field also he was crowned with glorious and astounding success. He simplified the ceremonial parapharnalias. His greatest achievement was the introduction of some innovations in the traditional religion by encouraging construction of temples which was never in existence before. The proselytizing activities of the Christian Missionaries since 1914 had thrown a challenge to the very foundation of the traditional and religious beliefs of his people. In order to defend and preserve the traditional religion and culture, he abolished many unnecessary and irrational taboos and superstitions, simplified the worship of God, encouraged the construction of temples for giving religious sermons, composed many religious hymns and other devotional songs and integrated the three tribes, the Zemeis, Langmeis and Rongmeis under the banner of Zeliangrong. In the western part of Manipur, the people felt the impulse of his movement. Sir Robert Reid states that in the hill portion of the Manipur state there broke out "Semi religious movement" which was launched out by Jadonang - a Kabui Naga. After he was arrested and hanged the flame of his movement spread to neighbouring districts.[41] The same author in another source says that Jadonang from his bamboo platform erected in his temple used to preach before the elders and followers about animistic religion which was based on their ageold beliefs. He encouraged the construction of temple for Gods. People worshipped him like the God. But the British instigated the villagers to demolish his temple as it was against the tribal practices. Inspite of this, his revival movement made a satisfactory headway to the best of his satisfaction.[42] Unfortunately, his movement was misrepresented as anti-Christian. While condemning it, Prof. Down, a church historian, stated that "The cult was an organized anti-Christian movement with no parallel elsewhere in North East India."[43] But this criticism seems to be baseless and unfounded as Jadonang's cult was revival of the traditional religion. The reformed religion of Jadonang came to be known as the *Haraka* (Pure) religion. According to Ursula Graham Bower, Jadonang enunciated a religion which was splendid blending of Hinduism and Cristianity.[44] But this view is hardly tenable. It can be fairly disputed. J. Johnstone has revealed the historical truth that "towards the middle of the 19th century a great Hindu revivalist movement of far-reaching importance broke out in the North-East of India, particularly Manipur and Naga Hills. Coversion to Hinduism on the Eastern frontier from Sadiya down to Chittagong was taking place. Hill tribes were admitted as Hindus by the Rajas after receiving the sacred thread of twice born castes called "Khetree".[45] Jadonang has appeared in the *Dictionary of National Biography as "Messiah"*.

According to N.C. Zeliang, after Jadonang was hanged by the British on 29th Aug. 1931 at Imphal, Rani Gaidinliu, his follower and disciple, undertook the responsibility of continuing the movement which was aiming at both political emancipation as well as socio-religious transformation. After Jadonang she became the torch-bearer of the movement. As a reformer she looked down upon the alien religion and made sincere effort to preserve the traditional Naga religion, culture, customs and usages of the Zeliangrong people. Her followers believed in one supreme God, prayers and sacrifice at the altar of God. Her movement was not a complete departure from the past but a reformed cult of the original religious and cultural traditions. The *Haraka* Bhakti movement was organized by her to save her community from the foreign influence and Christian dogmas. She raised her voice against western culture. In the western part of Manipur, the people felt the impulse of her movement. She kept this movement somehow alive between 1931 and 1932.[46] Pandit Jawaharlal Nehru, while visiting Assam in

1937, highly praised the activities of Rani Gaidinlieu. To quote him "...India does not even know of this brave child of her hills with the free spirit of the mountain in her. But her own people remember their Gaidinlieu Rani and think of her with love and pride. And a day will come when India also will remember her and cherish her and bring her out of her prison cell."[47]

Apart from social, political and religious reforms carried out by some prominent reformers, we have also got evidence of cultural and some other reforms in the hill-areas of north-east India. According to one dependable source,[48] in Manipur the various cultural organizations of the Thados, the Paites, the Hmars and other tribes played a vital role in the cultural development of the people. They published text-books and Gospel literature in their respective languages and promoted solidarity of their ethnic groups. Behind their cultural and social interest, the Prime-motive was to establish cultural superiority over the alien elements.

According to J.D. Baveja, in 1904 the revivalist movement percolated to Mizo Hills via Khasi and Jaintia Hills. The Mizos also started the movement for preserving their traditional folksongs, dances and hymns. They spared no pains to enliven the spirit of ecstasy and spiritualism. As a result of the subsequent revival movements of 1906 of ethical nature, 1913 of theological nature, 1919 which was an ecstatic movement and 1935 which was based on "spiritual gifts and mystical experience," significant changes occurred in northern, southern and eastern parts of the Mizo Hills.[49] "The movement ultimately developed into varied forms of mere striking charismatic gifts, trances and visions; prophetic utterances, speaking in unknown tongues and symbolic actions are some of the salient features." It also caused great dissensions in the Church and resulted in the birth of several deviationist bodies like Tlira Pawl, Khuangtuaha Pawl, Pa Pawl, etc.[50] The revival movement deviationist in nature started in 1935. It had a tremendous impact. Indigenous tribal songs, dances and prevalence of the practice of taking Zu (Rice beer) proved to be a counter movement against the growth of Christianity. Sir Robert Reid has correctly observed that "The Lushais are religiously emotional" Anything like "revivalism appears to them."[51] The movement of 1937 was also very effective. They used to love their traditional ways of living, religious practices and beliefs.

In Hill-Tipperah, some rulers of Royal family belonging to Tripuri tribe (Bodo-group having the admixture of Aryan and non-Aryan blood) are also stated to have evinced their interests in bringing about some remarkable changes in socio-religious fields. The period of Birchandra Manikya (1862-1896) marked the turning point in the history of revivalist movement. His reign synchronized with the 19th century Renaissance of Bengal. The ideology and philosophy of Raja Ram Mohan Roy left an indelible impression on his mind. He is credited with having abolished the institution of slavery and practice of Sati by a royal decree.[52] It is also supported by documentary evidence.[53] He also encouraged the remarriage of the widows.

According to some authentic sources,[54] during the reign of Birchandra Manikya a remarkable progress was made in the fields of astronomy and other branches of science, art of photography, oil painting and language and literature. After 1871 he introduced several reforms in different fields. According to documentary evidence,[55] great advancement in the field of education was witnessed. People were encouraged to take interest in education of the pattern followed in old institution known as Persian Maktab, Sanskrit Tole and Anglo-vernacular school at Agartala. The women education also received great impetus at his hand which was a kind of novelty. On the authority of other reliable source[56] we can point out that he was himself a great patron of art, music and literature. He himself composed several poems based on Vaishnava Padavali. His court was adorned by a number of gifted personalities.

The reign of Radhakishor Manikya (1896-1909) is also characterized by the spectacular progress in the field of literature, education, art and architecture. He built palaces, commodious buildings, Victoria memorial Hospital, Temple of Jaggannatha established museum, technical school, an art college, a n.umber of primary and secondary schools and reconstructed the Jail on more suitable site. He also helped the scientists and scholars and showed great favour to the ennobling course of education in general way.[57]

According to Roy Burman, in 1930's sincere attempts were made by the members of Noatia tribe to reorientate the tribal theology. A few converted Riangs abstained from any kind of sacrifice. A process of Syncretism ensued by which Hindu deities, Shiva Vishnu and Krishna were identified with their deities. No wonder, it also demonstrated that the tribes known as aborigines addicted to human sacrifice throughout Bengal had substituted a debased Hindu idolatry for the purer paganism of their ancestors.[58]

In Nagaland, the period 1866-1869 witnessed the dawn of socio-political and religious awakening especially among the Angami tribe. They raised the voice against their age-old practice of head-hunting. In 1866, as a result of the abolition of headhunting practice in the Naga Hills District boundaries which quickly disappeared, inter-village feuds came to an end and a new era of peaceful cultivation and trade began.[59] An ethnic association known as Ao (a Naga tribe) youth organization set up in 1918 introduced some useful reforms in various fields. This organization is credited with having established closer contacts between the villages and the younger generation. This organization also stimulated interest among the younger generation in conformity with the ideals which has got social and religious recognition. As a result of the partial abolition of the evil practice, head hunting, the people got considerable amount of freedom in daily life.[60]

There are some positive evidence to prove that the Kacharis, the Mikirs and other cognate tribes came under the proselytizing works of the Hindu priest.[61] According to L.W. Shakespear, Sambhudan, a great social, political and religious reformer of North Cachar Hills, started a movement in 1882 with the support of a good number of tribal followers for the preservation of their traditional religion and culture. He fought for political as well as religious unity. He kindled the spark of patriotism in the hearts of his followers.[62]

Roy Burman observes that the "Taimongal Association" founded in the united Mikir and north Cachar Hills by some of the ethnic minorities started a movement for religious reforms. They raised the voice for their solidarity with the Khampti and Singpho tribes of NEFA (present Arunachal), "Among the promoters of this movement a growing interest in Hinayana Buddism is also perceptible."[63]

It is also worth-mentioning here that some of the hill-tribes after coming under the influence of Shankaradeva's Bhakti cult of Vaishnavism based on the doctrine of monotheism as a result of the Vaishnavite Renaissance of the 15th and 16th centuries became his disciples and great religious preachers. Even in the 19th and 20th centuries, they practised their new faith quite unaffected by the western influence. Some of them, notably, Narottama of the Nagas, Govinda of the Garos, Balai of the Mikirs, Permananda of the Miris, Ramai of the Kacharis, Damodar of the Bhutias and Aghoria-Chandra of Gam Dafla tribe started preaching religious philosophy of Shankaradeva in every nook and corner of the hills as an ambassador of unity of the hills and plains.[64] Its effect during the later period was clearly discernible. R.M. Nath has also opined that the Kacharis, the Lalungs, the Garos, the Mikirs, the Nagas, the Daflas and other tribes were re-initiated and salvaged into the Hindu fold which was, of course, a great socio-religious change.[65]

In North Eastern Frontier Region (now Arunachal Pradesh), the attempts made by some of the tribes, notably, the Akas, the Miris, the Mishmis, the Noctes and Wanchos for preserving their traditional faiths during the period under discussion are of considerable importance. According to Dalton, the Tagi Raja of the Aka Tribe after becoming somewhat reformed started propagating the worship of Hari amongst the tribal people.[66] The Noctes and the Wanchos are also said to have taken all possible steps during the period concerned for maintaining their cultural identity with special references to their Vaishnava faiths without breaking away from the past. Here it was the force not the personality which was something vital. Though the historical authenticity of this fact can be doubted as it is not corroborated by any other contemporary source, but it can be deduced with great amount of certainty and conviction that it was an era of revivalism for them also. The traditional tribal institutions of this region have throughout played notable role in arousing a feeling in the hearts of their people for preserving, protecting and rejuvenating their traditional culture, religious faiths, beliefs, mythological and philosophical conceptions, the abstract ideas, hymns, prayers, rituals, taboos, customs, usages song and dances, etc. This revivalism became such a living force that it never faded away even in face of the rapid westernization in the last quarter of the 19th century and the first and second quarter of the 20th century. The available details alluding to the attempts made for the abolition of slavery are not satisfactory at all. But we find that in Sadiya region the practice of human sacrifice, which was very much in vogue during the medieval period (13th to 16th centuries) as testified to by many sources,[67] was discontinued.

On the basis of documentary evidence[68] it can be pointed out that the gradual process of conversion of animistic tribes to Hinduism and other faiths had taken place in different hill-regions of north-east India.

From the foregoing treatment of the subject it can be plausibly concluded that several attempts were made by the renaissance supporters and reformers in different parts of northeast India not only for the preservation and protection or revival and revitalization of their traditional region and culture but for the introduction of some reforms in social, religious, cultural, literary and other fields as well. It is true that the 19th century marked the beginning of tribal renaissance but it cannot be denied that in some hill areas the process began much earlier but it gained momentum during the period under notice. The 19th century Renaissance in Bengal and other parts of India and Vaishnava Movement in Assam (15th-16th centuries) profoundly influenced the tribals' socio-cultural renaissance in north-east India. Owing to the absence of any effective organization and systematic efforts in some tribal areas, the path of renaissance was never found smooth. Nor did it prove as a counterpart to and prototype of European Reformation Movement of the 16th century or the 19th century Bengal Renaissance. However, if it is judged in its totality and singularly with certain reservation, it can scarcely be denied that the period concerned witnessed the inauguration of a new era in the cultural history of the tribal people of north-east India.

Notes and References

Here I would like to express my indebtedness to U. Hipshon Roy and U. Kynpham Singh of Shillong for not only giving me the access to some valuable published and unpublished records, books, Journals, reports, letters, etc. but also for taking pains in translating and interpreting some passages form original sources (in Khasi) useful for my purpose and supplying me with some relevant information while I was at Shillong as a lecturer in the Deptt. of History, St . Anthony's college, form Sept. 1973 to July 1984.

1. *The Tribal People of India* (New Delhi, 1973) p. 17; see also *Nehru and the North East (Shillong,* 1989), pp. 1-11.

2. *Khasi Heritage* (ed. U Hipshon Roy, Shillong, 1979), p. 217.
3. Quoted in A.L. Rowse, *The Use of History* (London, 1947) p. 124.
4. Volume of letters issued to the Govt. Aug. 1864-65, Vol. 31; Volume of letters received from the Govt. Vol, 6 "A", Fort William, 6th June 1829; Aitchison, *A Collection of Treaties, Engagements and Sanads* (Calcutta, 1931), Vol. XII, pp. 74-75; BC Alien, *Assam District Gazetteer,* Vol. X. pp. 42-43; R.B. Pemberton, *Report on the Eastern Frontier of British India* (Gauhati, 1966), pp.232ff; William Robinson, *Descriptive Account of Assam* (Delhi 1975) p. 410; E. Gait, *History of Assam* (Calcutta, 1926), p. 302.
5. *Sneng Khasi* (The Journal of the Seng Khasi, its publication first began in 1901 and continued up to 1903. Again it was revived in 1977 by the editor Shree Hipshon Roy when he became Secretary in-charge, Literary Section, Seng Khasi, vide Resolution dated 14.10.1976), 1978, Vol. I, No. 4, pp. 57ff.
6. A letter written by Hormu Rai Diengdoh, dated 24.9.1902 to the Editor of the *Bengalee,* Calcutta, in connection with the publication of a controversial article in this paper as well as *Sylhet Weekly Chronicle,* Ref. to *U Khasi Mynta* (The monthly Newspaper in Khasi edited by himself), Risaw (Octob.) 1902; *Khasi Heritage,* pp. 62-66; for details see *U Khasi Mynta,* N. 65, Kyllalyngkot (January), 1902. pp.7-8; *U Khasi Mynta,* N. 78, laiong (April) 1903, pp. 3-4; *U. Khasi Mynta,* No. 93, Naitung (July) 1904, pp. 3-4; *U Nongphira* (The monthly Journal edited by Sibcharan Roy), No. 44, Nailur (Sept.) 1905, p. 88; *U Khasi Mynta,* No. 82, Nailur (Sept.) 1903, pp. 3-4; *U Nongphira* No. 33, Kyllalyngkot (Jan) 1907, p. 173; *Ka Pateng Khristan,* Vol. IV, No. 8, Aug, 1900, p. 60; *U Khasi Mynta,* No. 42, Kyllalyngkot (Jan) 1900, p. 3; *U Nongialam Khristan,* Vol. I, No. 2, Aug. 1902, p. 19; *U Nongpynim* (The Monthly Journal in Khasi edited by Sib Charan Roy), N. 18. Nailar (Aug.), 1929, pp. 16-17; *U Nongpynim,* N. 18, Nailar (August), 1929, p.6; *U Lurshai,* Vol. V, N. 5, May 1914, p. 3—Ref. to U Kynpham Singh, *Ki For Bad Ki Kam U Rash Mohon Roy* (Shillong 1979), pp. 30ff; *U Nongialam Khristan* (ed. Rev. Dr. J. Roberts and Rev. J.C. Evans),

Shillong, June 1908, Vol. VII, N.6; Sept. 1908, Vol. V, No. 9; Octob. 1908. Vol. VII, No. 10; Nov. 1908, Vol. VII, No. 11; *U Nongialam Khristan* (Ed. Rev. J. Jones & Rev. J.C. Evans), Dec. 1908, Vol. VII, No. 12; Jan. 1909, Vol. IX, No.l; *U Nongialam Khristan* (ed. Rev. E.H. Williams and Rev. R. Jones), Feb. 1909, Vol. IX, N. 2; March 1909, Vol. IX, N. 3; June 1909, Vol, IX, N. 6; July 1909, Vol. IX; July to Dec. 1909. Vol. IX; *Cherra,* 1910, Vol. X, Nos. 1 to 12.

7. W.W. Hunter, *Statistical Account* of Assam (London, 1879), Vol. II, pp. 207-8; R.C. Majumdar, *History and Culture of the Indian People* (Bombay, 1963), Vol. IX, pt. I, Ch. XXXII, p. 1038.

8. *U Khasi Mynta,* Nailur (Sept.) 1899; *U Khasi Mynta,* Jylliew (June), 1903; *U. Khasi Mynta,* N.89, *U Nongphira,* No. 16; *U Khasi Mynta,* Lber , (March) 1904; *U. Khasi Mynta, Risaw* (Octob.) 1902; *U Khasi Mynta,* Nailur (Sept.) 1902; *U. Nongialam Katholik,* Naiwieng (Nov.) 1902; *U Nongialam Khristan,* Aug. 1902; *U. Kahsi Mynta,* laiong (April) 1901; *U Khasi Mynta,* Lber (March) 1903; *Shillong Centenary Celebration Volume,* 1976, pp. 77-78.

9. *Ka Jingialang Kynmaw la U Babu Jeebon Roy,* Ha Ka 29th July 1932 (Shillong, 1933), pp. 7-8.

10. *U Khasi Mynta,* Supplement, Jylliew (June) 1903.

11. *U Khasi Mynta,* Jylliew (June) 1903.

12. *U Khasi Mynta,* Nailur (Sept.) 1896.

13. U Kynpham Singh, *U Jeebon Roy* (1838-1903), Pt. IV, P.32; *U Khasi Mynta,* Nailar (Aug.) 1899; *U Khasi Mynta,* Naitungl 1900; *U Khasi Mynta,* Nainohprah (Dec.) 1, 1900; See also *U Jeebon Roy, Ka Kitab Chaitanya Ne Lord Gauranga Charitara* (Shillong, 1900), pp. 1-6, 7,10, 11-13, 24-43; U Jeebon Roy, *Buddha Devcharitra* (1st Pub. 1901, Shillong, 1931), pp. 1-15, 19-30; U Jeebon Roy, *History of India (* in Khasi) (Shilong, 1900), preface; *Dictionary of National Biography,* Vol. Ill, ed. S.P. Sen (Calcutta, 1974), p. 556.

14. *U Khasi Mynta,* Naiwieng (Nov.) 1902.

15. *U Khasi Mynta,* Supplement, Jylliew (June) 1903.

16. For details see *Ka constitution Jong Ka Seng Khasi,* 23rd Nov. 1899 (1st revised printed copy, Shillong, 1913) Articles I to XIV; Extract form *U Khasi Mynta,* No.43 of March 1900 cf. Seng Khasi Miscellaneous File (Permanent Record, unpublished); Seng Khasi Annual Report, 25th Nov. 1900; Ka Report na ka bynta ka Seng kut Snem-23rd Nov. 1903; R.M Roy, *Ka Jingkrem ha Seng Kut Snem,* 23.11.1907; R.M Roy, *Ka Jingkren ha Seng Shiteng Snem,* 10th June 1911; R.M. Roy, *Ka Jingpyrta ha Seng,* 1912 (Unpublished); Seng Khasi Report 1915-16; RM. Roy, *Ka Jingkren Seng Shiteng Snem-23.5.*1915; Roy, *Seng Kut Snem*-27.11.1912-Ref. to Kynpham Singh. *Ki Por Bad ki Kam U Rash Mohon Roy* (Shillong, 1979), pp. 29f, 57-59.

17. Letter from Sib Charan Roy, dated Chatak, 27.6.1909 to the Secretary, Seng Khasi; Letter from H.M. Langblah, dated the 7th June 1913 to the Secretary, Seng Khasi; Letter from G.C. Rai Giri, Rtd. Executive Engineer, dated, Maulvi Bazar, Sylhet, 5.5.1914 to the Secretary, Seng Khasi; Letter from Abinanda Beri, Camp N. 2, Tezupani, Mishmi road, NEFA, 14-11-1913 to the Secretary, Seng Khasi; Letter from Dkhar Singh, Syiem of Khyrim State, 23rd May 1913 cf Misc. Files, Permanent Records and Proceedings Books, etc.

18. Report submitted by Nalak Singh langblah, vide letter dated, Dacca (Dhaka), 2nd Dec. 1911, to the secretary, Seng Khasi.

19. *U Khasi Mynta,* Rymphang (Feb.) 1902; *U Khasi Mynta,* Nailur (Sept.) 1903; *Shillong Centenary Celebration Volume,* 1976, pp. 80-81; *Ka Jingia Lang Kynmaw. la U Sib Charan Roy,* Jait Dkhar Ha Ka 28th April, 1952 (Shillong, 1953), pp.8,13; *Khasi Heritage,* pp. 93-94; Kynpham Singh, *Ki Kot Khasi Ba La Thoh Da Ki Khasi* (1896-1903) (Shillong, 1969), pt. II, p. 10.

20. *U Nongpynim,* A Monthly Journal in Khasi (ed. Sib Charan Roy), Kyllalyngkot (Jan.) 1939, N. 70, pp. 8-9, 13; *U Nongpynim,* Nai Jylliew (June) 1928, No. 4, pp. 22-24; *U Nongpynim,* Lber (March) 1929, No. 14, pp.15f.

21. *U Nongpynim, laiong* (Apr.) 1939, No.71, pp. 1-4.

22. *Shillong Centenary Celebration Volume,* 1976, p. 80.

23. *Ka Jingialong Kynmaw La U Sib Chadran Roy,* p. 34.
24. *Ibid.,* pp. 30-31; *Golden Jubilee Souvenir,* Seng Khasi (Shillong, 1971), pp. 30-32.
25. Seng Khasi, J.P. K 11-5-1921; *Ki Khubor Ka Skul Seng Khasi,* Lber (March) 1925, p 1; R.M. Roy, *Ka Shithi Shaka Seng Ka Seng Khasi* -1.1.1961; *U Khasi Mynta,* Jylliew (June) 1904, N. 92, p. 3; *U Lurshai,* Vol. XXIV, Nos. 7-8, July & Aug. 1924, p. 3 cf. Kynpham Singh, *Rash Mohan Roy,* pp. 64-66. *Amrita Bazar Patrika,* April 29, 1938; A letter (Unpub.) from A.V. Thakkar, Bharatiya Adim Jati Sevak Sangh, dated, Kinsway, Delhi, 5th July, 1949 to U. Rash Mohan Roy, Vide Misc. Files (Permanent Record) of the Seng Khasi; Unpublished Report of Rashmohon Roy, 15th Jan. 1961.
26. *Golden Jubilee souvenir of Seng Khasi,* 20th May 1971, pp. 28-29.
27. *U Nongpynim,* laiong, 1939, No. 71, p. 2.
28. *Shillong Centenary Celebration Volume,* 1976, pp. 78-79, 81-82.
29. Letter dated Shillong, 24.9.1902 to the Editor of the *Bengalee,* Calcutta; *U Khasi Mynta,* Risaw (Octob.)1902.
30. *Ka Syngkhong Jingtip* (The Quarterly Journal of the Khasi Cultural Society, ed. Theodore Cajee), April 1938, Vol. II, No. 5, pp. 2-3.
31. *Ibid.,* pp. 11-12.
32. *Meghdoot,* Sept. 18, 1976, Vol. II, p. 4.
33. *Golden Jubilee Souvenir* (1928-1978), Ramakrishna Mission Ashram Sohbarpunji (30th Jan. 1979), pp. 19, 41-42, 53. The author visited this Ashram on 8-11.1976.
34. *Golden Jubilee Souvenir* of Seng Khasi, 20th May, 1971, p.30. For detailed knowledge of the traditional religion of the Khasi see *Sneng Khasi* (The Journal of the Seng Khasi), Nov. 1977, Vol. 1, No. 1, pp. 3-9; *Sneng Khasi,* 1979, Vol. 7, No.7, pp. 132-142; *Sneng Khasi,* 1979, Vol. 6. No. 2, pp. 106-7; *Seng Khasi,* 1979, Vol. 2, No. 7, p. 122;, RT Rymbai, *The Cultural Heritage of the Khasi,* The International Association for Religious Freedom, *Souvenir,* 1977-78.

35. *Gazetteer of Bengal and North East India* (Delhi, 1979), pp. 488-89.
36. *The Background of Assamese Culture* (Shillong, 1948), pp. 104-05.
37. *Report on the Census of Assam for 1881* (Calcutta, 1883), (Report by C.J. Lyall), Tables III & IV, also p. 40; *Census of India* 1891 (Shillong, 1892), Assam (Report by E.A. Gait), Vol. I, p. 82, Vol. III, Tables V & VI; *Census of India* 1901 (Shillong, 1902), Assam (Report by B.C. Alien), Vol. IV, pt. I, pp. 46, 51-52, pt. II, Table VI; *Census of India* 1911 (Shillong, 1912), Assam (Report by J . Mcswiney), Vol. III, Pt. I, pp. 35, 38, pt. II, pt. A, Table XIII and p.84; *Census of India* 1921, Assam (Report by G.T. Llyod, Vol. III, pt. I, p. 50f; K.K. Das Gupta, "Spread of Brhamoism in the Khasi and Jaintia Hills", in *Sources of the History of India,* Vol. II, ed. S.P. Sen (Calcutta, 1979) pp. 268-74; see also *Golden Jubilee Souvenir* (1928-1978), Ramkrishna Mission Ashram (Sohbarpunji, 30th Jan., 1979), p. 39.
38. *American Anthropologists,* Vol. 58 pp. 264-65, Ref. to P.R.G. Mathur, *The Khasi of Meghalaya* (Delhi, 1979), p. 136.
39. *Op.cit.,* p. 137.
40. *North-Eastern Spectrum,* Jan. 1977, Vol. I, No. 7, pp. 32f.
41. *Years of Change in Bengal & Assam* (London, 1966), p. 111.
42. *History of the Frontier Areas Bordering on* Assam (1883-1941), (Shillong, 1942), pp. 168-69.
43. *Spectrum,* Jan. 1977, Vol. 1, No. 7, p. 32.
44. *Naga Path* (London, 1952), p. 41.
45. *My Experiences in Manipur and the Naga Hills* (Delhi, 1971), pp. 83-84.
46. *Hindu Vishva,* Chaitra, 1902, Vol. 15, No. 7, pp. 15-18.
47. *Collected Writings,* 1937-1940 (London, 1941), pp. 187-88.
48. Roy Burman, *Demographic and Socio-Economic Profiles of the Hill Areas of North East India (Delhi,* 1970), pp. 345f.
49. The Land Where the Bamboo Flowers (Gauhati, 1970), pp. 10, 40.
50. Roy Burman, *op. cit.,* p. 355.
51. *Years of Change in Bengal and Assam,* p. 112.

52. Somerset playne, *Bengal and Assam, Bihar and Orissa,* ed. by Arnold Wright (London, 1917), P 480; E.F Sandys, *History of Tripura* (compiled from authentic sources) (Calcutta, 1915, rept. Agartala, 1997), p. 97.
53. Foreign Deptt., Pol. Branch Consultation, Feb. 1879, Nos. 199. 5 dated, Indian Office London, 9th Jan. 1879 from Secretary of State for India to the Govt. of India; Foreign Deptt. Pol. "A" Consultation Dec. 1878, No. 266/70.
54. W.W. Hunter, *The Statistical Account of Bengal* (London, 1876), Vol. VI, pp. 470-71.
55. F.D.P.C.A., Dec. 1878, No. 266/70 of Pol. Agency of Hill Tipperah for 1977-78.
56. *Souvenir,* Purba Bhārat Sānskritik Sammelan, Gauhati, Jan. 6-15, 1975, p. 113.
57. Playne, *op.cit.,* p. 480; Sandys, *op. cit.,* p. 98.
58. *Op. cit.,* p. 107.
59. V. Elwin, *Nagaland* (Shillong, 1961), pp. 24-26.
60. *Ibid.,* p. 51.
61. SAA, Vol. II, pp. 400-01, Gait, *op. cit.,* p. 46; Dalton, *Descriptive Ethnology of Bengal* (Calcutta, 1872, rept. Calcutta 1960), pp. 82f; Frank, JASB, 1902, Vol. LXXI, pt. III, pp. 36, 37.
62. *History of Assam Rifles* (London, 1929), pp. 80-81.
63. *Op.cit.,* pp. 345f.
64. P. Chaliha, *The Outlook on NEFA* (Assam Sahitya Sabha, Jorhat, 1958), p. 45.
65. *Op. cit.,* p. 141.
66. *Op. cit.,* pp. 43, 77.
67. *The Journal of the Assam Research Society,* April 1938, Vol.VI, No. 1, pp. 4-11; B.K. Kakati, *The Mother Goddess Kamākhyā* (Gauhati, 1967), pp. 60-64; L.W. Shakespear, *History of Upper Assam, Upper Burmah and North Eastern Fontier* (London, 1914), p. 86.
68. Extracts from the proceedings of the Govt. of India (Home Dept. April, 1902), Shillong, 4th Feb. 1901, Nos. 175/433.

    For renaissance and reform movements of the tribal people in north-eastern India and other parts of the country see G.P. Singh, "Tribal Renaissance in India", *Manthan* (Monthly Jouranl of Deendayal Research Institute, New Delhi), Vol. IX, No. 8, 1989, pp. 21-41.

18

The Impact of Modernization on the Naga Society and Culture in the 19th and 20th Centuries : A Historical Perspective

While dealing with any aspect of the history and culture of the Naga people inhabiting the North East Frontier of India, one has to be conscious of his limitation becuase of their diverse social customs, traditions, beliefs, practices, dialects, etc. In this simple paper, I have attempted to focus only on those few relevant aspects of the subject concerned which find adequate reflection in some trustworthy imperial documents, contemporary accounts and standard historical texts.

Here it is worthy of remark that the nineteenth century constituted a significant landmark in the history and culture of the tribal people of north east India. It witnessed the transition from tradition to modernity. It was also a period of social transformation and cultural revolution. Like all other primitive oriental races, the tribal people of North East India too came under the impact of colonial rule. The impact of westernization and modernization on the Naga society and culture during the period under review does not only signify the spectacular progress, gradual development, miraculous changes in socio-economic, religious, educational and cultural fields, eradication of some evil practices such as head-hunting, slavery, human sacrifices etc. primarily based on superstitious beliefs and unscientific understanding but also denotes the gradual decline in tribal arts, crafts and other creative impulses, disappearance of traditional system of administration, Customary law and justice, social customs and traditions, abandonment of art of wood carving, destruction of indigenous industry and the extinction of popular social and political institutions. The alien culture dominated the indigenous culture which being detrimental to their tender sentiments greatly jeopardised their interest reflected in the age-old traditional system. The British policy of alluring the Nagas by introducing all the apparatus of western civilisation led to the crisis of faith, disillusionment with the traditional values, cultural neurosis, etc. Consequently, this necessitated the beginning of revitalisation movement and social-cultural awakening in the second quarter of the 20th century for reviving the archie civilsation and pristine glory of past and preserving all that was novel in their society, religion, culture, art, language etc. As a matter of fact, the conflict between two civilisations representing traditionalism and modernism ensued which marked a distinct phase in their history and culture.[1]

In an attempt to prove only the blessing of the colonial rule for the tribal people including the Nagas many occidental scholars have presented distorted picture of the subject. Some of their views are unbalanced and analysis very superficial. Both blessings and the curses of British rule should attract our attention in the treatment of the subject particularly in the context of all notable changes that took place in the modern age in various spheres of their lives. This fact should not be lost sight of that taking advantage of the contemporary tribal situation, the attempts which were repeatedly made by the British for westernization and modernization of the Naga society and culture were the means for the consolidation of their position and extension of political control over them and not the end. It was the circumstances not the motive which compelled them to accept all that which the British offered them. Actually, the tribals were the best medium through which the British wanted to change the socio-religious structure of India.

It is worthwhile to note that AJ. Moffatt Mills, the then judge of the Sudder Dewani and Nizamat Adalat, while submitting his account of the province of Assam to the government of Bengal in July 1853 emphasised the need for undertaking some projects for the development and progress in the tribal areas of Assam. The official records, particularly Lord Dalhousie's Minute[2] cast a clear reflection on the British attitude and policy adopted towards the tribals of the North East in terms of the interest and profit of the former and progress of the latter.

The dawn of modem civilization witnessed the educational advancement of the Naga at the behest of Christian Missionaries. But this fact should not be ignored that the education was the menas for the propagation of Christianity as well as indoctrination. Educational progress and conversion to Christianity went side by side. The credibility of this statement can be tested by the statement of John Butler which runs as follows: "Who shall say that the Bible will not be the means of changing the habits and ideas of these wild savages? The experiment is worthy of tribal."[3] The regular system of education included the religious instruction. John Butler in 1845 appointed school teachers for the Nagas of Hosanghajoo village to teach them Assamese language, Bible in Assamese language and other books. In course of time, many Naga boys and girls learned the first rudiment of the language and attained proficiency in Assamese language.[4] In 20th century, the opening of many schools in the Naga villages of Manipur and Naga hills paved the way for the educational development of the people.

One of the radical changes that took place during the period concerned was the conversion of Nagas to Christianity resulting in the gradual decline of their traditional religious system and faith. It is true that the Nagas by and large neither displayed any tendency nor showed any disposition towards being converted to Hinduism or Christianity as it is evident from the statement of Mr. A.W. Davis as well as the statistical figure supplied by him.[5] But the efforts made by the early Missionaries like Mr. Bronson, an American who worked in the Naga Hills between 1842 and 1852, Revd. Mr. Clark who worked from early sixties to 1898 among the Aos and their followers brought the Nagas within the pale of Christiandom.[6] Christian Missionaries going against the company's wish to protect the religion of the people taught by the fathers & mothers to their sons and daughters showing respect to the traditional and indigenous religious system of the country did their works, Lord Minto's letter to the chairman of the East India Company in 1807 afford a sufficient illustration of truth. The consideration of time and space compels to refrain from entering into detailed account of it but here I will definitely like to analyse though very precisely the politics of conversion of Christianity. While advocating the conversion of the Nagas to Christianity and justifying their attempts, the British created the false impression that the Nagas had no religion, they want a religion and only Christianity can make them civilised.[7] No better proof of this can be adduced than the statement of Mr. Johnston himself who pointed out that "The Nagas has no religion, that they were highly intelligent and capable of recieving civilisation; that with it they would want a religion and that we might just as well give them our own and make them in that way a source of strength, by thus mutually attaching them to us. Failing which...., following the examples of other hill tribes, they would sooner or later become debased Hindoos or Musulmans, and in the latter case as we know by experience, be a constant source of trouble and annoyance".[8]

There can be no greater mistake to assume that the Nagas like other hill tribes recieved a religion worthy of name only in modern age. They had of course a traditional religion known as Animism which was based on extra ordinary uniformity of principle common to them. No matter, it did not find a place in the four prominent schools of religion namely Hinduism, Buddhism, Islam and Christianity because of absence of prophets and preachings. Religion as a most powerful factor for testing the race also caught the imagination of Maxmuller. No doubt, the religious ideas and beliefs which the Nagas had been retaining from time immemorial underwent profound changes because of the imapct of modern civilisation.[9]

However, in all fairness it must be admitted that the Christian Missionaries proved to be a harbinger of progress to a considerable extent particularly in the tribal areas. They deserve the credit for stamping out certain "savage practices", putting down sanguinary and reprehensible customs and abolishing some evil practices and beliefs based on superstitions such as head hunting which was a symbol of honour, valour and manhood, tribal warfare, inter-tribal feuds, murder, human sacrifices' slavery prevalent among the Aos, infanticide prevalent among the Angamis and the Maos, polygamy of the Lothas and many other social abuses.[10] As a result of partial abolition of these evil practices a new era-an era of peace, progress, good neighbourly relation, freedom and security began. The progress of civilisation left its own mark on them. The period 1866-1899 also marked the beginning of peaceful cultivation, growth of trade and commerce and improvement in means of communication.

In the intercourse with the Naga people, the British persuing the policy of exercising control over them more by conciliatory measure than by coercion encouraged the trading activities of the Nagas by establishing haats or markets in the neighbouring areas. Both internal and external trade flourished, the Angamis, Lothas, Semas, the Western and Eastern Nagas started paying frequent visits to the neighbouring plain areas like Dimapm, Golaghat, Dibrugarh, Sibsagar, Jorhat, Gauhati and Cachar and exchanged their goods. The Samaguting and Kohima proved to be the emporia of trade. This practice accelerated the pace of their culture-contacts with the neighbouring people.[11] The improvement in the means of communication played a conspicuous role in the process of modernization. It conditioned the development of trade and commerce to a considerable degree. The road from Golaghat to Samaguting was completed some bridges were constructed, jungles were cleared and some roads were repaired in the last quarter of the 19th century under the supervision of P.W.D. of central Assam division.[12] Here I am reminded of what Mr. John Butler predicted in 1855. To quote him "it can't be deemed visionary to anticipate that the darkness and ignorance that now overshadow the land be speedily dispelled when our rule will prove a blessing to these benighted tribe who would hence-forth enjoy the fruit of their labour in peace and prosperity."[13] The prediction came to be true, so far, the progress and development in the Naga Hills under British rule is concerned.

But on the other hand the western culture and civilisation produced a disastrous effect on the socio-economic and political institutions of the Naga people. It resulted in the gradual decadence of the most popular social institution known as Bachelors Hall of the Semas, Lothas, Aos, Rengmas, Kabuis and other tribes. This institution was the centre of learning, spiritual and moral training, singing, dancing etc. for the younger generation. The spread of Christianity is greatly responsible for the decay and fall of this age-old institution. As a matter of fact this institution stood as a barrier in the way of the British so far the attempts at their westernization is concerned.[14]

The indigenous industry and arts and crafts of the Nagas were also adversely affected. The European goods stood in perfect competition with the fine manufactured products of the small scale cottage industry. The people started developing fascination for the European goods, as a result of which the art of weaving suffered a great setback. Karl Marx (*New York Daily Tribune* 1853) while reacting to the economic impact of the British rule of India observed that England has broken down the socio-economic structure and framework of India separating it from all its ancient traditions and past history. This is relevant to the tribal context as well.

The western civilisation also marked the decline of the authority of their chiefs or headmen and the autonomy and freedom of village council—a true republican institution. The traditional administrative system, customary law and the judiciary of the Nagas were too much affected because of external inteference of the British in their internal administration. The introduction of British system of administration and law failed to take any account of their needs and aspirations and eventually undermined the tribal solidarity.[15]

Their art and culture also could not escape the impact of the west. Their folk dance, songs, music, architecture, sculpture and the art of painting etc. based on their beliefs started fading away. The art of making the wooden images with the carving of the heads on them - monumental in character—the practice of erecting the Megalithic monuments and the custom of keeping the Morungs or Bachelors Halls in the village elaborately carved and ornamented with the figures of elephants, deers, tigers and life size figures of men and women gradually started disappearing.[16]

While coming to the most interesting and valuable aspect of the subject, I would like to add that Jadonang, a popular Kabui Naga leader, tried to reorientate the Naga society, religion and culture in the late twenties of the last century striking a balance between tradition and modernity.

Socially, he tried to integrate the three tribes i.e. the Zemi. Liangmei and Rongmei by putting an end to inter-tribal feuds and ill feelings. All the three tribes got combined under the banner of Zeliangrong. In the religious fields he tried to abolish certain unnecessary gennas and taboos and other superstitious beliefs. He simplified the ceremonial parapharnalia. He introduced some innovations in the traditional religion by encouraging the construction of temples which was never in existance before. He constructed the temples and installed the images of supreme deity Regang and his consort. While calling this movement as "semi religious movement", Sir Robert Reid[17] stated that Jadonang from his bamboo platform erected in his temple used to preach before the elders and followers about animistic religion based on age-old beliefs. But the British instigated the villagers to demolish his temple as it was against the tribal practices. Prof. Downs[18], a church historian misunderstood it as anti-christian movement". Actually Jadonang's cult was a revival of traditional religion. According to Ursula Graham Bower,[19] he enunciated such a religion which was a splendid blending of Hinduism and Christianity. But this view is hardly tenable. It can be fairely disputed. Mr. Johnstone[20] has revealed the historic truth that towards the middle of the 19th century a great Hindu revivalist movement of far-reaching importance broke out in the North East of India particularly Manipur and Naga Hills.

Rani Gaidinliu, his follower and associate, also started a movement for the socio-religious transformation. As a reformer she looked down upon the alien culture and religion and made sincere efforts to preserve the traditional Naga culture and usages of the Zeliangrong people. She introduced a monotheistic cult known as "Heraka" (Pure) religion for worshiping their supreme deity Ragg.[21] Her movement was not a complete departure from the past but a reformed cult conjoined with a new philosophy. She kept this movement somehow alive between 1931 and 1932 side by side with her political movement. Many became followers of this new cult but Kabui Christians called it "a heathen movement".[22] Pt. Jawaharlal Nehru, while visiting Assam in 1937, highly praised the qualities which she was endowed with. He commented that "India does not even know of this brave child of her hills.....a day will come when India also will remember her and cherish her...."[23]

From the foregoing treatment of the subject it can be plausibly concluded that the modern era was both a blessing and a curse for the Nagas. It was a period of both a progress and decay. It is in this line that the representatives of the two schools of assimilationists and isolationists have expressed divergent views and thoughts. Pt. Jawaharlal Nehru aptly remarked that "The so called European civilisation had the disastrous and paralysing effect on the tribal people. The march of modern civilisation destroyed the traditional way of their lives and put an end to their arts, culture and simple way of living."[24] O Malley dealing with the evil effects of the British rule on the primitive tribes observed that "Far from being of immediate benefits to the primtive tribes the British rule in India did much harm than the good. It is some what distressing record of the effect of an alien civilisation impinging on simple and backward peoples".[25] D.N. Majumdar,[26] H.B. Rowney[27] and Thackker have also expressed more or less the similar views. J.P. Mills also opined about the evil effects of Missionaries on the tribals of Assam. V. Elwin, a champion of both assimilation and isolation, also accorded, though unwillingly, his assent to the views of J.P. Mills. But Dr. Hutton[28], and Roy Bahadur, S.C. Roy, a noted Indian anthropologist, both advocates of assimilation and culture contact, highly praised the works of Christian Missionaries with reference to their impact on the Naga tribes. Mahatma Gandhi found Christianity "Synonymous with denationalization and Europeanization"[29]. Any way, the conflicting views of isolationists and assimilationists do not appear to be of much academic interest. Hence I close this discussion here. The best conclusion we can safely draw is this that during modern period the Nagas like all other tribes something gained and something lost. Their culture ultimately became a synthetic one retaining something what they found lovable in their tradition and adopting something what they found attractive in western and modern civilisation.

Notes and References

1. See my article, "Tribal Renaissances in India: A Historical perspective", *Manthan* (*Quarterly Journal of DD. Research Institute,* Delhi) 1983-84.
2. A. Mackenzie, *History of the Relation of the Govt. with the Hill tribes of the North East Frontier of Bengal* (Calcutta 1884) pp. 101-43.
3. John Butler, *Travels and Adventures in the Province of Assam* (Herein after abbrev. as T.A.P.A.) (London 1855), pp. 66-70.
4. John Bulter, T.A.P.A., pp. 66-70; See also Mill's *Report on the province of Assam* (Abbrev. as R.P.A.) 1854, pp. 26-28.
5. A.W. Davis, *Assam Census Report* (Abbrev. as A.C.R.) 1891, Vol. 1 pp 250ff. (In 1891 the number of converts were 211 and 579 in 1901).
6. A. Mackenzie, *op. cit.* pp. 92-99; A.W. Davis A.C.R. 1891, Vol. 1, pp. 250-52.
7. John Butler, *A Sketch of Assam with some account of the Hill Tribes* (Abbrev. as S. A. H. T.) (London 1847) pp. 149-52; Davis A.C.R.—1891.
8. *My experiences in Manipur and the Naga Hills* (London 1896), pp. 43-44.
9. E. Gait, *Census of India*, 1891, Assam. Report Vol. 1, pp. 92-95.
10. A.W. Davis, A.C.R. 1891 Vol. 1 pp. 241-49; Mills R.P.S., 1854, pp. CXLI-V; R. Brown. *Report of the progress in the Naga Hills*, 1874, pp. 27-9; John Butler, T.A.P.A., pp. 70 ff, SAHT, pp. 158-64; S.E. Peal, *Journal of the Royal Anthropological Institute* (J.R.A.I.) (London 1874), Vol. 3. pp. 770-84; Gait, *Journal of the Asiatic Society of Bengal* (J.A.S.B.) 1898, pp. 160ff; V. Elwin, *Nagaland* (Shillong 1961), pp. 24-26, 51.
11. Davis, A.C.R. 1891, Vol. 1, pp. 250-2; G.H. Damant, *Report on the Adm. of the Dist of the Naga Hills*, 1878-9, p. 11; Robinson, *A descriptive account of Assam* (London 1841, p. 244; Mill, R.P.A. pp. CXLI-III, John Butler S.A.H.T., pp. 187-8.

12. G.H. Damant's *on the Adm. of the Naga Hills dist.* 1878-9 pp. 10-11, Davis A.C.R. 1891, Vol. 1 pp. XXVII-IX.
13. John Butler. T.A.P.A., pp. 66-70.
14. R.G. Woodthorpe, J.R.AJ., London Vol. XI, pp. 52-73.
15. See Butler J.A. S. B. 1875, Vol XLIV, No. 4 ; See also S.A.H.T., pp. 164-72.
16. R.G. Woodthorpe's letter to Captain W.F. Badgley, dated Shillong 15th June 1876; John Butler. J.A.S.B. 1875 XLIV No. 4, pp. 144-7; Godwin Austin's *Report on the Naga Hills and Manipur* 1872-73, p. 86; R. Brown's *report on progress in Naga Hills,* 1874, pp. 13-15.
17. *Years of change in Bengal and Assam* (London 1966) p. 111; *History of the Frontier Areas Bordering on Assam,* 1883-1941 (Shillong 1942), pp. 168-69.
18. *Spectrum.* Gauhati. Jan, 1977, Vol. 1, No. 7, p. 32.
19. *Naga path* (London 1952) , p. 41.
20. *op cit.* (Delhi 1971), pp. 83-84.
21. *Hindu Vishva,* Chaitra, 1982, Vol. 15, No. 7, pp. 15-18.
22. *Quarterly Journal, Modernization in Tribal Culture*, Jan. March 1977, Imphal, p. 50.
23. *Collected writings,* 1937-40 (London 1941), pp. 187-88.
24. *The Tribal people of India,* (Delhi 1973), pp. 1-7.
25. *Modern India and the west,* pp. 417, 38; 442-44; G.S. Ghurye, *The Aborigines So called and their future,* pp. 178-198.
26. *J & Proceedings* A.S.B. 1929 , New series Vol. XXV, pp. 150-55.
27. *The Wild Tribes of India.* 1882, pp. 7-9. 14, 167-75. 216.
28. Cf. *Census of India Report* 1937.
29. *Young India,* Aug. 11, 1927 " Christian Missions their place in India," p. 101.

19

Contributions of the Tribal People of North-Eastern Region to the Making of History and Culture of India Through the Ages

"..history deals not only with the lives of great individuals; in a sense it may be said to consist of the sediment of the lives of millions of smaller men and women who have left no name, but who have made their contribution. Their lives make the materials of history as a coral-reef is built up out of the lives of millions of molluscs" (A.L. Rowse, *The use of History,* p. 17).

The tribal people of north-eastern region professedly made substantial contributions to the making of history and culture of India during all the three periods-the early, medieval and the British. The contributions were made in diverse fields-society economy, polity, religion, culture, philosophy, language and literature and art and architecture. Their contributions in the repulsion of the Muslims and the expulsion of the British are also not of mean importance.

The views generally held by scholars that in Pre-Āryan or Pre-Vedic period India was uncivilized and the "primitive men" had nothing to contribute appear to be untenable. The hitherto prevalent theory that the origin and growth of Indian culture and civilization can be ascribed to the Dravidians dwelling in Mohenjodaro and Harappa dating back to 3rd Millennium B.C. also cannot be taken as worthy of credence. As a matter of fact, the foundation of Indian culture was laid by not only the Āryans and the Dravidians but also by the Negroids or Negritos, the Australoids or Austrics (the Khasis and Jaintias), the Bodos (the Garos,

Kacharis, Chutiyas and Tipperahs), the Mongoloids (the Tibeto-Burmans, and the tribes of south-east Asian origin including the Nagas), the Kirātas (very often confounded with the Mongoloids) and other non-Āryan tribes. All of them played their respective parts in the gradual evolution of the composite culture of India. To quote Jairamdas Daulatram, formerly Governor of Assam, "Each section of our large population contributes to the making of the nation in the same manner as each flower helps to make a garden......" (quoted by V. Elwin in *The Tribal People of India* p. 18).

No doubt, the lessons of one culture constitute the materials for its successors to shape the pattern of another culture. The study of the tribal history cannot be conducted in isolation from the related features of Indian history and culture. The proper understanding of the subject will undoubtedly enable us to determine the exact nature of the genesis and growth of Indian civilization. The significant contributions made by the non-Āryan tribes of north-east India since the dawn of history to the various aspects of Indian lives, thoughts, beliefs and practices should in no way be underestimated. The view of Luigi Pareti is worth-quoting here: "Many features of History can influence developments in thoughts, science and culture not only among individual people but over wide section of humanity, sometimes even over the whole world. One group of people many be enabled to become leaders of progress; another may find its activities smothered or extinguished and be obliged to yield to its place to other groups. These processes often enlarge, restrict or drastically modify the zones from which culture radiates and exchanges between these two zones. Here a leap forward and there a leap backward or sometimes a people is driven by event into a dormant state which may be mortal but which could also be invigorating". (*History of Mankind-Cultural and Scientific Development,* Vol. II, p. 5).

The present line of inquiry, I am sure, will open a fresh avenue for conducting further historical investigation into the subject matter under our notice. The study of the subject is based on literary accounts, archaeological evidence, Persian annals, native chronicles, standard historical records, documentary evidence and other contemporary sources.

The Pre-historic period is marked by many significant contributions of far reaching importance made by the non-Āryan tribes of north-east India which in subsequent periods formed the basis of Indian culture. The non-Āryans like the Āryans by building up a distinctive advanced culture of their own came within the orbit of Indian civilization at a fairly early age. The fusion of various races *viz,* the Austrics or Nishads, the Negritos, the Bodos, the Dravidians, the Mongloids, the Āryans and the Alpine Āryans in both pre- and post-Vedic period and their cultural contacts with the Pundras of northern and central Bengal who had the Chalcolithic civilization like the dwellers of Indus Valley led to the evolution of the synthesis of cultures which profoundly influenced the various levels of Indian social structure. According to S.K. Chatterji, this may be looked upon as the great contribution of Assam in pre-historic period. *(The place of Assam in the History and Civilization of India,* pp. 6, 11).

The first remarkable and impressive record of their contributions begins with Neolithic period. According to K.L. Barua, the Khasi people made "several distinctive cultural contributions such as Megalithic burials, Neolithic shouldered hoe, terraced rice cultivation, iron-smelting and matriarchy, all indicative of advanced culture and civilization". (JARS, VII, 2, 1939, p. 35). The Ophiolatry, widely prevalent in most part of India, particularly southern India and eastern India, including Bihar, Bengal and Assam, may be originally connected with the Austrics. J.H. Hutton says that "the Austro-Asiatic Finnougrians clearly preceded the Medeterraneans in India and therefore ophiolatry is to be put down as the distinctive cultural contribution of the former" *(Ibid.* p. 37). Ophiolatry finds its reflection also in the sculptural art of the country.

The Neoliths and Phallic Megaliths of the Khasis, Jaintias, Garos, Kacharis, and Nagas associated with the worship of phallus-linga and yoni, later personified as Shiva and the Mother Goddess, cult of fertility, ancestor worship, Soul matter, magic, fetishism and animism led to the evolution of various minor and major religious cults and laid the foundation of socio-religious fabric of India. The ideas connected with the worshipping of memorial stones throughout the length and breadth of our country was brought to prominence first by the non-Aryans. J.H. Hutton informs us that the phallic worship (widely prevalent among the Hindus) is connected with the linga—a simple cone and yone—a triangular prism. Both are somewhat realistically presented by the Nagas and in the prehistoric monoliths of Dimapur *(Man in India-A Quarterly Anthropological Journal,* 11, 3, 1922, p. 150). L.W. Shakespear also observes that the chessman monoliths of Dimapur-"huge lingam (Shiva-Shakti principle) stones-are believed by some savants to be evidence of ancient phallic worship" *(History of Assam Rifles,* pp. 256 ff).

The religio-cultural and philosophical patterns of India distinctly appear as a curious blend or queer mixture of both the Aryan and non-Āryan elements The non-Aryans tribes' polytheistical belief, animistic belief, propitiation of both benevolent and malevolent spirits, supernatural objects, heavenly bodies, natural phenomena and other innumerable gods and goddesses having the anthropomorphic attributes based on magico-religious systems, eschatological belief or belief in life after death, and their ideas connected with monotheism or in the words of Max Muller henotheism, ritualism, priesthood, sacrifices, omens and divination, popular religious cults of Shaivism, Shaktism, and Tantricism associated with aboriginal forms of worship and other indigenous faiths further flourished after coming within the pale of Aryanisation. The Āryans further systematized, perfected and popularized the system. Most of the scholars are of the opinion that all the ideas connected with Hindu religion and culture conspicuous by their absence in the Vedas can be attributed to the non-Aryans. All the non-Aryan faiths and ideas were further assimilated into the Aryan religious system which further gave birth to intermittent character of Hinduism popularly known as "Proto-Hinduism" Several Upanishadic, Vedic and Pauranic doctrines and even the Vedantic philosophy have got pre-Aryan features. We find that the followers of three schools of religion—the Vedic, the Pauranic and the Tantric have thrived equally well among the people of non-Aryan races of the north-east who contributed to the building up of the Socio-cultural fabric of India. Their positive contributions in the long historic process of giving the concrete shape to Indian civilization appear to be the distinguishing hallmark of their history and culture. This truth can be confirmed by a number of reliable sources. According to S.K. Chatterji, "when the Aryans came into India the country was not a no-man's land—it was already populated by some races or people which had risen to a high level of civilization...... the credit for building up Indian civilization is not the Aryans alone, but that the non-Aryans in India had a share and that too, the larger share, in supplying the bases...... It is now becoming more and more clear that the non-Aryans contributed by far the greater portion in the fabric of Indian civilization, and a great deal of Indian religious and cultural traditions of ancient legend and history, is just non-Aryan translated in terms of Aryan speech....... The ideas of Karma and transmigration, the practice of Yoga, the religious and philosophical ideas centering round the conception of the Divinity as Siva and Devi and as Vishnu, the Hindu ritual of Puja as opposed the Vedic ritual of Loma-all these and much more in Hindu religion and thought would appear to be non-Aryan in origin" *(Indo-Aryan and Hindi,* pp. 32-34). Again, "These Kiratas or Indo-Mongoloids, i.e. Mongoloids of India, might very well have come to India before the Aryans and they contributed a great deal in the evolution of Hindu history and culture in N.E. and Eastern India".

Shree Ramdhari Singh Dinkar in his magnum Opus *Saṁskriti Ke Chār Adhyāya or Four Chapters of Culture* (pp. 49-50) and S. Radhakrishnan in his *Hindu View of life* have strongly supported this view P. Mitra in his *Pre-Historic India* (preface, IX) and S.K. De in his *"The beginning of Indian civilization" (in Monthly Bulletin,* Ramakrishna Mission Institute of Culture, II, 10, 1951, p. 152) have put forth the views that not only in the socio-economic sphere but also in the more important branch of the religious beliefs, nay in the whole field of Indian culture, the non-Aryans have really contributed to and laid the foundation of "Modern Hinduism" whether in India or Assam and many survivals of non-Aryan cults may still be traced.

N.N. Vasu has rightly remarked that Assam may be "'looked upon as a federation hall, where the most ancient and the most modern, the most antiquated and the most up-to-date are found to meet together upon terms of perfect cordiality. The followers of all the schools of philosophy-the Vedic, the Paurānic and the Tantric—have thrived here equally well; and people of all races, Āryans and non-Āryans, Hindus and non-Hindus have equally contributed to the building up of the social fabric of Kāmarūpa. In a word, with the ancient history of this glorious land is indissolubly bound up the social, religious and the national history of the whole of India" *(Social History of Kāmarūpa,* Vol. 1, pp. 1-2).

Atkinson has judiciously opined that "Forms of belief having their origin in or beyond the Himalayas have influenced the religious system of India from the earliest ages to the present day" *(Himalayan Gazetteer,* Vol. 1, pt. I, preface).

The non-Āryans' contributions to the growth of cults of Shaivism, Shaktism and Tantricism in gross forms can very well be established on the basis of trustworthy historical evidences. Shaivism, and Shaktism-a cult of Mother Goddess-identified with the active female principle (Prakrti) of Sankhya philosophy or with the Maya of Advaita

Philosophy co-existent with Brahmanas manifested in one or other forms of worship of Shakti or Shiva's spouse under various names Devi or Parvati, Durga and Kali in accordance with the rites prescribed in the Tantras became their prevailing religion in Pre-Vedic and pre-Bharata war period.

On the authorities of *the Kālikā Purāṇa, the Yogini Tantra,* B.K. Kakati's *The Mother Goddess Kāmākhyā* (pp. 10-16) and R.M. Nath's *The Background of Assamese culture* (pp. 4, 17, 95) we can state with great amount of confidence that the Kirātas installed the phallic emblem of their worship near the Austric *Ka-Mei-Kha.* No wonder, Kāmākhyā the chief sanctuary of Shaktism was an embodiment of the fusion of both the Āryan and non-Āryan beliefs and practices. They used to worship the Mother Goddess in the yoni symbol as opposed to the cult of Shiva worshipped in the phallic symbol in pre-Naraka period. The Kirātas lived in Prāgjyotisha containing the holy shrine of Kameikha (Kāmākhyā). Sir Charles Eliot has also observed that from historical standpoint "it appears to be compound of Hinduism with un-Aryan beliefs. It acquired great influence both in the courts and among the people of North-Eastern India but without producing personalities of much eminence as teachers or writers" *(Hinduism and Buddhism,* Vol. II, p. 274). These non-Āryan cults embodying cruder form of belief are as old as *Atharva Veda* which subsequently developed and later left its indelible mark on Buddhism. Dr. Bhandarkar is also of the view that all the thoughts and beliefs associated with the cult of Shaivism may be taken as the contributions of the Austrics and Negritos. The Archaeological Report of Dr. T. Bloch *(Report of the Archaeological Tour in Assam,* 1905) and the discovery of numerous objects in recent archaeological explorations clearly testify to the prevalence of Shaivism and the cult of Mother Goddess in North Eastern Frontier Region in ancient times.

Dr. D. Sharma (JARS, XVI, 1962, pp. 22-23) and K.L. Barua (JARS, VI. 1, 1938, pp. 8-9) placing their reliance on the views of John Marshall have tried to establish that the cult of Mother Goddess or the cult of Linga and Yoni are certainly of Pre-Āryan Dravidian origin. The Austrics and the Bodos, according to them, came under the cultural influence of the Dravidians the authors of the Pre-Aryan Indus Valley culture and perhaps copied this custom from them. These views are contradictory. As a matter of fact, whether the Austrics and the Bodos of north-eastern region borrowed or copied this custom from the Dravidians of Mohenjodaro and Harappa or *vice versa,* or some section of the Austric people of north-east India were dwelling in the Indus Valley and later on accepted the Aryanised faith; these are some of the questions which cannot be satisfactorily answered. But it can be definitely asserted that as a result of the mutual cultural contacts and fellowship between the Dravidians, Austrics and Bodos, the cult of Shaivism and Shaktism further flourished. N. N. Law has correctly stated that "the Mother Goddess cult is pre-Aryan element in the Indian culture. The cult of Linga and Yoni ('Saiva-Sakta principle') worshipped in anthropomorphic form is older than the Chalcolithic age of Mohenjodaro. Phallus worship played an important part in the religious and magical ideology of the pre-Aryan and Non-Aryan peoples of India. The cult of Linga became embedded in Brahmanism in the Epic period." (IHQ, X, I, 1934, pp. 14-20).

The non-Āryan cult of Tantrikism - a system of magical or sacramental ritual associated with magic, sorcery, witchcraft, exorcism, etc. conditioned the development of doctrine of Vedic Karmakanda, which after being accepted by the Aryanised people, further got manifested in *Vajrayana* cult of Buddhism. The Tantric form of worship is the resultant of the incorporation into Hinduism of a fertility cult which preceded it as the religion of the country. The theory of Nandlal Dey, that the Tantrik doctrines probably spread from the ancient Buddhist University of Vikramshila (near modern Bhagalpur in Bihar) in Kamarupa about the ninth century under the Pala rule (JPASB, X, 1914, p. 346), can fairly be disputed. Both E. Gait *(History of Assam,* pp. VII-VIII, 15, 58) and Charles Eliot *(Hinduism and Buddhism,* Vol. II, pp. 278-79) opposing this view have stated that the birth place of Shaktism and Tantricism, the two important sects, seems to have been northeast India which was inhabited by not Āryans but the people belonging to Mon-Khmer, Tibeto-Burman and Shan families. The north eastern tribal region was neither a land of ancient Brahmanic settlement nor a centre of Vedic and Puranic learning.

The Shaiva cult, which is one of the popular religious cults of Hindus, is admittedly of Kirāta origin. Shaivism, Shaktism and Tantricism the three different sects or forms of Hinduism are purely of non-Āryan tribal origin. The non-Āryan tribes of northeast India also made some contributions to the evolution of these three sects for faiths in ancient times.

The contributions of some of the tribes of north-east India to the linguistic and literary growth are also of considerable importance. According to R.S. Dinkar *(op. cit.,* pp. 24, 51, 75-76), the Austric or Mon-Khmer language (spoken by the ancient Khasis) got absorbed in Āryan language and literature. The stories as narrated in Hindu *Purāṇas* and Buddhist *Jatakas* are based on the folktales of the Austrics and Dravidians. Some scholars have presumed that even the story of Rama is also based on the popular folk tales of the Austrics. As a result of commingling of Aryans, Dravidians and Austrics, their folk tales were given recognition by each other which no doubt influenced the *Itihāsa, purāna* and Sanskrit literature. B.K. Kakati in his thesis *(Assamese : Its Formation and Development,* pp. 25ff) has clearly stated that both Austrics and Bodos have contributed words to Assamese vocabulary. Kāmākhyā and Kāmarūpa may be sanskritization of non-Aryan words *Khomoch* and *Kamrut* respectively. Accordingly to him, the

French Indologists, Przyluski, Block and Levi, and other scholars, notably Prof. T. Burrow have dealt with the Dravidian and Austro-Asiatic influences on Sanskrit.

From the Archaeological Reports of T. Bloch, 1905, *Annual Reports of Archaeological Survey of India,* 1902, 1903, and other evidence (L.W. Shakespear, *History of Assam Rifles,* pp. 263ff; JASB, XIV, 2, 1845, pp. 477-78; XVII, I, 1848, pp. 462ff; XLIII, I, 1874, pp. 1-6; LXXI, 3, 1902, pp. 37f) it is evident that the non-Āryan art and architecture was fundamentally based on Indian traditional system. Actually the tribal people laid the foundation of an artistic culture, non-Aryan in form, with little touch of Hindu art on which edifices of other schools of art and architecture have been erected. It further led to the evolution of various architectural and sculptural designs. A marked similarity between the non-Aryan art of this region and that of the contemporary Eastern school of Bihar, Orissa and Pala-Sena art of Bengal can be noticed. The tribal people of north-eastern region attained a high degree of perfection in the field of architectural, sculptural, iconographic and decorative arts as well as paintings and pottery or ceramic arts. They no doubt, contributed a lot to the enrichment of Indian art and architecture. Probably, the relics of Dimapur and Sadiya region - the two premier seats of Tibeto-Burman and non-Aryan culture - show their influences on Assamese art and the arts of other parts of India. S. Kramrisch has rightly observed that the various racial factors have determined the art history of India as a whole *(Ancient Indian Sculpture,* pp. 127-28).

In the political field, the early non-Āryan tribal conceptions of exogamous units, clans, families and villages laid the firm foundation of organized civil administration and it influenced the political evolution of the Vedic Āryans regarding the formation of groups, the family *(griha* or *kula),* the village *(grāma),* the canton or clan (*vis*), and the people *(jana).* This was rendered possible only due to their early mutual cultural contacts. Looking at over all picture of non-

Āryan tribal polity (including that in the north-east) it may be quite heartening to note that their age old and time - honoured self governing republican institutions, unaffected by manifold social changes and political turmoils in course of long passage of time covering many centuries or millenniums conserving and preserving their indigenous cultural patterns and practically escaping the fall into general complex dynamic process of transition from monarchy to aristocracy and on to democracy - a thesis, antithesis and synthesis - greatly influenced the Hindu and Buddhist polity and administration from the Vedic age down to 400 BC covering Brahmanic or Upanishadic period, Panini and post-Pāṇini Age as well as the general political system of India.

It is striking to note that some of the north-eastern tribes by offering vigorous resistance to the imperial authority of the Turko-Afghans and the Mughals for nearly six centuries (1206-1740) of Pan-Indian character not only stemmed the tide of the progress of Muslim rule in Eastern Bengal and Assam but also frustrated their sinister designs of planting the banner of crescent over the political horizon of whole North-Eastern India by bringing all the refractory tribes under their political sway and thereby they contributed to the changing of history, geography and civilization of the country to a considerable extent. The saga of their patriotism and gallantry indisputably constitutes an addition to the glaring examples set by their other tribal brethren, mighty heroes, illustrious fighters and victorious princes and monarchs of medieval Hindustan. On the basis of some reliable sources *(Baharistan-i-Ghaybi* of Mirja Nathan, 2 Vols; *Riyazn-s-Salalin* of Ghulam Hussain Salim; *Alamgir Namah* of Muhammad Quasim; J.N. Sarkar's articles in JBORS, vol. I, 1915 and vol. VII, pt 1, 1921, *Ahom Buranji* by G.C. Barua, *Kachari Buranji, Tripura Buranji', Rajamala* (royal chronicle of Tripura); C.U. Aitchison's *Collection of Treatis, Engagements and Sanads,* Vol. II; W.W. Hunter's *Statistical Account of Bengal,* Vol. VI; S.K. Chatterji's *Kirata-*

Jana-Kriti, E. Gait's *History of Assam,* K.L. Barua's *Early History of Kamarupa,* JASB, Vol. IX, 1840) we can get a clear picture of the roles played by the Khasis, Jaintias, Garos, Tipperahs, Kacharis, Nagas (of Assam during the Ahomi rule), Akas, Daflas and others directly or indirectly in the repulsion of Muslim invasions during the period concerned.

The roles played by the Khasis, Jaintias, and Tipperah rulers in the socio-religious reform movement of the 19th and 20th centuries may form part of the chapter, Indian Renaissance, in the history of modern period.

A vast majority of the tribal people and their chiefs took active part in anti-British movements. They struck blow after blow to the mighty British empire and fought battle after battle against the British in their struggle for freedom both at regional and national level. The parts played by the Khasis and Jaintias, Cacharis, Nagas and Kukis in the great Revolt of 1857, the Jaintias in the Rebellion of 1860-63, and the Garos, the Nagas and the Kacharis in the insurrections of 1871-1882, the Risings of the Lushais, 1890-1896, Kuki Revolt of 1917-1919, role of Khasi leaders during the Swadeshi movement 1905-11 and Non-cooperation Movement 1921-1922, and Jadonang's and Rani Gaidinliu's fight for Swaraj 1927-1932 can undoubtedly form the part of the chapter, Indian war of Independence, in modern history of India. Rani Gaidinliu's (contemporary of Mahatma Gandhi) role in the Freedom Movement of India has been highly appreciated by Jawaharlal Nehru in his *The Unity of India. (Collected writings,* 1937-1940, pp. 187f). All these tribes played historic roles in throwing off the yoke of British rule. The independent nature of these people animated by the spirit of patriotism may be taken as great contribution to the fundamental unity of India during the British Period. S.K. Chatterji has said : "The Spirit of Independence of various tribes may be taken as one of the contributions made to Indian culture and the complex Assamese culture composed of the same elements has got a stamp of independent character which added one more thread to the texture of Indian civilization characterized by its unity in diversities". The official records, reports and tour diaries preserved in National Archives, New Delhi, and in State archives at Shillong, Gauhati and Calcutta, and the Historical Records 1857-1942 are the principal sources for throwing light on anti-British tribal movements in north-east India.

Thus we find that the tribal people of north-eastern region made remarkable contributions to the socio-politico-cultural evolution of India right from the Neolithic Age till the dawn of independence. The above treatment of the subject whatsoever may lead us to dispose of the view of H.J. Mackinder that "Assam is a country which at most periods of its history has remained outside the Indian civilization" (*Cambridge History of India,* Vol. I, ed. E.J. Rapson, p. 10).

Index